SPANISH ANTICLERICALISM

SPANISH ANTICLERICALISM

A Study in Modern Alienation

BY

JOHN DEVLIN
ASSOCIATE PROFESSOR OF SPANISH LITERATURE

FORDHAM UNIVERSITY

JOHN DEVLIN

SPANISH ANTICLERICALISM

A STUDY IN MODERN ALIENATION

———

Manufactured in the United States of America by
COCCE PRESS

TABLE OF CONTENTS

INTRODUCTION 11

AUTHOR'S FOREWORD 13

CHAPTER I. MAIN CURRENTS OF ANTICLERICALISM
IN SPANISH LITERATURE PRIOR TO 1900 15
1. In the Early Years of the Literature 15
2. The Inquisition 20
3. Some Sixteenth Century **Erasmista** Controversies . . . 24
4. Toward the Modern Context: Other Developments in
Later Centuries 33
5. A Note on Interpretation 44

CHAPTER II. THE CLIMATE OF OPINION 47
Modern Thinkers and Institutions in Conflict
with Clerical Interest and Opinions, 1900-1939
1. The General Pattern 47
2. New Educational Trends and the Church 53
3. The Monarchy; the Directorate; the Church and the
Liberals 60
4. The Republic and the New Constitution 72

CHAPTER III. ANTICLERICALISM IN "BELLES
LETTRES" IN WRITERS FOR THE MOST
PART ASSOCIATED WITH THE
PRE-REPUBLICAN ERA 81

Benito Pérez Galdós (1843-1920) 81
1. Pérez Galdós and Liberalism 81
2. The Important Anticlerical Novels: **Gloria, Doña Perfecta, La Familia de León Roch** 82
3. Other Novels and Dramatic Works 92
4. Some Evaluations 94

Vicente Blasco Ibáñez (1867-1928) 96
1. Republican 96
2. Anticlericalism in the Valencian Novels 96
3. Anticlericalism in **La Catedral; El Intruso** and Other
Non-Valencian Novels of Social Protest 99
4. Best Sellers 108
5. Publisher 110
6. Concluding Remarks 112

Miguel de Unamuno (1864-1936) 113
1. Religion and Reason 113
2. The Extent of Unamuno's Anticlericalism 120

Pío Baroja Nessi (1872-1956) 123
1. Baroja and Iconoclasm 123
2. Baroja's Anticlericalism, Strictly So-called 125
3. Baroja's Reaction to Religion 126

4. Priests 128
5. Catholics, Protestants, Jews 129
6. Other Portraits; Jesuits 131

Manuel Linares Rivas (1878-1938) 133
1. **Aire de Fuera (Air from Outside)** 133
2. **La Garra (The Claw)** 135
3. The Extent of Linares Rivas' Anticlericalism 137
4. The Significance of Linares Rivas' Anticlericalism . . 139

José Ortega y Gasset (1883-1955) 141
1. Intellectual and Republican 141
2. Ortega y Gasset's "Implied Anticlericalism" 142
3. Ortega y Gasset and Religion 144
4. Publishing activities: the **Revista de Occidente** 146

Ramón Pérez de Ayala (1881-1962) 148
1. Writer and Republican 148
2. **Luna de Miel, Luna de Hiel** 149
3. **A. M. D. G.** 154

CHAPTER IV. ANTICLERICALISM IN "BELLES
LETTRES" IN THE ERA 1931-1936 161

Arturo Barea (1897-1957) 161

Ramón Sender (1902-   ) 168
1. Sender's Anticlericalism, Strictly So-called 172
2. Anti-Religious Anticlericalism Portrayed in Sender's
Work 174
3. Thoughts on Religious Problem in Sender's Continuing
Search 177

Rafael Alberti (1902-   ) 183
1. Alberti's Anticlericalism 184
2. Alberti's Insights and Contacts with Anticlericalism on
the Folkloric Level 188
3. Alberti's **Romancero** 190

CHAPTER V. THE AFTERMATH 193
1. Church and State and Freedom of Expression 193
2. Governmental Literary Policy 206
3. The Catholic Spirit in Modern Spanish Letters and the
Spirit of the "Catholic Revival" 214
4. Negative Spanish Evaluations of the Catholic Revival . 226
5. A Theological Evaluation of the Trends Studied in This
Chapter 230

CHAPTER VI. CONCLUSIONS AND IMPLICATIONS . . . 233
1. Conclusions 233
2. Implications 236

NOTES 243

BIBLIOGRAPHY 257

INDEX 269

INTRODUCTION

Gentle Reader:

You have in this book an objective account by an American Catholic of the reactions of liberal Spanish authors to the "confessional state" which was and still is Spain. John Devlin explains very clearly the difference in meaning between anticlericalism and anti-religious attacks on the Church in Spain, with special reference to the past century. He shows how Spain has suffered since her early days from the encroachment of the Church in politics and education. Perhaps the two most famous victims of the Church's power were Luis de León, the gentle mystic of the sixteenth century, and the contemporary Erasmus, Miguel de Unamuno. Because of their liberal positions both were ousted from Spain's once-great University of Salamanca. Devlin shows most eloquently how the state has suffered from ignorant and intolerant priests and politically powerful prelates. He deplores the fact that in the Spain of today he finds no such movement as the Renouveau Catholique in France, or the Catholic Revival in England. As far as religion is concerned in Spain, everything is black or white. There are no grays. All Catholic liberals, like Devlin for instance, are classed with atheists, anarchists, and communists by the devout. Even an *ateneista,* a member of the famous liberal literary and cultural club of Madrid, of which Alfonso XIII was once a member, is subject.

After giving a general summary of criticism of the Church in past centuries, Devlin goes into particulars of the anticlerical movement of the last hundred years. To name but three of the great liberal writers of this period, he shows how the mild and sympathetic Galdós was vilified, how the tragic and pathetic Unamuno suffered disgrace and exile, how the philosophic and subtle Ortega y Gasset went unheeded. He then traces the extremely revolutionary laws passed by the

11

Republican anti-religious leaders of the Left, which precipi-
tated the Civil War, and which culminated in the present repressive regime of Franco, with the Church more powerful
than it was before that blood bath. Alfonso, who blew hot and
cold in his attitude toward the Church, was far more liberal
than Franco. As Devlin points out, the failure of contemporary
reformers in Spain today is due to the fact that no distinction
is made by the ecclesiastical higher-ups between anticlericalism
and anti-Catholicism. The only hope for religious toleration
in contemporary Spain lies in the attitudes of liberal Catholic
leaders of the Oecumenical Council. They may be bringing
pressure on the medieval Spanish ecclesiastics, who, up until
now, have tried to turn Spain back to the ideals of the *Reyes
Católicos,* Isabella and Ferdinand.

SAMUEL M. WAXMAN

December 1, 1964
Cambridge, Massachusetts

AUTHOR'S FOREWORD

This study represents the confluence of three major interests — Spanish Literature, Theology, and Comparative Literature. All three fields are interrelated in my educational background, professional life, and intellectual and teaching experience.

After many years of reading and study in the literature of the so-called contemporary "Catholic Revival" in France, England, and Germany, I decided to extend the investigation to Spain. I soon found that the vein had run dry. Anticlericalism rather than spirituality appeared to be the hallmark of Twentieth Century Spanish Literature. Thus this work was born.

I am indebted to many people both directly and indirectly. And like most authors I cannot possibly mention them all. But three stand out. They are: Samuel M. Waxman, Professor Emeritus of Spanish Literature at Boston University. The work was largely conceived in his classes. Under his guidance as my mentor in my doctoral studies it achieved its first form. Secondly, I am indebted to Patricia, my wife, my favorite critic, and my typist. Finally, I must mention Father Francis S. Shea of the Archdiocese of Boston, my professor of Theology. Without his teaching the interpretations would have been difficult if not impossible.

The book has too many notes. But I tried to keep them to a minimum. I certainly have not tried to document every sentence, nor have I documented easily obtainable biographical or historical material, nor the type of facts which are part of the habitual knowledge of hispanists. Some references are clear in the text. The bibliography will be of help to anyone who may wish to pursue a fine point. Thus, I limited myself to direct or nearly direct quotations and to statements which I feel may be quite controversial. Certain references are combined, especially when they refer to passages within the compass of a few pages. The notes are set up according to the

MLA format, slightly modified by the exigencies of this work and with a few abbreviations explained before each grouping in which they appear. Since the work is written in English, the English system of capitalization is used. All translations are my own unless otherwise stated in the notes.

CHAPTER I

MAIN CURRENTS OF ANTICLERICALISM
IN SPANISH LITERATURE
PRIOR TO 1900

1. *In the Early Years of Literature*

> In Talavera, yonder, while the month
> of April still
> Some letters happened to arrive from
> old Archbishop Gil
> Wherein there was an order which created
> quite a shrill
> And if it pleased some one or two, two
> thousand thought it ill.
>
> "Intelligence I have of sin, wherefore I
> put this stated,
> That every priest or clergyman who
> has been consecrated,
> Shall not have concubine or whore,
> nor wife already mated.
> All those who disobey, henceforth
> are excommunicated!"
> As soon as all the chapter did
> this information learn,
> Young clerics flabbergasted were; old
> priests showed grave concern.[1]

These rollicking lines are from the "Cántiga de los Clérigos de Talavera" ("Song for the Clerics of Talavera") in the *Libro de Buen Amor (The Book of Good Love)*. The poet, Juan Ruiz, Archpriest of Hita, is the first major author in Spanish literature who can in any sense be termed "anticlerical." The jolly cleric, however, is not anticlerical in the sense in which the word is usually understood today, to wit "opposed to the clergy or to clericalism; especially in European

15

politics."[2] No, Juan Ruiz is simply a frank denouncer of the ecclesiastical immorality that existed fairly generally throughout Europe toward the close of the Middle Ages. The Archpriest is also not averse to having a bit of fun at the expense of the clergy of Talavera. *The Book of Good Love* is only one of many well-known literary or artistic works of this epoch which reflect or contain pronouncements on the unedifying state of the clergy. Similar awareness can be found, for example, in the *Decameron,* in the poetry of Hans Sachs, in *The Canterbury Tales.* The fact that this sentiment was shared by the late medieval community is further reflected by Juan Ruiz' sources. Another section from *The Book of Good Love* is entitled "How priests and laymen and friars and monks and ladies and troubadours went out to welcome Lord Love." It is even more devastating than the *Cántiga* and is a part of "The Battle that Lord Flesh had with Lord Fasting" which in turn is based on the Old French *La Bataille de Karesme et de Charnage.*[3] The solemn Easter ritual is satirized as follows:

> The streets overflow with large processions.
> Among them many ordained men who sell indulgences
> Secular priests and clerics;
>
> .   .   .   .
>
> The order of Santiago and the Hospital nuns are here
> The orders of Calatrava, Alcantara and Buenaval
> Holy abbots too are at the feast
> *Te, Amorem, laudamus!* *is their chant* — nothing else.[4]

The Archpriest's uniqueness — from the viewpoint of his criticism — is that he includes himself among those he condemns. Perhaps "condemn" is too strong a word. "There are bad priests," he admits in effect. "But we must remember," he chuckles, "that sin is a human phenomenon."[5] Juan Ruiz is utterly sincere. He is sincere in his simple yet lofty *loores* or praises to the Virgin; he is sincere when he stresses clerical inadequacy; he is sincere in the incipient humanism that pervades his work. This humanism is evident even in the passages I have cited. Juan Ruiz never scolds. His spirit is satirical, yes. But it is not really condemnatory. Consciously or unconsciously,

16

at the points where he is most satirical and "anticlerical," he enters a complaint and a plea. The complaint is against abstract theological moralizing — elaborate rules of conduct in a frame divorced from the human condition. The plea is for the recognition of the more earthly human composite. The Archpriest recognizes the supreme hypocrisy of the immoral yet "celibate" clergy of his predominantly coarse era. In protesting (under bawdy symbols for the most part) he strikes at an underlying unrealistic ascetic orientation of medieval thought that broke the human composite into two separate entities. The tendency had been passed down like an inherited plague from the Manicheans and neo-Platonists (including St. Augustine) and it continues to poison religious orientation in the contemporary world. The Spanish have wrestled with its puritanical implications throughout their history — but they are not alone. More broadly speaking, Juan Ruiz, like his great contemporaries Petrarch and Boccaccio, is opposed to what Arnold Toynbee has called "a solely other-worldly view of life" and to what the British Catholic philosopher, E. I. Watkin, has termed an exclusively "vertical" view of life which neglects the "horizontal."[6]

Similar in subject matter but vastly different from Juan Ruiz' pre-Renaissance tone are the anguished "anticlerical" outpourings of the Archpriest's Spanish contemporary, Pero López de Ayala. The gloomy Chancellor of Castile was also goaded by the clerical inadequacies of his day. But his ire was provoked. Unlike the Archpriest he finds no cause for humor. There is also no plea for human weakness in the devout lines of his *Rimado de Palacio* (*Rhymes from the Palace*). With knightly hauteur he speaks his mind: "If these are ministers they are Satan's ministers." Ignorance and malfeance rather than sexual exuberance sadden the Chancellor: "They don't know the formula for Consecration nor do they want to learn it. Not one in a hundred knows the words for Baptism." Prelates, even popes are subjected to his lashings: "Now the Papacy is rooted in the splendor of riches; there is no one to wrest it away; though old, the prelates don't lack vigor; no

17

one has ever seen a pope die in poverty."[7] Like Juan Ruiz, López de Ayala in no way steps outside the Church to level his criticisms. On the contrary, his poetry is pervaded by a piety which, for all his harshness, is traditionally medieval.

A spirit similar to the Chancellor's can be found in the *Dança General* or "Dance of Death." The Spanish *dança,* in resounding lines of *arte mayor,* dates from the early fifteenth century. The theme was used throughout Europe in both literary and pictorial expression, such as the *Totentanz* in Germany, the *Danse Macabre* in France, some of the etchings of Albrecht Dürer, and the *Last Judgement* of Hieronymus Bosch. In the Spanish version, death summons all; thirty-three victims, a layman always alternating with a cleric, are symbolic of the various ranks in society who are forced to leave the pleasures of the world and join in the dance. Among the clerics are a pope, a cardinal, a preacher. The anticlericalism of the *dança* is found only in the concept that clerics (as well as laymen) are transgressors of the law of God and have contributed to the dismal failures of late fourteenth century society. The prevalence of this *danse macabre* in this era strongly suggests a subconscious realization that a bizarre requiem was being sung for the death of an age.

Later fifteenth century expressions of this same typical, late medieval "anticlericalism" can be found in the *Corbacho* of Martínez de Toledo (the Archpriest of Talavara) and in the *Libro de los Gatos (Book of the Cats)*.

Outspoken criticism of clerical immorality and other failings continued in the sixteenth century. Francisco de Osuna in his *Abecedario Espiritual (Spiritual Alphabet)* castigated lax discipline in religious life and lamented that young priests "from the time they are ordained are left to follow their own whims."[8] Later the voice of Cisneros was heard in the realm. Indeed, such criticism, without any unusual overtones, continues down through the Council of Trent and beyond.

So far it will be noted that the word *anticlerical* has been set off in quotation marks. This is because I wish to make a strong distinction between general criticism of the clergy (on

18

such varied scores as sexual laxness, ignorance, materialism, or a too rigorous asceticism) from the specific definition which I have accepted in this study. It has been my experience that persons interested in religious controversy tend to label any criticism of the clergy as anticlericalism. Frequently a strong nexus actually does exist between "anticlericalism," that is, general criticism of the clergy, and anticlericalism in the more restricted sense. This nexus will be seen in later chapters. Failure to make the necessary distinction can easily lead to misunderstandings in a very sensitive area. Anticlericalism as it developed in Spain (and in Europe) in the nineteenth and twentieth centuries has the definite denotation of opposition to and criticism of the clergy and clerical pressures in the realm of politics. Almost always clerical pressure which stimulates anticlerical reaction has been exerted to secure a preference for the Catholic formula in mundane affairs. Very little has been written on the subject as such. But the term has been employed this way and accepted by historical authorities.[9] It is in this sense that this study is being chiefly extended.

A further note of caution is necessary. Anticlericalism definitely does not mean "hatred of priests because they are priests," as the late, brilliant Jesuit Terrence L. Connolly erroneously defined it.[10] On the other hand there are some rare cases, in Spanish literature at least, where a real hatred of religion seems to be combined with the accepted use of the word. Due note of this will be taken in succeeding chapters.

It should be noted also that it is entirely possible for a Catholic to be anticlerical. Antidiluvian Catholic apologists will resent and reject this statement. But the argument boils down to a battle of words. There are, to be sure, some semantic associations of the word that are unpleasant. Yet it was said of the late Georges Bernanos that "he was a distinguished Catholic author but at the same time a stern critic of various Catholic personalities and practises."[11] Later in this study specific references will be made to Bernanos' "stern criticism" of certain Catholic practises in the Spanish political cockpit. It will be seen that such criticism fulfills the strict definition of anticlericalism in every respect. Furthermore, I share the conviction of many who believe that anticlericalism is the result of clericalism. This, too, is a matter for later development. Suffice it to say now that from this point of view every Catholic has an obligation to be anticlerical.

2. *The Inquisition*

During the sixteenth century general criticism of the clergy became focused for the first time in controversies of a political nature. This era saw a new political situation, for with the Renaissance came the more fully developed concept of the national state. Thus, an historical and juridical situation was presented which was utterly different from the medieval polity where practical lines between secular and religious power were often difficult to distinguish. The achievement of a national unity in Spain was first accomplished, of course, in the reign of Ferdinand and Isabella. It was in connection with this unity that the Spanish Inquisition was established as a distinct function of the royal power.[12] Thus, historians are unjust to no one when they speak of a distinctly Spanish Inquisition. In the intentions of Ferdinand and Isabella the Spanish Inquisition was a weapon to be used against the Jews and Moriscos. The monarchs were convinced that these racial and religious groups jeopardized national unity. The first Spanish tribunal was set up in Seville. The "Catholic Kings" appointed two Dominicans, Miguel de Morillo and Juan de San Martín, as inquisitors in 1478.[13] Complaints of a grievous nature against the severe restrictive policies were soon heard; they proved to be well founded.[14] Nevertheless, the Inquisition continued to prosper and in 1487 Tomás Torquemada was confirmed as "grand inquisitor."[15] The movement spread rapidly to Córdoba, Villareal, and Toledo, the Primatial See. By 1538 there were nineteen tribunals. Actually the Spanish Inquisition represented a handing over of ecclesiastical and papal authority to a national state, for the Spanish tribunals were in reality royal councils — not ecclesiastical courts. Books were burned and thousands of accused persons were brought to trial for heresy and later turned over to the civil authorities for execution of the death penalty. The Spanish Inquisition was also exported to the Low Countries and its repressive policies, persecutions, tortures and cruelty did much to fan the flames of resentment and rebellion.

The Spanish Inquisition, of course, had its roots in a much earlier ecclesiastical policy of hunting down and punishing people whose beliefs did not conform to current orthodoxy. In the twelfth century in Provence in France a dualistic heretical sect known as the "Cathari" sprang up in and around the city of Albi—hence the term "the Albigensian Heresy." When various counter-measures, including the preaching of St. Dominic, failed to uproot this teaching, the Holy See decided to use force. Two crusades were launched, one in the reign of Pope Alexander III and a second under Innocent III. The crusades succeeded in eliminating the heresy by eliminating the people. A decisive factor was the formal establishment of the episcopal Inquisition in Toulouse in 1229. The local bishop was empowered to hunt down heretics, and, if they refused to recant, turn them over to the secular arm for punishment.[16] This local institution was transformed by Pope Gregory IX in 1233 into the papal Inquisition and the Dominicans were given official sanction to try cases. Soon tribunals were established throughout Europe. More than three centuries later the Roman Inquisition was established in 1542 by Cardinal Carafa, a southern Italian in whom the influence of the fanatical spirit of the Spanish Inquisition was strikingly reflected. Later as Pope Paul IV he wielded its awful power in the Counter Reformation.[17]

The Inquisition has always been a difficult historical area. Unquestionably, the German Catholic historian, Joseph Lortz, is correct in his assessment that "the Inquisition was a dreadful institution. It was responsible for the shedding of much innocent blood and much cruelty."[18] But many Catholic historians do not agree with Lortz. Many tend to minimize its historical significance and excuse it. For example, the following assertions are often made: In the medieval context in which the Inquisition emerged, the intimate union of religion and public order put heresy automatically in the category of a crime against the state. Even Lortz claims that "the lofty conception then held of the true Faith [was such that it was] not to be compared with anything else, even life itself."[19] The origin of the Inquisition during the Albigensian Crusade and the Crusade itself is defended — for example by Father Philip Hughes — by asserting that a new anti-Christian culture had been established which was actively and militantly hostile. Consequently the popes were required to treat the affair as urgent and grave.[20] One of the lesser defects of this argument is the belief that the Albigensians posed a real threat, or that a heresy which preached against copulation would really be taken seriously by the human race. (Certainly the record of ecclesiastical celibacy up to this time should have allayed fears of an Albigensian ultimate solution to the population problem.)

Another argument runs as follows: These were barbarous times. One must expect barbarous practises. Torture and burnings at the stake were also commonplace in various Protestant hegemonies, particularly in Calvinism (Servetius for example) and in England. This argument is of course pitiable. In its *naïvité* it ignores the fact that the opprobrium of failure is simply spread over the entire Christian community. Catholics can take cold comfort in the realization that other Christians have also spilt blood in the name of religion. It is more than disquieting to realize that Christians of any persuasion lost sight of Christ and the Evangelical principles to the extent that they condoned and sponsored religious persecution.

The Inquisition of course took no cognizance whatsoever of an individual's right to his good conscience. That this right is now vigorously upheld in many Christian circles (at least in principle) is a tribute to the modern popes — especially Pope John XXIII and his great encyclical letters — and the theologians and leaders of almost all denominations. Civilization is taking effect. The fact that it took so many centuries to come is one of the great tragedies of the human race and of Christianity. Grant for a moment the total weight of the various arguments excusing, minimizing, or defending the Inquisition within the historical processes and limitations of the epoch. Nevertheless, the Catholic and Christian conscience remains sorely troubled. The magnitude of the evil reaches the proportion of a mystery of Faith, as Christ, bleeding in His Mystical Body, is extended into history.

The origin, growth, and culmination of the Inquisition in the Sixteenth Century, with its systems of espionage, thought-control, and the expulsion of the Jews and Moriscos from Spain is echoed in the tones of cosmic tragedy by modern history. I refer to the rise of Hitler and his Third Reich in Germany. Here certain eloquent historians can accumulate fact after fact showing how the reasonable leaders in Germany and elsewhere were duped by Hitler's apparent prosperity and righting of previous wrongs. These historians point to the enormous popular vote against Hitler in 1933. But the fact remains that Hitler came to power by the aid of people; he also executed his theories with the co-operation of people. In addition to unleashing a horrible war, he caused the murder of many millions of Jews — one of the transcendental events in human history. At the crucial moments, responsible elements abdicated. A prince of the Church snapped out the Nazi salute. Anti-Semitism flourished in the Austrian Christian Social party and heavily Catholic Vienna.[21] As in the case with the Inquisition, the sensitive Christian conscience can contemplate these events only with the deepest sense of tragedy.

Unfortunately the effects of the Inquisition were lasting. So lasting, in fact, that they have not entirely departed from the face of the Church. The Inquisition lives on in muted form in the Holy Office and the Index — both very obviously unpopular with large segments of Catholic clerical and lay intellectuals. The effects of the Inquisition also live on in certain narrow, inquisitorial mentalities of a regional nature, as well as in certain facets of the external governing system of the Church. Thus, our age has witnessed the attempts of some

23

prelates to inflict their own narrow orthodoxy on the consensus of the entire Church.[22]

The Inquisition has also unfortunately survived in a mutated form in Spain. (This point will be developed in Chapter V.) Paradoxically, the "Catholic Kings" originally established the Inquisition as a direct arm of their royal power to rid the faith of contamination with impurities imported from Africa and the Near East — and thus aid the establishment of their national state. Yet it is possible that Spain's long contact with various Arabic peoples (some of whom were unquestionably limited in civilizing experience but well-schooled in the arts of cruelty, deceit, and torture) explains why the institution flourished with such vigor on the Peninsula.

3. *Some Sixteenth Century Erasmista Controversies*

In the sixteenth century in Spain the Inquisition was of course alerted against the doctrines of the Reformation. But these had a short life. Of much more significance to literature and thought was the part that the institution played in the so-called *erasmista* movement.

Desiderius Erasmus of Rotterdam had become the most powerful figure in European learning in the first decade of the sixteenth century. Throughout his career he projected his Christian-humanistic synthesis in sharp and bitter controversy against the weaknesses and abuses of the clergy and the decline of the interior spirit of Christianity. His powerful criticism was the most penetrating, caustic and intelligent heard up to that time. His critical spirit, however, was in no way disloyal to the Church and he continued to enjoy the intimate friendship of persons such as St. Thomas More of England, the Dutch Pope Adrian VI, and Pope Paul III, one of the leaders of the Counter-Reformation, who wished to make him a Cardinal. Up until recently it was almost impossible to find Catholic bibliographical material on Erasmus that did not treat him as suspect or heterodox. Today, thanks to a more enlightened scholarship and greater good-will, that attitude has been almost completely reversed. Erasmus has become "rehabilitated" and is now considered one of the great lights of the Church. This fact, of course, makes the entire *erasmista* controversy in Spain look slightly ridiculous. An added irony is the fact that some of the initial, solid, re-evaluation of Erasmus was done by competent Spanish scholars.[23]

The ideas and works of Erasmus found immediate fertile ground in Spain and just as immediately became suspect in official, inquisitorial circles. In 1527 a *junta* in Valladolid was held against some of his writings. The presiding officials were among the leading inquisitors, but the convocation was suspended shortly with no findings, because of an outbreak of the plague. Actually, a finding would have been most difficult, because opinion within the *junta* was violently divided. Many of the officials were themselves humanists and favored Erasmus' cause.[24] More or less vindicated in Spain, Erasmus fared poorly in France. On Dec. 17, 1527, thirty-two of his propositions were condemned by the Sorbonne after Natividad Bedda accused the humanist of being the ultimate cause of Lutheranism.[25] The absurdity of this charge is historically proved by Erasmus' many works refuting Luther's doctrines. Later, some of Erasmus' works were put on the Index.

Many of the followers of Erasmus were persecuted for adherence to his doctrines. To name but a few: Juan de Vergara, the eminent humanist and secretary to the Archbishop of Toledo, was summoned before the Inquisition and imprisoned in 1533 for favoring Erasmus.[26] Juan's brother, Francisco de Vergara, author of the first Greek grammar in Spanish, was likewise imprisoned.[27] Fray Alfonso de Virués, the favorite preacher to Charles V and translator of the eleven *Coloquies* of Erasmus, was incarcerated in 1533 for four years for favoring the doctrines of the celebrated Dutchman.[28] In 1537 the venerable theologian and scholar Pedro de Lerma was imprisoned and forced to recant sermons which he had based on the writings of Erasmus.[29] Other eminent followers of Erasmus who were persecuted were Juan de Mal Lara and Antonio Nebrija, the noted grammarian.[30]

The *erasmistas* were not alone in incurring the displeasure of the sixteenth century inquisitors. On guard against any and all innovations which, in their opinion, seemed to be heterodox, they hounded the mystics and the religious reformers. Ignatius of Loyola was imprisoned twice.[31] Santa Teresa was denounced and her *Concepts of Divine Love* proscribed.[32] Fray Luís de León, as is well known, was incarcerated on trumped-up denunciations engineered by his enemies and rivals; St. John of the Cross was harassed and imprisoned. In fact, there is hardly a name among the great galaxy of Spain's Renaissance writers, intellectuals, and religious leaders, etc. who was not at some time harassed or imprisoned by the Inquisition.

Actually, the Inquisition did not constitute precisely the same situation that was to attract the anticlerical spirit in the nineteenth and twentieth centuries — although there are striking parallels and the socio-intellectual results were much the same. In the modern historical framework, anticlericalism is directed (as I have alluded) against interference of the clergy in public affairs and more specifically (as we shall see in detail) against the desire to establish a single predetermined opinion in matters of public policy and administration. In the inquisitorial context the emphasis was inverted and matters of conscience and opinion were constituted as public policy. Also, in the more modern context, many of the anticlerical writers lost patience with the Church; in the sixteenth century the victims of the Inquisition were frequently the most illustrious and devoted children of the Church in Spain's greatest age.

Despite the pressure from the inquisitors, men of letters did not cease to inveigh against what they considered to be the defects of Christian society. The Valdés brothers, for example, both *erasmistas*, attacked the Inquisition by indirection in their works, some of which are also strongly critical of conditions in Christian society in general. Alfonso, in the introduction to his *Diálogo de Lactantio,* writes with as much critical acumen as a twentieth century author (such as Bernanos, whom he strongly resembles in this context). He carefully distinguishes between his objection to abuses and his own loyalty to the Church. "It is my desire," he writes, "that my words be able to reach all intelligent, real Christians. Should there be any error in this *Dialogue*, . . . let the blame be laid to my ignorance . . . for I submit entirely to the Holy Church, which I confess as my Mother."[33] He then makes a similar distinction between the legitimacy of some of Luther's criticism and the actual heresy (from the Catholic point of view): "If you had corrected the things that he had at first rightly pointed out, perhaps he might never have come to the writing of his later heresies."[34] With his position toward the Church firmly and clearly established Alfonso de Valdés then attacks, in a vein similar to Erasmus, all manner of abuses (but with the unfortunate and dubious political bias of attributing the sack of Rome in 1527 to the scourge of Divine Providence). He considers "the sale of offices, benefices, *bulas,* indulgences, and dispensations" to be "a scandal to the Christian faith." He finds money too intimately linked to the administration of the sacraments of Christ, "who praises poverty and invites us, with his perfect example, to follow." Similarly, he resents the Church's greater partiality to the rich than to the poor. Like Erasmus, he felt that too much emphasis was being placed on externals. "A person who submerges his soul in the virtues which Christ commanded . . . does a better and truer service to God than one who builds a church, even though such a church were built of gold and as big as the Cathedral of Toledo." Alfonso also had comments to make on clerical sexual laxity. Warrior churchmen he also found hard to take. But false relics he singled out for special scorn. "If St. Christopher's shoes were preserved in a golden reliquary in one part of a church, and the Blessed Sacrament (to which any comparison would be less than useless), in another, we would find the faithful in prayer in front of the shoes."[35]

In a letter to the papal nuncio, the famous Baldassare Castiglione, Alfonso de Valdés reiterated that his denunciations were against the abuses which impede the flourishing of Christian life. On the political level he made the same distinction that Catholics in the nineteenth century had to make when fighting on the side of the *risorgimento*: "I could not avoid criticizing the Pope, whom I revere and respect as much as any good, faithful Christian."[36] The famous Castiglione, however, while justly refusing to accept Valdés' explanation for the sack of Rome, was either unwilling or incapable of understanding the distinction drawn between respect for religion and criticism of its ministers. After having read the *Dialogue* thoughtfully several times he found that it contained "many impious thoughts totally contrary to the constitutions of the Church."[37] Likewise he was unable to accept Valdés' declaration that criticism is not the same as Lutheranism. "It suits your disposition to lutheranize and introduce novelty into the Christian Religion."[38] The author of the famous *Courtier* is unable to keep the discussion on the high level of a Renaissance disputation. He seems to shake with rage and descends to the most violent personal invective, thus showing an aspect of personality that is rather unexpected and unknown in this celebrated Renaissance author:

You were simply born bad. And you were formed by nature to such perverse condition that you can't avoid speaking bad and evil things, obedient to your instinct. Evil inhabits your heart. I have seen it in you without your opening your mouth. I have seen it written in the pallor of your pestilent face and in your poisonous eyes and in your false smirks . . . You are an impudent, damnable sacrilege of a man! How can you dare raise your eyes? How can you dare show yourself among respectable men? . . . Don't you fear that God will send down fire from heaven, that the most bizarre spirits inhabiting the depths of the abyss are going to carry you out of this world? Get ready, for divine justice will not leave such abominable sins unpunished. Believe me, your malicious eyes will be dug out of your head by crows . . . and your evil tongue . . . will be chewed by dogs.[39]

Castiglione understood well Valdés' veiled references to the Inquisition and brandished the long arm of that institution. An *auto da fe* would soon be prepared for Alfonso; and he would meet his death dressed in a "San Benito," a sort of clerical garb worn by the condemned on which were painted devils being devoured by flames.

The Lord Inquisitors will not be lacking in their office in your regard —the very ones whom you, in the beginning of your dialogue, called superstitious pharisees, saying that you knew in advance how they would judge your work. I know that they will make a most accurate judgement of you . . . In the last part of your dialogue you called upon the Archdeacon to go to San Benito and present your thoughts on religion. I think here is an indication that a San Benito will come to you; so dressed you will end your life . . . With your obstinacy you prepare the way for punishment, nor do you show any purpose of amendment that would suggest mercy.[40]

This dispute took place in 1528. In 1529 Alfonso left Spain in the retinue of Charles V, in his capacity of the latter's secretary, for the diet of Augsburg. He died in Vienna soon afterwards, a victim of the plague. His brother, Juan, the author of the famous *Diálogo de la Lengua,* departed for Italy where he became a member of the Waldensian sect and remained until his death. Thus, both brothers escaped the processes of the Inquisition which opened against them in Spain in 1531 and against various examples of their work, such as the *Lactantio* and the *Diálogo de Mercurio y Carón* by Alfonso, and the *Diálogo de la Doctrina Cristiana,* by Juan. In the nineteenth century, the arch-conservative critic Menéndez Pelayo evaluated Alfonso as being most likely a heretic in disguise and more *erasmista* than Erasmus himself. He speaks of Castiglione, in connection with the letter cited above, as "a man of most gentle genius, an excellent Latin poet, a friend of Bembo and of Navagiero, an artist with both a heart and a head, and as cultured and gallant a cortesan as the ideal model that he etched in his beautiful book."[41]

Another writer who spoke out against the Inquisition was the famous Francisco Sánchez, known as "el Brocense," (1523-1600). He is a most interesting and pitiful case. An *erasmista* and humanist, he was one of the best classical scholars of his day. He was also a man of piety and obvious loyalty to the Church. The father of twelve children, he was reported to have been seen frequently at Mass. "El Brocense," however, had several idiosyncracies that eventually got him in trouble with the sentries of sixteenth century thought-control. One was the delight he took in shocking his audiences, particularly by paradoxes and overstatements that did not literally conform to the official thought of the day.[42] One anonymous denunciation at an inquisitorial hearing in 1593 reads as follows: "I have heard many references to his paradoxical opinions . . . he has a personality always inclined toward the opposite of the commonly held opinion."[43] It was probably his direct and implied criticism of the Inquisition, however, which merited him the most displeasure. The anonymous declaration continued:

Item: the said *maestro* Francisco Sánchez was in the habit of saying that neither the jurists nor theologians of Salamanca knew anything, and that he could teach them all theology; he said he had written a theological work and had sent it to Italy to be printed because there was no one there who could understand it.[44]

The inquisitors duly noted that "the proposition manifests a very great temerity and argues that the person who made it must be suffering from the sin of pride."[45] One Juan Pérez, a student, went on record with other quotes from the master's lectures and conferences:

Speaking of Erasmus the said master Francisco said, "anyone who speaks ill of Erasmus is either a friar or an ass" . . . and the said master added that if there were no friars in the world the works of Erasmus would have been considered good and nothing forbidden would have been found in them.[46]

In rebuttal to this the inquisitors indignantly replied that: "The proposition is a great temerity; nay more, it is an error against our faith to the extent that it approves the errors of Erasmus which the Church has condemned."[47] The propositions are among several others of little import dealing with biblical details and the artistic representation of biblical subjects.

"El Brocense," who had appeared as a witness for Fray Luis de León in 1573, was summoned to testify in his own defense in 1584. He was released with the warning that "in this and all the other matters he deserved to be reprimanded and punished for having flaunted personal opinions in areas outside his competence."[48] Aubrey Bell remarks that it was probably the scholar's friendship with Pedro Portocarrero, Bishop of Cordoba, Calahorra, and Cuenca, and later Inquisitor General from 1594-1600, which saved him from more serious trouble at this time. Portocarrero died September 20, 1600. Five days later "el Brocense's" books were seized and he was again instructed to appear before the Inquisition at Valladolid. A long, detailed process was instituted; the treatise, *De los Errores de Porfirio,* was included among his suspect work; he was put under house arrest at the home of his son. As in the case of Alfonso de Valdés, death relieved "el Brocense" from further harassment. Knowing that his end was near he wrote a long letter, ringing with sincerity, to the Inquisitor. He recanted no errors for he had none to recant. He reiterated his loyalty and devotion to Christ's Church and asked that his books be printed in benefice for his children. He also requested burial according to the dignity of his office and the holding of the customary honors for him at his University at Salamanca. Evidently this request was not honored. His burial was relatively unattended and his passing was overshadowed by a pall of disgrace and disfavor.[49]

The cases of the Valdés brothers and of "el Brocense" are particularly fascinating both for their human interest and for the light they shed on the inquisitorial mentality and self-righteous thought-control. Of course there were many other cases, such as the well-known condemnation and imprisonment of Fray Luis de León, to which I have already alluded. Another was the case against Pablo de Céspedes (1538-1608), the Cordoban humanist and writer on esthetic problems. He was one of the lesser figures who spoke against the Inquisition. He was tried in Valladolid for having allowed a treatise by him to appear among the collected papers of Archbishop Carranza. The treatise contained material derogatory of the Inquisition and of the Inquisitor General.[50]

Parallel to these tendencies critical of the religio-political situation, the more general spirit of criticism and satire continued to exist. Judging from the frequent, varied nature of such manifestations in the sixteenth century, the spirit seems by this time to have become rooted as a commonplace among

31

the psychological manifestations of the Spanish temperament. In the drama before Lope, for example, Juan del Encina, himself a cleric, in his *Égloga de Cristino y Febea*, has as his protagonist a shepherd who has become an *ermitaño* and later had hung up his garb at the imperation of the god of love, who caused him to be tempted by the beauty of a nymph.[51] The *ermitaño,* or hermit, represented a type of person who lived a solitary life, withdrawn from the pleasures of the world, often spending long hours in ascetic practises and not usually ordained. Hence the tone of this delightful *égloga* is at once another plea in favor of Renaissance humanism and a mild criticism against a too rigorously ascetic interpretation of life. The humanistic note, however, was frequently combined with caustic satire in other contexts. The *argumento* of Gil Vicente's *Comedia Rubena* runs as follows:

> In the land of Campos, way off in Castilla
> There lived an abbott; he had his house there.
> And a daughter he had; much he loved her,
> She was passing fair, indeed a great wonder.
>
> A young cleric who served the abbot
> Fell in love with the girl:
> With him she had quite a whirl
> That really should never have started.
>
> Her name was Rubena.
> She was pregnant; the young
> Cleric left town in a hurry . . .[52]

Similar incidents can be found in the plays of Lucas Fernández and Torres Naharro. Finally — to mention another deeply Spanish *genre* — every one who has laughed (and cried) at the plights and pranks of Lazarillo de Tormes is familiar with the author's uncomplimentary, caustic, and devastatingly satiric treatment of the priest, the Mercedarian friar, and the seller of indulgences (*budero*). History, of course, is sad witness of the types the author satirized — a fact born out by the Council of Trent which tried to legislate a more respectable life for the clergy and a less offensive method of collecting money in connection with pious practises.

It would be a mistake to think, however, that either these critical sentiments or the religio-political criticism fomented by the Inquisition (despite its towering importance), or the two combined, set the entire tone of Spanish religious life in the sixteenth century. A glance at the array of mystical writers, unique in Spain, should be sufficient proof to the contrary. The mystics and many others loved God and loved the Church as a manifestation of God among men. For the most part they patiently suffered the lashes of the Inquisition. Indeed, for a time the liberal *erasmista* spirit penetrated the fiery portals of the Inquisition and mitigated its horror. Evidently certain of the early humanists felt that if they had the administration in their own hands they could keep the bad effects at a minimum. Thus, there were such figures as Pedro Portocarrero, the protector of "el Brocense," the Archbishop Manrique, and the professors at Alcalá who helped save Erasmus from condemnation at the *junta* at Valladolid. Many years later, in the late nineteenth century, the arch traditionalist critic, Menéndez Pelayo, stated categorically that the Inquisition was "very tolerant."[53] He refers scornfully to the liberal inquisitors as "a whole conclave of *erasmistas.*"[54] Furthermore, Gerald Brenan notes in his book *The Spanish Labyrinth* that during this era an amazing harmony existed in the relationships between the lower classes of society and the rural or poorer clergy who supported the people against the encroachments of the upper classes and the State.[55]

4. *Toward the Modern Context: Other Developments in Later Centuries*

In the literature of the later Golden Age, controversies involving prominent men of letters cease, for the most part. The towering figures of this era were too closely associated with the solidified concept of Spanish "theocracy" to admit any intrusion of a strong anticlerical spirit. Cervantes has been pointed out as a notable exception, especially by the distinguished critic Américo Castro in his famous study *El Pen-*

samiento de Cervantes (*The Thought of Cervantes*). In this work Castro developed the idea that Cervantes' *Don Quijote* and other works were deeply impregnated with thinly disguised *erasmismo* and other heterodox positions. Cervantes, Castro claims, was a sort of hypocrite who dissimulated his real beliefs to escape the claws of the Inquisition. I will have to bypass this interesting and controversial idea. Suffice it to say here, that I do not agree with Castro. A large number of the world's greatest cervantine scholars also disgree with him, and Castro himself is retreating from this position in his more recent work, particularly his *Hacia Cervantes* (*Toward Cervantes*).

If anticlerical controversies are lacking in the Baroque era, the popular spirit of satire and criticism (initiated by Juan Ruiz) continues in the full flowering of the picaresque novel. Mateo Alemán, alerted by the furor which the *Lazarillo* had encountered with the inquisitors, made a pretense of enshrining the adventures of his *pícaro* amid much moralizing. Anyone who reads between the lines of the *Guzmán,* however, cannot fail to note the caustic satire; for example, the treatment of the Italian Cardinal in Book II, Chapter VII. Quevedo, however, with his massive sardonic approach, paints in bold strokes the "card-sharping" hermit among the types of the age. My strong predilection for Quevedo makes it impossible to refrain from quoting some of this scene:

We bumped into a hermit riding on an ass. His beard was so long that it dragged in the mud. He was withered, dressed in a spotted habit . . . and told his beads on balls of woods so large that every Hail Mary sounded like a falling log.

When they arrived at the inn the hermit said:

Let's have a little fun; idleness is the mother of vice. Let's play *avemarias*. So saying he slipped a pack of cards from his sleeve. I was on my guard and suggested other games. The hermit, not wanting to be a spoil-sport agreed. He said he had some money from the vigil oils that amounted to two hundred *reales*. I confess that I had thoughts of becoming a bit of a coin collector and sucking him dry. But the best laid plans so oft go awry. The game went on to the bitter end. The

good hermit said he didn't know it and asked us to teach it to him
. . . I ate my nails and the friar kept his own busy relieving me of
my money.[56]

With the coming of the eighteenth century the messianic
re-embodiment of the medieval theocratic concept in the Renaissance national state of Charles and Philip had passed. The increasing absolutism of the Bourbons was directed toward secular problems of centralization. The State, which remained
Catholic, continued to rely on the Church for the furtherance
of its own ends. Parallel with this development was the growth
of a legitimate secular spirit in the realm of the mind. The
ideas were imbibed particularly from the eighteenth century
French enlightenment and, to some extent, from England and
Italy. The history of political events in early eighteenth century Spain abounds in efforts made to spread these ideas and
the measures exerted to prevent them.[57] As is well known, the
century produced few writers of major importance who exhibited the characteristic literary savor which had come to be
known as typically Spanish. Rather, the period is marked by
the ideological struggle with new ideas.

Not all the thinkers who were influenced by the enlightenment absorbed only those ideas which could be interpreted
as inimical to religion and Christianity. One of the most brilliant men of the age was Padre Feijóo, a Benedictine monk.
He was completely orthodox and had read deeply in the French
tradition. In his monumental *Teatro Crítico* (*Critical Essays on
Universal Topics*) he displayed remarkably advanced ideas,
on such subjects, for example, as the rights of women and
the stupidity of false relics. He was, of course, subjected to
heavy criticism throughout his long career and was the object
of a galaxy of *impugnadores* and *anticríticos*. Menéndez
Pelayo was very restrained and reluctant to praise him too
highly.

The Inquisition continued on with its *autos da fe* in its effort to rid Spain of heterodox impurity. Usually, however, the
persons who were now being burned were relatively unknown

recalcitrants. A few examples taken from the year 1724 will illustrate the activities of this institution:

Beatriz de León y Contreras, a native resident of the area of this Court. A widow, fifty-eight years old. Died in prison. It was decreed that she be represented in the *auto* in the form of a statue, clothed in a "San Benito" with a crown of flames. Her bones were exhumed and burned with the statue. She was a negative, convinced, proselytizing Jewish heretic.

Juan López, a native of the city of Berganza in the realm of Portugal, and a resident of the area of this Court. Widower. Occupation: silk-weaver and keeper of a tobacco stand. Age: eighty years. Reconciled for Jewish tendencies in the Inquisition of Coimbra of said realm, in the year 1667. He was condemned to go out to the *auto* in a "San Benito" and a crown of flames for the crime of being a relapsed, convinced, proselytizing Jewish heretic. His person was handed over to the Legal Power and the secular arm. Having become penitent, he was strangled and his body burned.

Ana Núñez Márquez, a native resident of the area of this Court. Occupation: teacher of girls. Unmarried. Fifty-five years of age. She was condemned to go out to the *auto* in a "San Benito" and crown of flames for the crime of being a negative, convinced, proselytizing Jewish heretic. Her person was handed over to the Legal Power and the secular arm. Having become converted on the way to the pyre, she was strangled and her body burned.

Manuel Custodio de Soto y Herrera (alias Manuel de Guzmán Castro y Herrera), a native of the city of Granada, stepson of Francisco de Robles, and a resident of the area of this Court. Bachelor. No occupation. Nineteen years of age. He was condemned to go out to the *auto* dressed in a "San Benito" and crown of flames for the crime of being a proselytizing, negative, and convinced Jewish heretic. Impertinent and tenacious of his errors and blasphemously heretical. Maintaining himself so and not wishing to recant his body was tied to a stake and he was burned alive.[58]

Gerald Brenan notes that as time passed the Inquisition gradually "ceased to inspire terror but continued to exert great political power."[59] Examples of this religio-political pressure exerted in sustained efforts to superimpose conformity are not wanting, for churchmen continued to look upon the medieval inquisitional mechanism as a solution for modern problems. Having had few real ideological challenges during the seventeenth century, the tribunal's activities were now

focussed upon the Spanish representatives of the French influence. There were a number of important cases involving
men of letters: the naturalist, José Clavigo y Fajardo, was denounced for "philosophism"; Benito Bails, a noted mathematician, suffered a similar experience.[60] Perhaps the most celebrated writers of the day to be involved in processes were the
poets Tomás de Iriarte and Samaniego. They, too, were guilty
of philosophism. Menéndez Pelayo quotes examples of their
fables and satirical writings which flow from their encounters
with the inquisitors. The poetry is acridly anticlerical and
strongly indicative of personal irritation.[61]

In addition to this anticlericalism, emerging now in the
strict sense, the more general spirit of criticism continued. In
the late years of the century Leandro F. de Moratín, in his
El sí de las niñas (*The Young Girl's Marriage Promise*) contributed a work which certainly would not be classed as strictly
anticlerical. Yet, as a comedy of manners, it extends implied
criticism of unwholesome consequences of a socio-religious
practise in the nation. It criticizes marriages arranged — not in
heaven, but in a conventual atmosphere. Also, the play being
a comedy, it is obvious that some of the nuns' names were
assigned in a spirit of slightly irreverent humor.

The eighteenth century also saw the birth in a modern context of economic problems which were to be the plague of
the nineteenth century and enter into the formation of clerical
and anticlerical patterns in the twentieth century. The most
acute problems were in the agrarian area. The famous Jovellanos busied himself with his noted study on the agrarian
question at the same time that he was functioning as a most
effective adjunct of the Inquisition in vigorous examination of
suspect or heterodox books.[62]

The nineteenth century saw the end of the Inquisition.
Napoleon suppressed it in 1808. In the next fifteen years it
underwent several abolitions and revivals attendant upon rapid
changes in momentarily ascendant liberal and conservative

ideologies. All chances of its revival *per se* ended in 1834 when Queen Cristina reluctantly allied herself with the moderates.

Although the Inquisition had ended, its "mental formality" had by no means died. Cristina's move toward the left was dictated by the necessities engendered by the Carlist controversy. Ferdinand VII, it will be recalled, had died and left the throne to his infant daughter; Cristina, his queen, became regent. However, Ferdinand's brother, Carlos, claimed the throne — hence the Carlist controversy. But the essence of this very violent dispute was much deeper. The exterior political issues merely served as a focal point through which was drawn a line dividing into bitterly opposed camps the forces of moderates and liberals and reactionary conservatives. Around the standard of the Carlists gravitated those forces which had looked upon the Inquisition as a norm of political and religious action. Cristina had no other choice than to follow the moderates. The Carlists wanted to root out all liberalism and reestablish the Inquisition. Their ranks were swelled by many bishops, secular priests, and religious orders. A civil war began which lasted seven years. The conclusion of hostilities in 1840 did not see the end of the controversy. There were major uprisings in 1845, 1855, and 1873 and the short-lived liberal Republic was unable to cope with Carlist pressure. Indeed the Carlists have never died in Spain. Their spirit moved into the twentieth century and found expression in virulent, arch-reactionary newspapers. The Carlists still have a claimant to the throne in the person of a certain French-born Don Carlos, the husband of Princess Irene of the Netherlands. At past midpoint twentieth century the Carlists still represent a potent force. Up until the present writing they have been loyal to the present regime.[63]

Carlism in the nineteenth century was a political expression of the attempt to apply medieval solutions to contemporary problems, or, to express the same idea in historical terms, "to use against liberalism the same weapons that Philip II had used against Protestantism."[64] The clerical attitude of mind, which is so often encountered in controversies over liberal

ideas in the twentieth century, is exhibited in clear foreshadow-
ing in the alignments on the legitimacy of Don Carlos' claim.
Conversely, those of us who have been nurtured on the thought
that the mentality of the generation of '98 was formed entirely
under the shadow of loss of empire can listen with profit to
Unamuno. He wrote, "My civil conscience dates from the day
in which twenty bombs were laid in Bilbao, my native city,
by the absolutists of Don Carlos de Borbón. Fifty years have
passed since then."[65] Unamuno undoubtedly speaks for others
of his generation.

Despite the extreme antagonisms generated by the Carlist
question, anticlericalism, in the more exact meaning of the
word, does not emerge into the exuberant growth in *belles
lettres* that it found in the twentieth century. A steady strength-
ening of the tendency can be noted, however. Emilio Castelar
(1832-1899) provides a most interesting case in point. He had
been formed in the liberal humanitarian tradition of Kraus and
was an executive of the Republic of 1873. Therefore it is not
surprising to find certain aspects of his thought that were de-
cidedly left-of-center — a fact which is evident in his cor-
respondence which reveals cordial contact with practically every
European non-conformist and rebel of his day. Today he is
remembered as a competent and powerful orator. Among his
many *discursos* there is one which is of special interest for this
study. It will be seen that a strong dose of anticlericalism in-
termingles with the author's liberal political views on the structure of the modern state — a situation which will be seen
duplicated again and again in many of the major writers who
will be examined. The *discurso* in question was delivered at the
Cortes on April 12, 1869 in a rebuttal to ideas that had been
advanced by a priest named Vicente Manterola. Judging by
Castelar's references, the priest had gone on record solidly in
favor of tradition and the old regime. In his refutation Castelar
first reiterated a basic tolerant atitude: "I have attacked no
belief, I have attacked no religious practices, I have attacked
no dogma." But he goes on to a clarification of his principles
with regard to Church and the clergy in the realm of politics.

"I did say that the Catholic Church, organized the way you organize it, organized as a function of the State, can only bring us great unrest and great conflicts." He continues with a description of the Church in the Spanish context of his day:

The Catholic Church with its ideal of authority, with its ideal of infallibility, with its ambition to extend these ideals over all peoples, in the organism of free states, is unable to be less than a cause of continual unrest to all consciences, a cause of constant threat to all rights.

Castelar then goes on to point out that Manterola's own words are proof of his uncompromising attitude:

His speech, absolutely every word of it, is nothing more than a complete confirmation of my words: whatever I have said, Señor Manterola has demonstrated in detail. For example, did he not say that the doctrine of national sovreignty, expressed in most modest terms by the commission, is inadmissible since the clergy recognizes no other dogma that the sovreignty of the Church,

The author then embellishes his argument by citing the lack of religious spirit and devout observation of Sunday among the "slave nations," namely Spain and France. He finds the true religious spirit in the "free nations," England and Switzerland, and speaks glowingly of "Sunday celebrated with extraordinary severity, a severity which is astonishing" —a rather remarkable Puritan sympathy for a Spaniard. He scores tellingly when he underlines the danger of supporting or enforcing matters of religious conviction or observance by recourse to the power of the state. Such a policy, he maintains, is dangerous and ultimately subject to the whim of governments. Did not Henry VIII overnight change the official religion of England from Catholicism to Protestantism? Did not the French revolutionaries impose for a time the cult of the goddess of reason? He concludes this section of the discourse with the following argument.

Thus, Señor Manterola had absolutely no right to demand — in the name of Catholicism, in the name of Christianity, in the name of a religious idea — the coercive force, the coercive support of the State. This would be a great step backward, because, Gentlemen, we either believe in religion because our conscience tells us to, or we don't believe in religion because our conscience tells us to. If we believe in religion because our conscience tells us to, the protection of the State is useless — completely useless. If we do not believe in religion because our conscience so dictates, it would be a vain effort for the State to impose belief upon us.

After this thought provoking passage the remainder of the discourse is devoted to polemics with Manterola concerning the vitality and numerical strength of Catholicism in areas such as the United States, England, and the Orient. He concludes by citing some of the more unsavory examples of Catholic intolerance in history. Upon finishing his speech an editor's note reads: "Frenetic and prolonged aplause. Members from all sides of the chamber approached Señor Castelar to give him warm words of congratulation."[66] Two days later Castelar asked for a few additional moments to provide documentation for instances of Catholic intolerance that he had previously cited.

In this very interesting debate, many elements of the twentieth century anticlerical controversy are foreshadowed in miniature. On the one side was the liberal exponent of the secularist concept of government, which, emerging in the Latin countries in the nineteenth century, collided with the old order represented by the "confessional state" (a concept which will be fully treated in the next chapter). Furthermore, the author was an enthusiast for foreign ideas and customs, a sure sign of the Spanish iconoclast. Finally, he was anticlerical, both in the strict sense, as regards the specific political issue, and in the extended sense in that he surrounded the nucleus of his argument with the more general criticisms which at times are pertinent to the specific issue and at times are not. In many ways, therefore, he was a prototype of the modern anticlericals. On the other side was Manterola, the priest, also a prototype He undoubtedly reflected the majority view of the other clerics seated in the chamber and spoke for them. He represented the old order and was not likely to be convinced by his opponent's eloquence. He was obviously unshakable in the position which the orator ascribed to him, namely that the new governmental concept under discussion was "inadmissible." One is forcefully

41

reminded of another controversy, sixty-two years later, when the Cardinal Primate of Toledo disappointed liberal Catholic political leaders and wrote a pastoral letter rallying opinion against the newly born Second Republic which was working upon the mild reforms of the First Draft of the New Constitution. (The controversy will be examined in the next chapter.) Castelar was speaking in the second half of the nineteenth century. His ideas must have seemed shockingly advanced, for example his argument concerning the futility of coercing belief and the inviolability of conscience. This argument appears constantly in the anticlerical writings of the twentieth century. Yet it is nothing more than the "pluralistic" concept of our own time which is in substatial agreement with the thought of contemporary Catholic theologians, philosophers, and political scientists, such as John Courtney Murray, S.J., Jacques Maritain, and Conrad Bonacina. In succeeding chapters I intend to examine this question in order to obtain, from a Catholic point of view, a balanced interpretation of the anticlerical controversy.

On the other hand, Castelar's thought lacks some of the precision of the contemporary pluralists. For example, his assessment of Catholic authority is too sweeping. He fails to distinguish between authority in religious matters as expounded in traditional Catholic teaching and that same authority extended as a power of the state in a particular historical setting. Here his grasp of the dubious theology of the confessional state is as limited by time and space as the understanding of the theologians who expounded that doctrine. Later writers, such as Pérez Galdós, Unamuno, Ortega y Gasset, Arturo Barea, and Ramón Sender all are in varying degrees aware that the Church's authoritarian discipline and dogma—in the abstract—are internal to her own organization. Explicitly or implicitly they limit their objections, at times begrudgingly, to the demand for exclusive external favor and support for the Catholic formula. Whether he realized it or not, Castelar's too facile evaluation of authoritarianism in Catholicism would vitiate any participation of the Church in the free, pluralistic society which he envisioned. Only writers such as Blasco Ibáñez and

Rafael Alberti in his communist period, attack Catholicism (and all religion) in its vitals. Castelar's overall high moral tone excludes him from such company. He was a pioneer. He scaled the heights and saw into the future. But his vision remained of necessity somewhat clouded.

Finally, it is not at all unlikely that Castelar furnished some of the ammunition of the "big guns" of anticlericalism in the twentieth century. For example, he draws an overgeneralized distinction between contributions to social progress and social inertia made respectively, supposedly as a result of differing religious mentalities, by the Indo-european and Semitic peoples. This sounds suspiciously like Pío Baroja, who undoubtedly devoured Castelar in his youth.

I have yielded to the tantalizing temptation to anticipate slightly my further developments. Now I must return to the development of the other threads weaving toward the all-important twentieth century pattern.

Anticlericalism can be found in the works and activities of other literary figures of this era. Pedro Antonio Alarcón as a young man directed for a time the anticlerical newspaper *El Látigo* (*The Whip*). Later he became a strong traditionalist. Leopoldo Alas (Clarín) put the novel to use in criticism of society that included the clergy. Similar in many ways to Pérez Galdós, he presents in *La Regenta* a priest, Fermín de Paz, whose vocation is insincere, who falls into sinful love, and who abuses his power over consciences. Although this critical emphasis is not directed specifically against clerical pressure in political areas, the interior shortcomings are concomitant with what Alas considered to be strong clerical opposition to modern progress and the advancement of Spain. José Echegaray is another late nineteenth century writer tinged with anticlericalism. A noted economist, politician, road builder, and engineer, he thus possessed personally the secular and scientific skills with which the anticlerical authors (as shall be seen) frequently endowed their protagonists. Echegaray addressed himself to the problem of tolerance in *La Muerte en los Labios* (*Death upon the Lips*) and, more pertinent to our investigation, in *En el Pilar y en la Cruz* (*On the Pillar and on the Cross*) which dealt (unsuccessfully from the theatrical standpoint) with Protestantism under the Renaissance Inquisition. Finally, to mention another *genre,* the noted essayist Ganivet was sharp in his condemnation of clericalism even while asserting the importance of Catholicism in the life blood of Spanish culture.

The more general spirit of criticism also continued in the nineteenth century, particularly in some of the more important novelists. Juan Valera in his most famous work, *Pepita Jiménez,* stresses the idea that love of God need not always find expression in rigorous asceticism. The simple unlettered clergyman of unbending but limited convictions projects an implied generalization. Also, Valera's essay "Los Jesuitas de Puertas Adentro" ("The Jesuits of the Inner Doors") is truly anticlerical. It is found in the collection *A Vuela Pluma* (*The Random Pen*). Armando Palacio Valdés, a sincere Catholic, likewise exhibits a critical attitude toward wrong emphasis on the "vertical" side of life; in *Marta y María* he points out the dangers of false mysticism; in *La Hermana San Sulpicio* he suggests, in passing, that true religious devotion can be found apart from profession in the religious life. Both authors draw unattractive pictures of clerical "types" in the natural development of their plots: the former with the village curate who condemns Pepita's love as basically sinful; the latter in *La Hermana San Sulpicio* with his sketch of the priest who tries to prevent Sanjurjo from meeting Gloria. Of the two authors, Valera was unquestionably more anticlerical.

5. *A Note On Interpretation*

Before proceeding to a study in depth of the anticlerical controversy of the twentieth century and its expression in literature, some explanatory remarks are necessary. First, it should be noted that some of the authors to be examined in later chapters — such as Pérez Galdós and Blasco Ibáñez —

belong aesthetically to the nineteenth century and did much of their writing in the latter part of that epoch. Their pertinence to this study, however, belongs to an historical context that culminates in the twentieth century. Hence they are included in what is essentially a study of a phenomenon of the twentieth century, though the roots extend back to the nineteenth and beyond, as has been seen. Secondly, it should be emphasized that the critical tendencies and unattractive portraits which I have examined so far — and will continue to examine —do not, from my point of view, in any way suggest an all-inclusive evaluation of religion in Spanish life and literature. Unattractive portraits and critical themes can be counteracted in some eras by many motifs of the opposite coloration. On the other hand there can be no denial that anticlericalism has deep roots in Spain. And Spaniards criticize their clergy freely— particularly in the context of, or in the wake of religio-political controversy. It is a strong stream in twentieth century Spanish letters. In the next chapter the climate of opinion in which this spirit evolved will be examined in depth. In the third and fourth chapters the important writings of the most prominent men of letters who reflect this spirit will be treated. The fifth chapter will take note of certain related literary trends which are the aftermath of a bitter Civil War. The sixth chapter will draw some general conclusions and evaluations in the light of Catholic theology and recent developments in the Church.

CHAPTER II

THE CLIMATE OF OPINION

*Modern Thinkers and Institutions in Conflict with
Clerical Interest and Opinions, 1900-1939*

1. *The General Pattern*

The struggle between the old and the new which, we have seen, is reflected in literature, became greatly intensified in twentieth century Spain. The anticlericals continued to be identified with the so-called liberal movements which represented the new. An extremely important element became injected into the scene and contributed to the intensification of the struggle. This was the major and continued national unrest centered largely in the agrarian question and in the social and economic problems normally attendant upon the growth of industrialism within nations. Serious agitation against the status quo was felt in pressure from groups of varying ideologies such as the communists, syndicalists, socialists of motley brands, anarchists, and advanced Catholic movements like the *Federación Nacional de Sindicatos Católicos Libres.* Frequently violent anticlericalism was associated with the extreme leftist organizations and expressed in the radical periodicals, for example, the *Solidaridad Obrera.* On the academic level, democratic and liberal thinkers of various convictions voiced general theories of basic reform combined with republican aspirations. Here too, as will be seen in men of letters, a definite but varying pattern of anticlericalism — usually academic and speculative — was intermingled with the theories. On the right, as frequently happens in history, the wealthier classes sought alignments to protect their traditional interests. Their political expression gravitated to anti-republican, pro-monarchist parties; it was felt that tradition and the *status quo* were best represented in these organizations. Waves of uprisings, church burning (since Carlist times unfortunately associated with social and political protest) strikes and disorders spearheaded by the more violent segments of the left were followed by reaction and retaliation from the right. On the governmental level, differences of a shade of political coloration among parties on both sides (reflecting the traditional Spanish inability to compromise) emasculated most efforts toward fundamental reform. Prime ministers followed each other in and out of office with alarming rapidity. This situation existed both during the Monarchy and the later years of the Second Republic. The governmental changes during the Monarchy frequently represented nothing more than *rotativismo,* shoddy trading between venal leaders of both right and left. Some sincere coalitions were repeatedly tried; they repeatedly failed. A segment of the left would be called to form a government; alliances would be sought from the left side of the right. Similarly, when the right was forming a government, the leaders would seek cooperation from their "righter leaning" colleagues on the left. Support crumbled at the real tests. The center parties, gradually developed from the unstable coalitions, served to mark time, to the increasing dissatisfaction and violent remonstrations of both extremes, as was the case for example after the November 1933 elections during the Second Republic. From 1902 until 1921 there were 23 completely different governments. During the Second Republic there were at least as many.

If the political scene was amazingly complex the underlying pattern was clear: the underprivileged were developing a pattern of protest against exploitation and the forces of established tradition and reaction which cut them off from participating in the fruits of the earth. Their voices and the voices of their champions were being heard; their cause was gathering strength in the various social movements and political organizations, which ranged from violent subversion to the utterances of the most high-minded idealists, often associated with the republican movement. The right was not always blind to the legitimacy of this protest. There were, for example, the liberal reforms in the second decade of the twentieth century under Eduardo Dato, a minister usually associated with the Right. He failed utterly to close the gap between the real and the ideal. Yet the sincerity and far-reaching implication of the reform laws passed during his ministry should refute the charge that there were absolutely no people on the Right who were aware of the legitimate claims of the poor and the workers.

More frequently, however, the voice of the lower classes was feared and misunderstood; political movements to the Right expressed these misapprehensions; their leaders were frequently driven by fear and often by their wealthy and reactionary supporters to contradict absolutely the liberal demands, often with repressive tactics.

The Church in Spain was intimately involved in this conflict. We have seen that through a variety of circumstances a considerable segment of the clergy and clerical opinion in general had favored the forces of conservatism in past centuries. In the twentieth century this tendency continued. Clerical opinion largely gravitated toward the Monarchy because here was found the sure guarantee of the "confessional state." The tensions flowing from this situation were accentuated by the fact that many members of the hierarchy (as in 17th century France) were allied to the nobility and the wealthy classes.

At this point it is necessary to consider briefly the term "confessional state." Here and throughout this study I use it in the sense that the distinguished theologian John Courtney Murray, S.J., has defined and descibed it:

To the historically realized concept and political ideal of *libertas civilis* there has been opposed that concept and political ideal of *libertas civilis* which was realized in the post-Reformation "confessional state," the nation state with predominantly Catholic population, wherein Catholicism was legally recognized as "the religion of the state" and wherein it was considered "logical" as well as politically necessary that legal restrictions should be imposed upon other religions, notably on their propaganda.[1]

Father Murray throws additional light on the concept in the following passages:

The so-called 'confessional state' wherein the freedom of the Church expressed in the concept of "the religion of the state," is represented as entailing what Pius IX called "the logical and juridical consequences of such a situation" in constitutional law . . . In its historical realization it was, in Sturzo's exact judgement, "formalistic and equivocal," especially in its post-Reformation revivals. It initially represented a desperate attempt to rescue out of the wreckage of political and religious disruption some national fragments of religious unity and political order. Later it represented an attempt to heal, by the so-called Union of Throne and Altar, the cleavage between the religious and political order that had opened at the Renaissance . . . On the premises of the confessional state therefore it is conceived to be politically logical that there should devolve on the throne the function of preserving, by the use of governmental power, the unity of the religion at whose altar the whole nation knelt.[2]

Father Murray then focuses his attention on the concept of the confessional state within the Spanish context:

That [the concept] has a status is certainly true; but what status it has is another question around which there is controversy among Catholics . . . The question is not whether the total politico-religious organization of contemporary Spain is an apt means, defensible from a political and religious stand-point, for saving or restoring Catholic unity in Spain and the national values of *Hispanidad* . . . For the theologian, the basic question concerns that situation itself. Is it or is it not the theologically necessary, permanently valid, unalterably ideal realization of Catholic principles on Church-state relationships, in such wise that any constitutional situation which deviates from it can be the object only of "toleration," not of approval in principle — a concession to the exigencies of an "hypothesis," prompted by expediency, and not the embodiment of a "thesis" warranted by theological and political doctrine? In other words, the question is whether the concept of *libertas ecclesiastica* by intrinsic exigence requires political embodiment in the concept of "the religion of the state" with the "logical and jurisdical consequences" that have historically followed from that concept.
Surely the answer must be no.[3]

Another contemporary Catholic thinker of similar views is Conrad Bonacina, a political scientist and formerly a member of the People and Freedom group formed around Don Luigi Sturzo when the latter was in exile from Mussolini's Italy.

He formulates his question in a general way without specific reference to Spain:

Why, it will be asked, does [the Church] always seem to lean so heavily to the Right? How are we to explain the fact that, in modern times, at all events, the Catholic Church has been in almost permanent alliance with Conservative politics? Why, for example, in the political struggles of . . . Europe was Catholicism, by and large, the bulwark of reaction? Why do we so often find it the prop and stay of rotten monarchies, oppressive administrations and inequitable social systems? How comes it that the Liberal and progressive movements . . . for free democratic institutions, for the abolition of privilege, for social and political emancipation, found so little favor in Catholic eyes, that almost every democratic victory was won in the teeth of fierce clerical opposition?[4]

To these questions, Signor Bonacina provides some answers, which also can be applied to the Spanish situation:

It is important to remember that the Church's relations . . . were enormously complicated by the fact that she was herself — I am speaking of course of Catholic countries — an organic and highly privileged part of that very structure of society against which the new democratic spirit was in such violent revolt. Thus in the conflict between the old order and the new, between the aristocratic and semi-absolutistic systems of the *Ancien Regime* and the Democratic Revolution, the Church was not and could not be a disinterested party, since any attack on the established order was bound to include in its objectives some at least of the immunities, and spheres of jurisdiction she enjoyed as a social and political institution. The Church had in fact a vested interest in preserving the *status quo,* and it is idle to pretend that her quarrel with the Democratic movements was due entirely to spiritual causes, and that her dislike of their ideological principles was not a little intensified by the threat they constituted to her material interests. Even had these movements been of a professedly Christian inspiration, it is difficult to see how they could have effected the democratic transformation of society without challenging the Church to readjust her relations with the State on an entirely new and less favored footing; in which case not all the soundness of their principles would have saved them from her anathemas. Never yet has the Catholic Church yielded a temporal position without a struggle.[5]

Clerical opinion, in the first half of twentieth century Spain, certainly, was no more attuned to the type of thinking represented by Signor Bonacina and Father Murray than it had been to the earlier foresighted liberalism of Emilio Castelar.[6]

51

(Indeed, this line of reasoning, which has now received special new emphasis since the reign and teaching of Pope John XXIII, has not yet received wide-spread recognition on the Peninsula.) A patched reform of the *status quo* was, consequently, the most that was tolerated as the Spanish situation worsened in the advancing decades of the twentieth century. But as Signor Bonacina noted:

These forces [of reform] were none the less morally, historically, and sociologically justified in many of the causes they stood for, and their revolutionary challenge to the established order should have evoked from the Church a more creative response than a succession of fiery anathemas interlarded with scholastic homilies on the right order of a Christian Society, resurrected from the text books of an obsolete feudal tradition. Political and civil liberty, free democratic institutions, social and economic justice, the equality of men in natural rights — these broadly speaking were the four head causes for which the forces on the Left . . . were doing battle.[7]

The attitudes which Conrad Bonacina and Father Murray express on these politico-religious questions (and the related problem of the liberty of the individual's conscience) are, of course, found in the thought of other eminent Catholic writers and scholars, among whom may be mentioned John Cogley, Franz Joseph Schoenigh, Emmanuel Mounier, Etienne Gilson, Yves Simon, Father Yves Congar, of the famous review, *La Vie Intellectuelle,* and the encyclical letters of Pope John XXIII, especially *Peace on Earth.*

It was in an atmosphere such as Bonacina describes — the hurling of anathemas interlarded with scholastic homilies — that the psychological relationship between certain writers and the Church developed. I have observed that the authors were stimulated to their anticlerical stand chiefly in three inter-related areas of the general pattern:

1. educational programs and intellectual movements
2. the status of the Monarchy and the Directorate
3. the Republic and the New Constitution.

In order to understand the position of the anticlerical writers, I intend to examine in depth the climate of opinion in these areas. They provide most of the major "keys" to Spanish anti-clericalism.

2. New Educational Trends and the Church

There had long been a feeling among Spanish intellectuals that a reappraisal of education was both desirable in itself and necessary as a means to stimulate movements toward general reform. This opinion, expressed in varying ways, is common among the writers of '98. Long before this generation, however (1876 to be exact) a group of discharged university professors, liberal thinkers, and scientists had founded the *Institución Libre de Enseñanza*. The school developed rapidly and became a potent force in the twentieth century. Giner de los Ríos was for many years its soul and guiding spirit; Manuel B. Cossío continued the work of Giner.[8]

The *Institución* had certain obvious affinities with the *erasmistas* of the sixteenth century and with the critical spirit of the eighteenth century. But the educational philosophy of Giner and his followers both in the *Institución* and the later allied programs stemmed, with several admixtures, principally from two sources: Germany, particularly the ideals of Kraus, spread previously in Spain by Sanz del Río; and England, especially the cherished tradition of freedom of debate and expression. Under Giner's mild but forceful personality, the various eclectic elements of the program were welded into a productive unity. The school refused State support to avoid the dangers of having to accept a prescribed orientation and dedicated itself to the task of providing a harmonious, humanistic education apart from any extrinsic predetermined formulas. The educators insisted upon inculcating in their students skill in the scientific areas combined with the spirit of free and impartial investigation followed by its inevitable concomitant, the moral stamina of arriving at independent conclusions. The entire program was suffused with the concept of the development of a personality which combines within itself artistic taste, and above all, a capacity for humanitarian idealism.

Beneath these aims there are others extending to the practical and political order with an eye toward the renovation of all Spain, this program to be built upon liberal and lay bases. It was hoped that the *Institución* could prepare its students to become scientists, men of letters, doctors, lawyers, men of industry, etc. As Giner said: "The Institution does not pretend to limit itself to instruction. Rather it cooperates in the formation of men useful for the service of Humanity and the fatherland . . . Only in this fashion, by directing the development of the student in all respects, can we sincerely aspire to a truly educational action in those spheres where the need of redeeming our spirit is most acute."[9] The reformers succeeded, in a limited way, in their task. The flourishing life of the *Institución* in the early days of the twentieth century stimulated reforms in other areas. Richard Pattee, hardly a strong partisan of liberal movements, writes: "The influence of the protégés of Giner de los Ríos can hardly be underestimated .They filled the school system and entered the universities; they gave tone and note to the new reviews that appeared and set the pace for much of the intellectual production of Spain. The far reaching consequences of this program can be seen during the Second Republic when so many of them came into positions of direction in public affairs."[10] Among the excellent results of the *Institución* was the foundation of other educational organizations for the furtherance of educational vitality. A prominent expression of this vitality was centered in the *Junta para Ampliación de Estudios*. The *Junta* functioned by submitting proposals for the use of State funds in education. The first director was Ramón y Cajal; José Castillejo served with distinction as permanent secretary for thirty years, beginning with the initial foundation in 1907. It was hoped that the *Junta* could aid in breaking the monotony of Spanish education which had been engendered by uniform patterns. New ideas were anticipated as the result of scholarships abroad; research organizations were fostered, and experimental schools and colleges were founded. In addition, the *Junta* published books which by 1921 numbered nearly four hundred. These books included scientific papers, results of original research, and translations of important books printed in other languages. Thus, a series of institutes and laboratories grew up. Among them were: the *Centro de Estudios Históricos,* mostly for Spanish Language, Literature, and Art; laboratories of Geology, Botany, Zoology, and Biology; the Cajal Institute for Histology; the Physiological Laboratory; the Institute of Physics and Chemistry.

Experimentation in secondary education was represented by the *Instituto Escuela,* founded by the Ministry of Education and entrusted to the *Junta* in 1918. The *Instituto* provided a training ground for teachers to enable them to grow in advanced methodology combined with interior competency and the spirit of research. The children were grouped according to mental ability and experiments were made in free vocational selection. The *Residencia de Estudiantes* opened its doors in Madrid in 1910. Its guiding spirit was for many years Alberto Giménez. As the son-in-law of Manuel B. Cossío and husband of Natalia Cossío de Giménez, a translator of Milton, he naturally had strong affinities for the tradition of Giner. The *Residencia* and the *Grupo de Señoritas,* a similar organization devoted to women, both show strong influences of English education. John B. Trend in *A Picture of Modern Spain* devotes an essay entitled "Oxford and Cambridge in Madrid" to these groups. The two organizations aspired to providing facilities for further study, research, recreation, and exchange of ideas among students of various universities. Social life was stimulated; libraries were provided, books were published (including some of the works of Unamuno and Ortega y Gasset), medical facilities were set up — all in an atmosphere of the "amplification" of Spanish intellectual life. The *Grupo de Señoritas* was long under the patronage of María de Maeztu y Whitney, another exponent of the English tradition.

The Ministry of Education was constituted as an independent department of the government in 1900. Although many of its officers were motivated by a desire for outstanding reform, contributions to the thoroughly new educational directions did not go beyond cooperation with the proposals of the *Junta* in such programs as we have noted. The level of illiteracy, which was sixty per cent of the electorate in 1870, continued to remain extremely high after World War I, with estimates as high as fifty percent.[11]

The *Junta* and its allied programs and, in general, the reform movements initiated by Giner, found stubborn opposition. Chief among the antagonists were disgruntled candidates, the universities which believed that the "super-university programs" were a waste of money which they could have used more wisely, and the Church. In the words of José Castillejo:

Neither the Church nor the parties of the left took up his [Giner's] challenge. Their intolerance was derived from fear. Both thought that faith runs risks of being lost if it is not isolated from other ideas. They did not trust their own strength. Only so can be explained the insistent and fierce campaign against a tiny and friendly school like the *Institución* in a country where undenominational schools scarcely existed, and where the Catholic Church owned half the secondary schools and controlled religious teaching in all the elementary and secondary state institutions.[12]

It is of course a mistake to think that Giner, although not himself a practising Catholic, was opposed to either religion or the Church. When taking Catholic children on trips he never failed to have them attend Mass. He believed that schools need a religious spirit to augment the instruction given at home and in the Church of one's choice. He was vehemently opposed to the anti-Catholic bias that sprang up in certain "lay schools" during his life. He was also strongly opposed, with regard to the Church, to what has been described as the tendency of some Catholics "to politicize dogma and religious energy."[13] He opposed Catholics who would, in the educational controversy, "apply the necessarily authoritarian nature of the Church to the experience of the State."[14]

Menéndez Pelayo was quick to spring to the defense of immemorial tradition. Probably stimulated by the growing impact of Giner to write his monumental *Historia de los Heterodoxos de España,* he castigated the work as leading to a "kind of lodge or mutual aid society, a tribe and a fraternity."[15] Further expressive of his opinion, "fiery anathemas interlarded with scholastic homilies" began to be hurled from the pages of newspapers and periodicals edited by leading Spanish churchmen. To cite instances, in May, 1910, the following comment on the work of the *Institución* appeared in the Jesuit periodical *Razón y Fe*: "In our country a silent campaign is being waged — a campaign no less effective for its silence — to dechristianize the teaching Majesterium. One does not have to be a party to privileged information to know what is being wrought here by the *Institución Libre de Enseñanza*, a focal point of Krausism and other similar ideas."[16] The traditional Spanish concept of regulation of education by the state, but exclusively according to the Catholic formula, was reiterated in the Augustinian review, *Ciudad de Dios*:

. . . intervention in education can be reduced to the following points:
1. organizing it in all its phases by law.
2. awarding degrees, after the proper examination.
3. preserving the official teaching of these faculties that cannot, through no fault of their own, be paid for through individual initiative.
4 establishing free centers, particularly of secondary education . . .
But these centers must be submitted precisely to the same conditions as all other schools.[17]

Official favor for the Catholic formula was demanded in an episcopal letter of the Archbishop of Valencia: "We need academic freedom in teaching against the monopoly of the State. It must be Catholic in all schools in conformity to the law."[18] The following passage is a detailed example of the uncompromising confessional demands in the realm of education:

1. Let religious tolerance be restricted to that very limited degree permitted in the basic law severely prohibiting public manifestations of dissident cults. . . . And since the school is not a part of religious cult, let every non-Catholic school be prohibited with equal vigor.
3. Academic freedom in teaching in favor of the Church, without being subjected to official educational centers.
4. Let the instruction in the universities, secondary schools, seminaries, and public and private schools of whatever class be entirely in conformity with the Catholic Religion, which is the Religion of the State;

and let the Bishops be efficaciously on watch for compliance with this accepted formula.[19]

In the pursuance of these ends clerical intervention was commended. A statement in the *Ciudad de Dios* outlines certain "injustices of the Spanish State." It is an example of "politicizing dogma and religious energy." The author commends "the intervention of the wise prelate from Jaca in the discussions of the Senate, in the period of the last legislature; an intervention not limited to defending the rights of the Church . . . but extended to other questions with reference to relations between the Church, the State, and education."[20] Any alternative to the universally prescribed religious approach was considered utterly immoral and atheistic. "We believe that without religion . . . neither morality, nor integrity, nor conscience is possible, and that the atheistic land of necessity must become a people of either victims or hangmen."[21] It was charges of this nature leveled at the liberals — charges of atheism and immorality — that Pérez Galdós vigorously contradicted. The charges were repeated constantly. A review of R. P. Laberthoniere's *Le probleme de l'Education* has the following note: "The author, who thoroughly understands modern theories on education, clearly demonstrates the purposes and ends, at times dissimulated, of these procedures; they are directed principally at forming a young generation devoid of all religious ideas and feelings, thus preparing a future anti-Christian and atheistic society."[22] The distinction between anti-religious and neutral education was not admitted: "The school without God, *despite whatever neutrality with which it masks its atheism,* is an unworthy mutilation of the human understanding."[23] English influences was another focal point of denunciation. The volumes of Catholic periodicals for the year 1900, for example, yield ample documentation. An article in the *Revista Contemporanea* demonstrates a profound lack of understanding of American and British tolerance. There is an extended series of articles entitled "Catholic and Protestant Nations" in the *Ciudad de Dios*. The author laments the secular tradition imported from England to Spain. "The Church has no influence on the politics and government of the nation; secularizing policy has reigned supreme. And lo its work! To this has come the thriving, prosperous Spain of Isabel the Catholic and Philip II."[24] While the moderns and their influences were being condemned outright, there was no lack of sermonizing on the accomplishments of tradition: "But above all there is need of practical teaching of religion and morality, which has always been the true generating cause of progress."[25] The battle was joined on the very concept of liberty of conscience. The "Crónica General" of La Ciudad de Dios yields a denunciation of a Minister of Education who sponsored a circular expressing a desire to have "liberty of conscience" substituted for "tolerance" in Article II of the constitution. The proposal was condemned as "inspired in an obviously sectarian spirit, against which various Prelates have rightly protested."[26] In the "Variedades" of Razón y Fe an author expresses concern lest there be lack of respect for the "limit expressed in our codes of law against the free circulation of ideas."[27]

Space does not permit, nor is it necessary, to present further documentation of the clerical climate of opinion in the realm of educational and intellectual reform. The articles quoted indicate the trend. In general, between 1900 and 1910 each volume of Ciudad de Dios and Razón y Fe yield between five and ten articles, reviews, and other major references of the type we have noted. At times there are that many in a single issue. Examination of other periodicals such as the Revista Contemporanea, Religión y Cultura, and Revista de Estudios Franciscanos yields parallel material. Most of these periodicals, commenting on history as it was being made, frequently carried digests of a wide range of other periodicals, giving still further indication of the type of opinion sampled.

Yet, despite the opposition, the modern trends initiated by Giner, overshadowed by his spirit, and carried on by his followers continued to make some headway in the early decades of the twentieth century. Influential men such as M. B. Cossío (long intimately associated with the Institución), Ortega y Gasset, Azorín, Antonio Machado, Juan Ramón Jiménez,

Joaquín Costa, Unamuno (later strongly opposed to some of the trends) — all these, to mention but a few, were directly affected by the new educational trends, had contact with the leaders, or were actually educated in the *Institución*.

3. The Monarchy; the Directorate;
The Church and the Liberals

Despite the tradition of conservatism with which the monarchy had long been associated, Alfonso XIII showed considerable early affinity for the liberals. From the time of his accession in 1902, the first ten years of his reign were marked, like the history of the era, by fluctuations between the two tendencies. Whether his occasional leanings to the left were motivated by personal convictions or political expediency, I will not venture to analyze in this study.

Evidences of Alfonso's liberal side were manifest as early as 1903. The Conservatives were in power and remained so until 1905; nevertheless, during 1903 the *Comisión de Reformes Sociales,* set up in 1883 to study social conditions and recommend reforms, was reorganized. Alfonso favored this action even though the commission was able to effect little, due to the unhealthy *rotativismo.*

In 1905 the Liberals came to power. It was during this period that Alfonso approved of the establishment of the *Junta para Ampliación de Estudios.* Further interest in reform in education during these years was evidenced in the plans for the huge University City of Madrid.

The Liberal government was followed by a return, under Maura, of the Conservatives. After Maura's hasty retirement in the wake of the Ferrer case, the Liberals returned under Canalejas. This Minister was at once a solid Catholic and a sincerely convinced liberal. During his years in office the King exhibited his strongest tendencies in favor of liberalism and reform. The influence of Canalejas is to be strongly presumed when in 1910 Alfonso addressed himself to the understandable problems created by the heavy participation of the very large number of religious orders in secular affairs. In a speech from the throne the King proposed a reduction and control of the areas of influence of the orders. At the same time he emphasized their autonomy in matters of a spiritual nature. Diplomatic tensions with the Vatican followed, but Alfonso, when Canalejas offered his resignation, graciously refused to accept it.

Another item on Canalejas' liberal agenda aroused the white heat of clerical controversy. It was the Royal Decree of June 10, 1910 granting greater freedom of worship to non-Catholics. The Decree read in part:

Placards, symbols, flags, announcements, signs and other exterior devices designed to designate buildings, ceremonies, rites, observances and customs of religions other than the religion of the State are not considered "public manifestation"; therefore, their use will be authorized.[28]

This move was hotly denounced: "What could there possibly be to justify this innovation? What legal, social, or political necessity in the experience of the Spanish people? What interior or exterior policy of the State has imposed the duty of adopting such a resolution? . . . None. Absolutely none."[29] Canalejas stated that the resolution was necessary because many foreigners felt that they were unable to attend their churches with the same liberty as Catholics. "What sort of a reason is this?" was the reply. "Doesn't the Government have more urgent matters to attend to?"[30] Canalejas had noted in *A.B.C.* of June 2 that he would not yield on principle in this matter, even though it should lead to tensions with the Vatican prelates: "The die has been cast. If the reply from Rome makes an accord between us impossible I will get along without it because I intend to bring about this necessary reform. The Spaniard is master of his own house."[31] This provoked a reply which was practically a call to arms against the forces of Satan: "In other words, order and subjugate the Church, deprecating its spiritual sovreignty . . . Let Catholics judge whether or not a truly urgent task, in behalf of the welfare of religion, has been imposed on their faith and zeal . . . It

61

certainly is necessary to organize an active campaign, not only to resist the advance of the anti-religious resolution, but to cause it to retreat, to storm the positions already taken, and to wrest away its evil weapons of combat."[32] Indeed, Church-sponsored rallies against Canalejas were held and were well attended: "The public meetings held to protest the anticlerical policies of Canalejas have been magnificent. There were 8,000 men and 9,000 women at the one held in Carrión de los Condes . . . Catalonia had never seen such a spectacle . . . The Bishop of Toledo, etc. . . ."[33] The possibility that Canalejas could remain a member of the Church and maintain his position on this issue was denied by an author writing in *Razón y Fe,* in an article entitled "Has Rome permitted freedom of religion in Spain?" "Permit us to make the observation that the Canalejas case is truly strange, like many other people who call themselves Catholics and anticlericals, trying to distinguish between clericalism and Catholicism."[34] These words were written in Nov., 1910. Some twenty-five years later Jacques Maritain, one of the most eminent Catholic philosophers of the twentieth century, fearlessly made the same distinction during the tensions of the Spanish Civil War.[35]

During Canalejas' term in office and afterwards, the King showed considerable tolerance, if not interest, in the arguments in favor of republican government. The political formation of the intellectuals of republican leanings had been forged in the midst of the increasing problems of the previous century. Together with the top of the professional classes — doctors, lawyers, professors, writers, and scientists — they owed their stature to the education they had received in the *Institución Libre de Enseñanza*. Their headquarters was the *Ateneo* in Madrid, a renowned literary and political club. For over a hundred years it numbered among its members most of the distinguished figures of Spanish intellectual life. Alfonso was a member of the *Ateneo* and did much to further its growth.

The King's concessions to the liberals continued to be viewed with alarm by the Church. Symptomatic of this attitude was the reaction when, as late as 1921, Alfonso tried to ease the long-standing tension created by professional restrictions upon non-Catholic teachers:

We have a new reason to congratulate the previously mentioned minister [minister for Public Education, Silió] . . . concerning whom there was mention in the *Gaceta*, July 1st of the current year, concerning dispensations from study and teaching of Religion for Mohammedan and Jewish students in the Normal Schools. Public opinion very rightly became alarmed and expressed itself in complaints against a Royal Decree that would prejudice the unquestionable rights of the Catholic Religion. The Most Eminent Cardinal Primate, in the name of the entire Spanish episcopate, addressed the Minister, asking that said Royal Decree be revoked. A clarification left those rights intact. Accordingly, Mohammedans and Jews are prevented from exercising the teaching magisterium among people who are not their co-religionists; and in the zone of our protectorate of Morocco, education in State schools will continue to be the task of our national teachers.[36]

The year 1912 marks the end of Alfonso's liberal period. Canalejas, after showing firmness in the railroad strike, was slain by a terrorist. At a loss for another forceful leader Alfonso again began to play one politician against the other and the unhealthy *rotativismo* of the early days of his reign returned. Actually, the King's basic aspirations, as history later attests, seemed to lie on the side of conservatism. His early experiences had taken place in his mother's court which had been dominated by clerics of the old school, and his education had been entrusted to the Jesuit father, Montana, an arch conservative. The Conde Romanones gives a revealing account of the first cabinet meeting presided over by the King. At this meeting he lost no time in assuming the autocratic tendencies that had long been associated with the Spanish throne. The Conde maintains that the frequent changes effected through *rotativismo* were in part the result of intrigues of the King "who seemed to enjoy changing frequently the persons to whom, more or less completely, he gave his confidence."[37] During the first four years after the termination of the Regency there were no less than fourteen political crises and eight prime ministers. Thus, *rotativismo* brought about a desired change of political atmosphere, a sop to popular demands. But governments lacked the power to progress; the *status quo* was thereby effectively maintained.

It was under the Conservative Minister Maura that the King blundered badly and foreshadowed the mistakes which were to come after Jaca at the end of the Directorate. We have reference to the Ferrer incident, which became an international *cause célèbre*.

Francisco Ferrer was a theoretical anarchist who had founded the *Escuela Moderna* at Barcelona. Unlike the *Institución,* this educational movement was vehemently doctrinaire. The children were instructed to believe in liberty and equality but were also indoctrinated with an abiding hatred for the Church, and scorn for all forms of religion. Thus, Ferrer's movement, both in his school and in his publishing and adult education program, embodied the trends of fanaticism so uncompromisingly condemned by Giner. Ferrer and his schools were violently catapulted into the public eye in 1909 when riots and strikes took place in protest against Morroccan conscription. Violence was violently suppressed and Ferrer was shot as one of the ringleaders.

It is extremely difficult to find unanimity on every aspect of the Ferrer case. Commementators and historians disagree on many of the facts and interpretations. Certain features of the case, however, are clear and sufficient to establish the larger historical significance. At the time of the uprising, for example, Ferrer was not residing in Barcelona. There was, furthermore, no evidence to show that he was implicated in the conspiracy. But, as Gerald Brenan writes: "He was generally regarded as having been the instigator of an attempt on the life of the King three years before by a pupil of his called Morral and the opportunity was taken to get rid of him."[38] The execution caused a furor throughout the world. Ferrer had enjoyed considerable popularity outside of Spain in various circles and various countries. Public opinion was shocked by an execution which, in its absence of a legal case *ad rem,* had all the earmarks of the mentality of the Inquisition. Inside Spain the Conservatives were forced to resign and Maura had to relinquish leadership of his party.

Clerical opinion was violently arrayed against the cause of Ferrer. The writers in the Catholic reviews, understandably hostile to his educational themes, were unable to call upon the evangelical precepts which demand charity for the man himself, irrespective of his views and of any degree of guilt. Rather, the execution was enthusiastically approved. Father Montes, O.S.A., wrote the following vitriolic comment in the pages of *Ciudad de Dios*: "If ever a man were born for crime, with instincts so depraved as to do evil for the sheer sake of evil; if such a born criminal ever existed, Ferrer is a precious example . . . A novelist's imagination could not invent a more monstrous criminal, a lower creature, a more evil human being."[39] Similarly bitter condemnations of Ferrer are found in other issues of this period as well as in the corresponding volumes of the Jesuit *Razón y Fe*.

The condition of the laboring classes and the agrarian question had produced Ferrer and the other patterns of protest. As the Monarchy continued down the road to ruin, the problems of the poor became even more acute. Pope Leo XIII's encyclical on the condition of the working class, *Rerum Novarum*, had been issued already late in the hour in 1896. He had fearlessly condemned *laissez-faire* capitalism and castigated the apathy and criminal exploitation in the rich. There is evidence, however, that Spanish Church officialdom in large numbers refused to promulgate the letter. At most, the years immediately following the encyclical produced little more than platitudes. A review of an article from an Italian periodical, *Civilità Catolica,* attempted to center the distribution of guilt in the problem of the equitable distribution of wealth. It is an excellent example of what Conrad Bonacina calls a "scholastic homily:"

The worker exaggerates what is entailed in his work and asks that his salary be increased; the owner, in turn, wants low costs and high profits — the eternal battle between capital and labor. To remedy such a grave evil, it is not sufficient to raise the worker's salary nor to make life easier for him, to the extent that this might be possible. The evil is much deeper. First of all pity must be aroused in the hearts of the owners. Secondly, the moral condition of the worker must be rectified. His heart, led astray by the love of riches, must be purified by the love of virtue, and his beclouded intellectual faculties . . . ."[40]

Similarly, during these years, there was a general fear of what was called *democracia liberal*. In such a democracy "envy, hate, despair, and anarchy" reign supreme. In *"democracia cristiana,"* however, "all is love, harmony, peace, prosperity, and well-being . . . There are no class wars or enmities between the elements of society."[41] This dream of Utopia appeals to the necessary hierarchy within nature for its justification. Inequities within this hierarchy — the nucleous of the problem, it would seem — are ignored: "[Christian democracy] does not try to share the wealth. Rather, it admits and defends the right to private property — the hierarchy of classes — as a most effective bulwark of liberty and necessary cause of progress."[41] The author continues with quixotic idealism: "Some people look upon Christian democracy with misgiving. It can be essentially defined as that civil disposition in which all the social, juridical, and economic forces in the fulness of their development cooperate proportionately for the common good."[42] And always the return to the homily. "The worker's condition in Christianity is touched by something sacred. His work is respected. There is something majestic in its inevitability; in its religious overtones something august and expiatory."[43]

On the other hand, as years went on there is some evidence of a more practical attitude. Enlightened groups tried to put some of the social reforms suggested by Pope Leo XIII into action. Evidence of clerical effort on the level of applied theory can be found in the pages of the *Ciudad de Dios*. For example, in 1921 there is an article evaluating the cooperative movement in various localities.[44] In the same issue a long series of articles begins on the functioning of "consumers' cooperatives."[45] The leading article of the following volume contains a long, detailed analysis of "the Catholic agrarian

Syndicates in Viscaya."[46] The most common remedy attempted was the association of workmen together with employers. Frequently the gap between classes was too wide and the associations were most unsuccessful, sometimes becoming additional organs of oppression.[47] There were some admissions of failure. Father Teodoro Rodríguez, O.S.A., for example, wrote: "One of the most competent and experienced members of the Catholic-agrarian Confederation admitted to me, candidly and bluntly, that in some sections ninety percent of the cooperatives founded by the Confederation have failed completely."[48] These words, written in September, 1921, admitting failure in a specific effort, are vastly different from the confidence of twenty years previously when a writer in the same periodical stated unequivocally that "only in Catholicism can be found the true solutions for the real crisis that societies are passing through."[49]

Some social legislation was attempted on the governmental level. The greatest effort was made in the last years of the second decade, under the conservative Minister, Dato. It was the first real if slight progress since the resuscitation of the ineffective *Commission on Social Reforms* in 1903. The Dato government succeeded in at least getting on paper provisions for workingmen's insurance, compensation for accidents, and regulation of women's and children's work. Like Canalejas, Dato was rewarded for his efforts by being slain by a terrorist. In general the lag between law and reality widened. Drastic changes were necessary but not forthcoming. Catholics objected to any plan to break up the enormous landed estates called *latifundios*.[50] The desire of the reformers to break up the huge "agrarian trusts" is a policy long advocated and practised by many Christian democratic parties in many countries. The Catholic historian, Richard Pattee, in his study *This is Spain* sides with the conservatives and severely criticizes the efforts of the reformers in this area.[51]

In 1917, while Cambó was Prime Minister, the failure to find a solution for growing economic distress was reflected in a general strike. The breaking of the strike helped to set the stage for what was to follow in the political directions of the Monarchy. Cambó, anxious to avoid a revolution, was drawn over to the King; he called upon the Army to end the strike. Many people were killed and thousands wounded or imprisoned. In the King's mind it was the Army which had saved the throne against a largely republican inspired demonstration. From then on, he looked upon the military arm as the only real power in the country. Committees of Defense were formed and increasing power was given to them. Originally conceived as a bulwark against army abuses, "they took a weapon from the arsenal of syndicalist labor and turned against the State the force which the State had entrusted to them."[52] The King appeared anxious to govern through them. As their power rapidly increased they caused the dismissal of one government and forced Dato to pass a law granting them a legal status. As increasing rapidity of governmental changes grew apace, Alfonso became the only symbol of governmental stability. In 1920 the *Juntas* forced another government out of office. The atmosphere was being created for a military *coup* and the Morrocan defeat was the last straw leading to the establishment, in 1923, of the unconstitutional Directorate.

History attests to the initial successes of the Directorate. Primo de Rivera was a man whose background enabled him to understand the problems of the poor. He immediately began huge public works projects to relieve unemployment and extended his hand to Largo Caballero, the powerful Socialist leader. History also attests to the fact that almost all of Primo's accomplishments were made in the context of shallow material gain, and this during a period coincident with the post World War I boom that lacked interior vitality. They were also made at the expense of intellectual freedom and independence. Before the Directorate people could at least say what they wished and did not shrink from outspoken criticism. Unamuno, for example, in a public address in 1922, referred to Alfonso as a "Palm Beach Monarch."[53] Primo changed all this with his constant battle against the intellectuals. Unamuno and others soon were forced into exile or left the country voluntarily. Free speech and free expression of opinion were eliminated; the Dictator censored and suspended newspapers; the *Ateneo* was repeatedly opened and closed; public meetings and banquets were well attended by spies. Leaders of thought were fined, imprisoned, and exiled for the mildest disclaimers; associations were abolished; universities were suspended indefinitely; the board of the *Junta* was packed and interfered with; religious tests were imposed upon State officials and recalcitrants were dismissed. Satisfaction with economic improvement soon yielded to dismay when, at the end of five years, the old problems came back; the value of money declined, and the country seemed even less stable than before.[54] The continued opposition of the Church prevented any deep probing of the agrarian problem and the *latifundios*. Large sections of public opinion became outraged at the sustained reliance on the Army which, although it usually avoided violence, caused a most oppressive political atmosphere. By 1925 the Dictator's days were numbered, yet the King in December of that year wrote a letter to the General: "Fully appreciating the crisis in which Spain finds herself, I consider it essential to persist in the work of the revival which the Directorate has set itself. I give you full authority to form a government and to preside over it. Appoint whom you will as Vice-President."[55] It was vain hope. The Dictator's last two years were marked by an almost universal cry against him. The brief governments of Berenguer and Aznar saw the country become progressively worse. When elections were finally held the Monarchy had ended.

The Church continued to support the tottering Monarchy throughout its last few years. Rebukes were reserved for the King when, as we have seen, he seemed to favor the liberal cause either out of sincere motivation or as a gesture of appeasement. In 1921 the editor of *Ciudad de Dios* wrote the usual platitudinous amenities on the occasion of the birthday of a Monarch already discredited with a large segment of his nation. "The birthday of His Majesty the King was celebrated amid the customary solemnities and spontaneous proofs of affection that the people of Madrid offer, at all significant moments, to our beloved Monarch. We associate ourselves with the spirit of those manifestations of sympathy and we beg Our Lord that . . ."[56] Seven years later, during Aznar's brief hegemony, and on the eve of the country's repudiation of the Monarchy and the election of the Second Republic we read: "His Majesty the King, Alfonso XIII, continues to be the strongest man in Spain, the man who once again has saved the Monarchy."[57]

Throughout these troubled years serious efforts were made to use Catholic organizations to maintain the appearances of the triple alliance of Religion, King and State. An example of this was the *Confederación Nacional Católico-agraria de Madrid,* one of the ineffectual reform organizations. Concerning the sixth general assembly, at which the Cardinal Primate designated the Bishop of Plasencia as presiding prelate, we read: "The *C.N.C.A.* is known and valued by the Monarch who lends it great prestige by his enthusiasm and support. It demonstrates its powerful vitality in the fact that *caciquismo* [bossism] views the organization as a formidable enemy, and considers agrarian syndicalism a battering ram that shortly will demolish its destructive work."[58] Another Catholic organization used as a monarchical prop was the *Federación de Sindicatos Femeninos,* directed by the reactionary Vásquez de Mella. The *Ciudad de Dios* of May, 1921 reports on a series of conferences held in the *Teatro de la Princesa.* Señor Vásquez de Mella spoke on organizing Catholic opinion as a political arm of action.[59] Still another Catholic organization was the *Confederación Nacional de Estudiantes Católicos.* Their political orientation is rather strongly etched in the following: "The celebration in the Royal Theatre by the *C.N. de E.C.* was brilliant. It was held in honor and thanksgiving to the King for having graciously accepted the title of honorary President of said organization. . . . The entire, august royal family was present at the festival."[60]

In the "Crónica de España" of *Ciudad de Dios,* so fruitful a source for Catholic comment on the processes of history, the *coup* of Primo de Rivera went uncommented. But articles of the type I have cited throughout this chapter continued. For example, Silió, a Minister of Public Education, had ordered the restitution in all schools of the Crucifix and the picture of the King "which symbolize the unity of the country."[61] This move was of course resoundingly commended. Teodoro Rodríguez wrote an anti-intellectual article against the growing dangers of *Intelectualismo*.[62] As time went on the negative, condemnatory, or platitudinous articles increased in volume. The slightest mention of republicanism was viewed with alarm. For example, derogatory notice was taken of a political dinner. Among the speakers was Alcalá Zamora, the future Prime Minister of the Republic who later resigned in protest to Article 26 of the New Constitution. The cavalier notice reads in part: "Our readers will be amused (for it merits only a laugh), if we take note of the prestigious banquet held in the Palace Hotel in Madrid by a concentration of liberal forces. . . . The gentlemen already mentioned spoke, with the exception of Señor Salvador, and we will not record what they said so as not to annoy our patient readers by repeating addlepated thoughts that have been heard and read a million times."[63] On the other side of the political spectrum, a letter of Primo de Rivera condemning a proposal for the creation of a national assembly was published with approbation.[64] The uprising at Jaca and the subsequent executions of Fermín Galán and Hernández were the occasion of frenzied outbursts reminiscent of the Ferrer incident.[65]

Such is the pattern of the Church's attitude toward the Monarchy, the Directorate and the problems which plagued the era. Spanish churchmen continued to face the present and future in the light of the past, tenacious of the Church's traditionally favored status. In Conrad Bonacina's words, they engaged in "an anachronistic endeavor to find a medieval solution for a modern problem."[66] Unquestionably, a considerable percent of the negative criticism I have adduced stemmed from the atmosphere created by Pope Pius IX's condemnation of theological modernism in the nineteenth century. This proclamation — pertinent as it may or may not have been for Catholic theology — unnecessarily spread a cloud of negativism over the minds of Catholics engaged in the changing problematic areas

71

of later decades. William Clancy, a modern Catholic intellectual, sums up the situation in the following passage:

The work of Pius IX in the area of modern culture was essentially negative . . . we know what is not possible. We are plagued by ambiguous attitudes to what is possible . . . No effort was made to distinguish what is valuable from what is perverse. Pius IX named what the Church could *not* reconcile with her own spirit. He did not attempt to explore nor to understand what the Church *could* accept.[67]

It would be an enormous understatement to say that this passage completely describes the situation in Spain. It merely suggests part of the spectrum of vast, tragic misunderstanding.

The ineffective concepts of reform, combined with continued opposition to the moderns and alignments with the *status quo,* created tensions with the intellectuals which are reflected most especially in the works of Blasco Ibáñez, Ortega y Gasset, and Unamuno.

4. *The Republic and the New Constitution*

During the elections which ushered in the Second Republic in 1931, the cause of the Monarchy was even more strongly identified with the Church. In the pulpit and press the Republican candidates were denounced as the paid lackeys of Moscow.[68] When the Republic became a fact, an embarrassing shift of opinion became inevitable. Editorials now stressed the Catholic moral teaching that the faithful must respect any legitimate authority. A large percentage of the hierarchy issued a joint declaration easing cooperation with the new regime, although, as Mendizábal notes, this position "was made all the more difficult on account of their previous campaign."[69] It is of course indisputable that communist and other unsavory influences were long at work in the extremist segments of republican opinion. This influence grew and contributed notably to the failure of the new form of government, as I shall note below. On the other hand, overemphasis upon communist infuences and the false and facile equating of Spanish republicanism and communism — to this day still repeated, for example, in the American Catholic press — undoubtedly intensified the misunderstandings and confusions of the year 1931. As Alfred Mendizábal wrote: "In the electoral campaign the attitude of the Catholic Press and numerous ecclesiastical authorities was one of frank opposition to all Republican candidates. This stirred up the hate of the enemies of the Church and placed Catholic Republicans in a difficult position, for they saw themselves included in the anathema hurled against the whole of Spanish republicanism by people who considered it to be sold for money from Moscow."

Of course there were many enlightened Catholics of republican persuasion. Many priests voted for the Republic. Spanish Catholic intellectuals such as Mendizábal and other governmental leader were as loyal to the republican aspirations as they were sincere in their Catholicism. José María de Semprún y Gurrea in 1931 wrote in his *República, Libertad, Estatismo*:

Religious liberty, neutrality of the State, and its separation from the Church have nothing in common with any form of persecution or hostility. Religious liberty and the neutrality of the State mean that the State can neither oppose any religious standpoint nor impose one. That is to say, that if the State is neutral and secular, it can force no one to believe in God, nor persecute, discredit or victimize anyone because he believes in God.[70]

This concept of independence of church in the spiritual realm and of the State in the temporal order was accepted, even by some Catholics who were not Republicans. Professor Minguijón, a traditionalist, referred to the anticipated release of the Church from patronage as a situation which "may raise the dignity of the Church in the eyes of the people."[71] Many agreed with Mendizábal who claimed that "the old system was not ideal for Catholicism."[72] Maritain wrote: "for centuries in Spain religion had become confused with clerical power."[73]

The Cardinal Primate, Monseñor Segura, did not share this view of the "liberal Catholics." In an article in the *Sol* (May 8, 1931) he lamented the departure of the King to whom he owed his elevation to the Primacy. He went on to the following reaction to the situation created by the new governmental structure:

If we unite our forces and prepare to fight with perfect cohesion and discipline, without vain parade, but with faith in our ideals, with abnegation and the spirit of sacrifice, we shall be able to look at the future confident of victory. . . . If we leave the road open to those who are attempting to destroy religion or expect the benevolence of our enemies to secure the triumph of our ideals, we shall have no right to lament when bitter reality shows us that we had victory in our hands, yet knew not how to fight like intrepid warriors, prepared to succumb gloriously.[74]

E. A. Peers speaks of this letter as "nothing less than a call to battle."[75] Gerald Brenan refers to it as "a violent militant pastoral."[76] Alfred Mendizábal characterizes the letter in the following statement:

The Archbishop's dislike and mistrust were as evident as his distress. So that whilst viewed as a private matter his action was unassailable, officially it was inopportune as well as dangerous for the future relationships between Church and State. Had not the Cardinal himself avoided any contact with the civil authority in Toledo, although the post of Governor han been given to Señor Semprún just becaose he was a Catholic, and in a desire to keep on good terms with the Archbishop.

Certainly Cardinal Segura, a prelate whose austerity was always exemplary, did not show himself possessed of the diplomatic talents to be desired of an ecclesiastical leader at a moment so serious for the future of the Spanish Church. Entirely unnecessary difficulties resulted from his attitude, and these were inexorably exploited by the partisans of anticlericalism.[77]

Serious disorder and violence followed this letter which appeared simultaneously with favorable articles on Alfonso in the strongly Monarchist and traditionally Catholic paper, *A.B.C.* The anticlerical spirit was, consequently, in ascendant flux when shortly afterwards the *Cortes* began debate upon the first draft of the New Constitution.

The battle was indeed joined on the field of religion. Redefinition, delineation, and restriction of clerical influence as it touched upon matters of public, political, and national interest was expected; religious instruction in the State schools was a burning question; liberty of conscience for non-Catholics and non-believers was high on the priority list; the influence and number of religious orders was intimately associated with the entire question. The Consultative Juridical Commission set up to prepare the Rough Draft of the Constitution attacked these problems with moderation. When the proposals came up for debate, however, Señor Azaña insisted upon much more stringent measures which were regarded not as neutral but as aggressively anticlerical. Thus, the most bitterly contested proposals were embodied in the following units of the New Constitution: Article 26 prepared the way for the expulsion of the Jesuits in 1932 and placed the other orders on a precarious footing; Article 27 prescribed Christian burial only upon explicit request; Article 43 legalized divorce; Article 48 heavily reduced the teaching program of the Church and necessitated a vast scheme of immediate educational reorientation and a building program of huge proportions.

In the light of the events that had gone before, these moves were not unexpected. But sincere liberal opinion was understandably badly disappointed and fearful of the far-reaching nature and possible future implications of the statutes, especially Articles 26 and 48. There was apprehension that the intent was not so much to eliminate clericalism as to isolate the Church from participation in Spanish life and culture. Intransigeance was being replaced by a different brand of the same commodity. Practically all fair-minded major commentators agree on the following points:

1. Article 26 was a violation of liberal principles and a retaliation.
2. Article 48 was unnecessarily broad and unrealistic. It imposed an impossible task upon the infant Republic's resources.
3. The tone of all four measures aroused the conservatives to divisive tactics and stiffened reaction.

Señor Manuel Azaña further alarmed public opinion when he boasted openly that his stand in favor of these articles was frankly illiberal and vindictive. His unfortunate remark that

"Spain is no longer Catholic"[78] was widely misunderstood and misinterpreted. He qualified the statement by affirming that there were "millions of practising Catholics" even though Catholicism had "ceased to be the expression and guide of Spanish thought."[79] But people tended to remember the core of the statement.

The passing of an agrarian reform measure (without any real machinery of implementation) and important concessions of autonomy to Catalonia were the chief steps taken in a truly liberal direction during the first two years.[80]

These "two years to the Left" were followed by the elections of 1933. A strong reaction to the Right was registered. It was the inevitable backlash to the frankly illiberal measures of the New Constitution. José Ortega y Gasset, one of the foremost Republicans, voiced the growing disenchantment. Speaking of the authors of the New Constitution, he said: "These Republicans are not the Republic."[81] Progress which could have been made toward reform was halted. An unstable Center coalition marked time for upwards of two years and uneasily balanced the tensions between Right and Left, while constant shuffling of cabinets revived memories of the worst years of *rotativismo* under the Monarchy. The agrarian problem remained unsolved.[82]

In 1936 Azaña rallied most of the highly diversified and shattered elements on the Left into the Popular Front. His victory at the polls was the beginning of the end for the Second Republic. Faced with staggering problems and seething unrest, the new Government at first busied itself with the vulgar removal (on trumped-up charges) of Alcalá Zamora from the office of President. Azaña filled the vacancy. Furthermore, although the Popular Front had undoubtedly shown a new swing to the Left, the victory was far from overwhelming and was reflected only by a narrow majority in the *Cortes*.[83] Yet the Government — supposedly committed to democratic principles — further risked its parliamentary insecurity by reviving the stringent anticlerical issues that had contributed largely to the trend toward reaction and loss of faith in republicanism. Some attention was given to the Agrarian Law, but the Government was unable to prevent disorderly seizure of land by the peasants. Effective government, in short, was lacking and the country was gripped by a daily mounting toll of strikes, counterclaims, and disorder. Churches once again became the object of popular violence, but this arson merely provided additional opportunity for "the inactivity of the forces of law and order."[84] E. Allison Peers comments: "Being unable to control the extremists on its own flank, the Government endeavored to oblige its opponents by rounding up extremists on theirs."[85] The rapidly growing *Falange* became more vociferous and contributed to the mounting obstruction. On the other extreme, communist influence was waxing within the Popular Front.[86] A notable example was the powerful old socialist leader, Largo Caballero, who became a full-fledged convert to communism. Spain had become a cockpit of bitter, warring intransigeants. The Civil War infinitely deepened this chaos and the welter of confusion of issues. The legitimate dream of an orderly entrance into the modern world was lost in the shuffle, and liberalism ended for the time being in Spain.

Just as I have examined the dominant shades of Catholic opinion during the years leading up to the coming of the Republic, a similar investigation during its decline and the onset of the Civil War should prove valuable.

There were, first of all, those people who, despite their feelings toward the new constitutional position on the Church, believed in the basic ideas of the Republic. They believed that time would heal wounds and they remained loyal. Alcalá Zamora typifies this attitude. He resigned as Prime Minister in protest to Article 26. Yet he later presided over the Republic as President. During the agonizing years of marking time with the Center coalition, he steadfastly refused to allow the Right to form a government under the then reactionary, Gil Robles. Alcalá Zamora's views were shared by people such as Alfred Mendizábal, to whom I have so frequently referred. Other prominent Spanish Catholics of republican sentiment were, to

77

name but a few, Señor de Irujo, a Basque Cabinet Minister; José Antonio Aguirre, leader of the Basque National Catholic party; José María Semprún y Guerrea, professor of law at Madrid; Enrique Moreno, a lecturer at Oxford; Canon Rocaful of the Córdoba Cathedral; Father Leocadio Lobo, a priest of Madrid; José Bergamín, director of *Cruz y Raya;* etc.[87]

Outside of Spain there was Jacques Maritain, who, in his Introduction to Senior Mendizábal's *The Martyrdom of Spain,* referred to the Republic as "a government sprung from the people and charged with its hopes."[88] It should be carefully noted, however, that Maritain and Mendizábal are referring to the early ideals, while analyzing the illiberal attitudes on both sides that dashed the early promise to ruin. Georges Bernanos, a leading figure of the French Catholic Literary Revival, should be included in this listing, even though he was by personal inclination a monarchist. His book, *Les Grands Cimetières sous la Lune,* is in accord with the Maritain-Mendizábal outlook; his views, however, are expressed with a polemic far removed from the serenity of socio-philosophical disputation. The book is invaluable as source material for eyewitness accounts of the early developments in the Civil War. His reliability as a witness is beyond question.[89] Pro-Republican sentiment of this nature was shared by certain liberal segments of the American Catholic press largely in the *Commonweal.*[90] The fact that this thoughtful Catholic opinion existed should have helped to dispel the charge that the entire Republican movement was directed toward a "red dictatorship" or that the Civil War was a "holy war." The late William Cardinal O'Connell of Boston expressed such false views to the New York papers in March, 1938.[91] The issues, as we have seen, were far too complicated to admit such facile classification.

On the other side of the spectrum were the proponents of the *nueva Catolicidad.* The "philosopher" of this movement was Ernesto Giménez Caballero. His work, largely in essay form, appeared in the pages of *La Gaceta Literaria.* Later these were gathered together in special collections under flowery titles that spoke of "the Genius of Spain" and "the New Catholicity." His leanings were frankly "roman," combined with the worst interpretations of Nietzsche, culminating in his proclamation of Mussolini as the leader of the New Catholicism. Fascism was explicitly equated with the Spirit of Christ. Giménez Caballero's thought, consequently, was not only heretical but psychopathic. Nevertheless it served as a reservoir of energy for the youthful elements that were rallying around the Falange.[92]

Between the progressive and liberal Catholics and the hard-core fanatics of *nueva Catolicidad* stood the larger elements of Catholic opinion before the Civil War. On the political scene they generally supported the Center coalition but continually struggled to come to power on the Right. Their organ of opinion was the strongly pro-Catholic newspaper, *El Debate*. As time went on various Catholic organizations grouped together under Gil Robles and formed a party known as the *Ceda*. Throughout the remaining years of the Republica, *Ceda* sought to bring its leader to power. During the campaign they identified their political aspirations with the cause of Catholicism, despite the fact that a warning had been issued against such tactics by the Spanish Hierarchy.[93]

Opinion varies on the political philosophy of the *Ceda*. Gerald Brenan implies that it was "fascist";[94] E. A. Peers defends it against this charge;[95] Alfred Mendizábal writes that it rendered disservice by "accentuating all the values which characterize a conservative regime with fascist methods."[96] The *Ceda*, at the outbreak of the Civil War, went over to the insurgents.

In 1937, after the outbreak of hostilities, the Spanish Hierarchy issued a joint pastoral which made "an unreserved choice of the national side . . . on the empirical plane."[97] But, as Jacques Maritain wrote: "the intention of the bishops . . . [was] certainly not and could not be to impose such a choice on the whole world."[98]

It does not fall within my purpose to continue the analysis of Catholic opinion into the period of the Civil War. In this highly sensitive area much has been written and much remains to be said when the time and altered world situations have diminished the heat of controversy. Insofar as this study is concerned, certain tensions were created by the various involvements and opinions of Catholicism in the 1930's. These tensions are sufficiently delineated by the Republican controversies. These tensions are reflected par excellence in the anticlerical writings associated with the era and especially in the works of Arturo Barea, Ramón Sender, and Rafael Alberti.

CHAPTER III

ANTICLERICALISM IN "BELLES LETTRES"
IN WRITERS FOR THE MOST PART ASSOCIATED
WITH THE PRE-REPUBLICAN ERA

BENITO PÉREZ GALDOS (1843-1920)

1. Pérez Galdós and Liberalism

Pérez Galdós is the best loved and greatest Spanish novelist since Cervantes. He figures in the great nineteenth century cluster including Tolstoi, Dostoiewski, and Balzac and offers striking parallels to Dickens. At past mid-point twentieth century, only Gironella has approached his stature. He evoked and plumbed the nineteenth century and its particularly Spanish context almost in its entirety. He also foreshadowed the Generation of '98 and prophetically intuited the latent elements of the tragedy of the Civil War.

He came to Madrid (from Las Palmas) at about the age of twenty to study law, but like so many creative geniuses soon abandoned these efforts. Travel to France broadened his knowledge of French literature, especially Balzac. Returning to Madrid he plunged into the literary currents of a most turbulent, colorful epoch. He attended *tertulias,* began life-long association with the liberally-inclined *Ateneo,* wrote articles for liberal newspapers, and soon embarked upon his career as a novelist. He remained on cordial terms with José María de Pereda, his ideological opposite, and with Marcelino Menéndez Pelayo, the traditionalist critic. Except for a few journeys and for holidays, Madrid became his home. He made several forays into liberal politics and his name became a household word, beloved by the humble and respected by the nobility, (including Alfonso XIII) and the rich. In some circles, due to the controversial themes of some of his novels, he was thoroughly disliked. The Carlist newspapers gloated at his death. The most obvious of the author's anticlerical works were written a quarter of a century before 1900 and were pertinent to their own day. At the same time they clearly foreshadowed the conflicts that were to become the increasing preoccupation of Spain's twentieth century.

Pèrez Galdós was close to the spirit of Giner de los Ríos.[1] His anticlericalism is intimately associated with his liberalism. It pivots largely on matters of an intellectual nature involving the acceptance of modernity, the "key" of which, as we saw in the last chapter, is found more under education than under monarchical problems or republican controversies and aspirations. He was convinced that there were forces for good struggling beneath the surface of Spanish life and that these forces were being frustrated by various reactionary attitudes, especially clericalism. He fought these attitudes vigorously, wherever he found them, and, as we have seen in the previous chapter, his position was historically justifiable. Unlike some writers who will be studied later, Pérez Galdós' anticlericalism is not antireligious. This fact is proved by his many characters who represent the author's anticlerical position and at the same time proclaim belief in and practise religion. Again, the author does not usually paint all his "clericalists" and clergymen as vicious, malicious scoundrels. Rather, in keeping with the artistic demands to depict life, he portrays the persons associated with the clerical position in a spectrum ranging from true interior dedication to the hard-bitten, *carlista* outlook.

2. *The Important Anticlerical Novels*: Gloria, Doña Perfecta, La Familia de León Roch

The novel *Gloria* offers a glance at many of the various colors of the author's anticlerical palette. Juan de Lantigua, Gloria's father, is a *cristiano viejo* (an old Christian) as his name implies.[2] He is too gentlemanly to be openly fanatical, but he is rooted in the sincere convictions of the particular brand of Catholicism which he inherited. "The contemplative turn of his mind led him to look upon religion not only as the governing principle of the individual's conscience, but as an official regulatory instrument which ought to direct all human affairs in their external manifestations."[3] It would be difficult to find a more concise statement of the clerical mentality.

Don Angel, a bishop and Juan's brother, is of a different religious disposition — at least on the surface. "He was a man whose natural sentiments led him to see the good in everything. His studies and his work in the confessional had taught him that there were evil people in the world . . . In dogmatic matters he professed the doctrine of tolerance."[4] While Juan de Lantigua is firmly convinced of the necessity of the union of the Church and secular power, Don Angel tries to avoid getting involved in matters related to the political arena. He leaves this to his aides, Rafael Horro and Rev. Señor Sedeño. López Sedeño is the "ambitious ecclesiastic."

[Don Angel] held his secretary, Doctor López Sedeño, in such high esteem that he never touched any serious problem without consulting him, for Sedeño was an eminent theologian and a great scholar of canon law. For some time the secretary had devoted himself assiduously to political affairs and reading on politics. At first this displeased Don Angel. But soon he became accustomed to it and ended up by praising it, considering the fact that the times demanded taking up arms. . . . Others said that Sedeño was very proud and had aspirations to become a bishop . . . when Don Angel would be transferred . . . to a metropolitan see . . . and receive the red hat.[5]

Still another type is the curate of Ficóbriga, Don Silvestre. He is neither all good nor all bad. He is worldly and boastful; he is anti-intellectual, engages in political pressurizing, and is not generous with people whom he considers weak. On the other hand, he is brave, hard working, and not unkind to the poor. The author leads us to conclude that Don Silvestre's type was not uncommon; that he belonged among those clerics whose vocations were stimulated by the material considerations of certain surviving medieval customs. "One day his father's voice penetrated his ears and caused him to realize the advantage of not losing the income of certain chaplaincies. Silvestre stuffed himself with Latin and became a priest. Things went quite well with him. He had forgotten a lot over the years, but not his congenital passion for hunting."[6]

Pérez Galdós' anticlericalism can be isolated in the general area of Church-State relationships as they impinged on the educational-intellectual atmosphere. But its many facets both reflect and dart out against a variety of aspects in Spanish life. *Gloria,* by reason of its richness in characters, dialogue, and situations, affords a fairly composite view of the author's complex ideas on many overlapping areas. For example, a conversation between Don Horro and Padre Silvestre illuminates at least three matters related to anticlericalism: the Church's reliance on political power, her uneducated clergy, and religious hypocrisy. Don Horro is a "whitened sepulchre." Like Don Juan he believes in the necessity of intimate rapport between Church and State. But Juan would at least use the State to further spirituality. Rafael Horro, however, believes that spiritual practises help to further his particular type of state, even though his own personal beliefs are practically nonexistent. He says to Don Silvestre: "Let's understand one another, my good Father. I believe that society is impossible without religion. Where would the frenzy of the stupid, ignorant masses bring us were it not for the restraint of religion on their evil passions." Don Silvestre, despite his worldliness and ignorance, ventures that "in matters of belief there is something more than a restraint placed upon the ignorant." But Don Rafael insists that though he may "have some small doubts about what the catechism teaches" . . . he believes that "the Masses, sermons, offerings, and all the other rites and religious customs that have been invented should continue to assist the great work of the State and to surround with safeguards the powerful and intelligent classes." Don Silvestre agrees with the political principle but is too intellectually atrophied to enter another plea for spiritual value. His arguments dwindle off in the inane remark that he "could answer point by point" if he could remember what he had read in his books.[7]

Pérez Galdós speaks his mind on education proper when

dealing with Gloria and her contacts with her father. Gloria had received a stereotyped education of some years in a high school named after one of the most pious titles of the Blessed Virgin. She came back home with complete mastery of the catechism, a smattering of history (mostly Church history), and some confused notions about Geography, Astronomy, and Physics. She could mumble some French, without really having understood the basics of Spanish. She could recite "The Duties of Man" by heart and knew how to play the piano. Juan de Lantigua decided to regulate his daughter's reading habits with his own thoroughgoing censorship. He recommended the great Quevedo's theological writings, but forbade his picaresque novel, the *Buscón.* Gloria — showing some of the latent fires of her personality that were to bring her to tragedy — rebelled and even managed to read *La Pícara Justina,* a novel about a woman of "easy virtue." In her long conversations with her father she gave further signs of the natural impulses she would later follow. Don Juan recommended the mystical writers of the Sixteenth Century. But Gloria found them not very interesting; she felt they never could be a guide for ordinary people because they were too difficult to understand.[8]

The vital nucleus of Pérez Galdós' anticlerical position emerges in a conversation that the de Lantigua brothers have with Daniel Morton. Daniel is an English Jew who becomes Gloria's lover through chance. Using this conversation the author first isolates and then castigates what Conrad Bonacina called "the dogmatization of political energy."[9] Morton first describes the Spanish Church as many have seen it:

In no other country in the world is there less belief. And it should be noted that in no other country is there more pretending that there is belief . . . Belgian and French Catholics, Protestants, Jews . . . Mohammedans practise their faith with more fervor than the Spaniards . . . I am amazed at the lack of religion in the majority of well-educated people. With rare exceptions the entire middle class is indifferent . . . Women give themselves to devotions but men flee from the Church . . . Don't you understand that this gives you no right to say 'We are the most religious people on earth?'[10]

Don Juan is forced to agree. But he feels that the remedy lies in the realm of politics. He claims that the weakening of religion is due to "revolutionary excesses and the influence of foreigners who are jealous of the most religious nation on earth." The Church could easily cure the situation if it could "find a government pious enough to aid" in this work.[11]

The central theme of the book, of course, is the inability of Gloria and Daniel to marry because of the conflict between their respective religious traditions. The de Lantigua brothers are unable to find an effective compromise. Daniel is admired for his excellent intellect but pitied for the impending damnation awaiting all Protestants. Gloria seeks out the advice of her uncle in the confessional. Don Angel advises her to "cast away this senseless passion, to suffocate it with an aspiration toward the one sovereign love." He refuses her absolution on the grounds of "latitudinarianism," or belief that non-Catholics can achieve salvation. When Daniel later says he is a Jew, the conflict reaches its climax and a terrible scene, with good splashes of Galdosian melodrama, ensues. Don Angel and Don Juan burst in. The father drops dread in shame; the bishop drops his genial mask of benevolence, and bares his claws and fangs. "Get out of here, you God-murderer!" he shouts.[12]

In the anticlerical novels the author does not espouse any specific political cause. His position is limited to his objection to the extension of the influence of clericalism — or, indeed, any denominational attitudes which tend to separate mankind — in the conduct of human affairs. But he accurately observes the various nuances of the contemporary political scene. For example, republicanism was a *bête noire* in his early years as well as in the twentieth century. In *Gloria,* Bartolomé Barrabás, a village republican, was regarded with dark suspicion by the de Lantigua contingent. Horro pointed strongly critical remarks in this direction declaring that "a huge filthy, leperous pestilence was spreading over the social system. It is the so-called modern spirit, a dragon of one hundred deformed heads, that is fighting to dash down the standard of the Cross."[13] In the second part of the novel a religious procession is described. The various external trappings of confessionalism are portrayed amid barbs of satire:

Don Silvestre wore his pluvial cape with mundane elegance. Father Poquito, serving as deacon, was imprisoned in the dalmatic. Juan Amarillo went a bit behind, swollen with pride in finding himself in the fullness of his municipal functions. . . . He represented human authority protecting and fostering, with its guarding arm, divine authority. It was essential that his person should be equal to such a distinguished role . . . When they passed by the casino the town band began to cut the throat of the Royal March.[14]

Pérez Galdós' *Doña Perfecta* is perhaps even more widely read than *Gloria*. In *Doña Perfecta* the author's anticlericalism is double-pronged with two separate yet interwoven ideas:

1. The perennial conflict between liberalism and reaction.
2. The portrayal of a *beata* — that type of woman whose "piety" is out of proportion to her calling in life and occupied rather exclusively with the letter rather than the spirit.

The first theme is achieved by the plot of the story. Pepe Rey, in love with Perfecta's daughter, is the protagonist. He represents the modern struggle toward a new Spain which would rely upon the contributions of modernity and break away from narrow, intolerant provincialism and a mode of life which has passed into history. He is frank in his espousal of science which he has made his profession. Doña Perfecta, like the de Lantiguas represents the reaction against the modern spirit. In her mind Pepe's science is destroying faith and the life of the soul. Consequently, she equates his modernity with atheism. Unlike the de Lantiguas she does not have a good bone in her body. Pepe is not irreligious, but if his religious needs find fulfillment within the Catholic formula, it is certainly not the brand of Catholicism represented by Perfecta. In his second meeting with Rosario and in other scenes he firmly expresses his religious beliefs which seem to reflect the influence of Kraus and, in general, the optimistic pluralism of Giner and his followers, without much reference to any particular sectarian context. Dona Perfecta is determined to thwart Pepe by using her clerical friends. Chief among them is her confessor, Don Inocencio, a typical sacerdotal "lounge-lizard." He is a man of narrow views, inquisitorial, and intolerant, and he is not averse to using insinuation and half-truth. In the last analysis he is the ultimate cause of the conflict between Pepe and Perfecta — he wanted Rosario to marry his nephew, Jacinto.

The general lines of the conflict between Pepe and Perfecta, together with the nuances of the forces they represent, is summed up in the following conversation:

"Ah, the fine understanding of your German mathematical and philosophic mind is not able to grasp the subtle thoughts of a prudent mother . . . Ah, my boy, one does not get inside the human heart by railway tunnels, nor plumb its depths by mine shafts. The conscience of another person cannot be read with the naturalist's microscopes nor can the guilt of one's neighbor be decided by balancing ideas with a theodolite."

"For the love of God, dear Aunt!"

"Why do you use God's name if you don't believe in Him?" Perfecta said in her solemn tones. "If you believe in Him, if you were a good Christian, you would not dare make wicked judgments on my conduct. I am a pious woman — do you get that? My conscience is at peace — do you get that? I know what I do and why I do it — do you get that? . . .

"You are a mathematician. You can see what's in front of you and nothing else. You can see brutal nature, and nothing else — lines, angles. weights, and nothing else. You see the effect and not the cause."[15]

This clash of seriously misunderstood value patterns brings about the tragic denouement. Perfecta's fanaticism mounts in intensity until she finally incites the braggart, Caballuco, to kill Pepe with a blunderbuss:

Doña Perfecta moved forward a few paces. Her harsh voice vibrated with her terrible intent. She spat out these words. "Cristóbal, Cristóbal . . . kill him." A shot was heard. Then another.[16]

As can be seen from the foregoing, the author's picture of Doña Perfecta is unrelieved in its stark horror. Still possessing the remnants of physical beauty, the woman is despotic, cold, intransigeant, and fanatical. "She seemed like an anathema made into a woman."[17] Yet, she is wax in the hands of the "penitenciary," Don Inocencio. The author wants to impress on his readers that the substructure of her character was an intense and terrible pride and he wishes to point up the effect of religious exaltation in a hard character which is devoid of native goodness. Rather than devoting herself to improving her spirit by meditation upon the beauty of the truths of her religion, which are beyond time and place, she seeks to arrange her own life and the lives of others by narrow formulas bounded by the limits of her own highly restricted horizons. This is what Pérez Galdós means when he appends these final lines to the novel: "This is about all we are able to say about people who seem good but really are not."[18]

Objections have been made that the author erred artistically in this study of a *beata*. Critics have claimed that he created a character without any shades of psychological color — in short, a monster of abnormality. It has also been stated that this lack of proportion extends to the other characters and consequently to the book as a whole. Perfecta and the priest on the one hand, Pepe and Rosario on the other, become little more than opposing ideas thought out ahead of time and subsequently personified. The result is a stark contrast of black and white, lacking the ingredients of at least some good with evil, some imperfections with the good. César Barja asks, "What kind of a novel is a work in which good and evil are divided into absolute qualities?"[19] And José Balseiro, speaking of both *Doña Perfecta* and Pereda's *Don Gonzalo González* (intended as a "reply" to Pérez Galdós' work) asks, "Is life as simple as presented to us in either work?"[20] In *Gloria* there is gradation between the separate individuals and much more psychological nuance within each character. And as will be seen in *La Familia de León Roch*, a *beata's* religious fanaticism can be complicated by very worldly wants indeed. Certainly, in *Doña Perfecta* Pérez Galdós has not probed as deeply into the psychological motivations of a *beata* as the contemporary Catholic author, François Mauriac. Mauriac, in his *La Pharisienne*, very competently analyzes deep, distorted religious convictions and self-righteousness that wreck the lives of many people.[21] Certainly, also, Pérez Galdós has stacked the cards ahead of time. Perfecta and her clerical friends are entirely bad; Pepe and Rosario are all sweetness and light.

On the other hand, it should not be felt that Doña Perfecta's "execution" of Pepe Rey is beyond credence. Georges Bernanos, the late Catholic author, cites a real incident illustrative of the lengths to which the "beatific" spirit can go. The time and historical context are vastly different; the place is Mallorca; but it is a real example of fanaticism leading to crime as in the Inquisition:

Yes, I have seen some strange things. There was an unmarried girl, thirty-five years old, who belonged to that inoffensive group that are called *beatas* down there. She was living quietly with her family after having left the novitiate. The time she did not spend in church she dedicated to the poor. Suddenly she fell victim of an unexplainable nervous terror; she spoke of possible reprisals and refused to go out alone. A very close friend of mine, whom I cannot name, took pity on her and hoping to restore her confidence, took her into her home. Sometime later the pious young lady decided to go back to her family. The morning of the day of departure her charitable hostess said to her affectionately: "See here, dear girl. What can you possibly be afraid of? You're one of the Good Lord's little lambs. Who could be evil enough to wish death to a person as truly inoffensive as you?" "Inoffensive? You don't know what you're talking about, dear lady. You think I am incapable of rendering service to religion. And everyone thinks as you do. Make no mistake about me. Here's a bit of information for my lady. I have had eight men shot, Madame." Yes, there can be no doubt. It has ben my lot to have seen strange, interesting things.[22]

La Familia de León Roch is another of Pérez Galdós' hard core anticlerical novels. Here the plot is centered in the tensions between a man and his wife — tensions that have been aggravated by religious fanaticism. A complicating factor — sometimes overlooked by critics who see it as a purely anticlerical work — is the presence of a "triangle" situation. León had never ceased to love Pepa Fúcar, even though he tried to disguise this love and sublimate it to the platonic level. He and María had been drawn to each other by strong physical attraction. When this ceased to be compelling, the religious problem rose to plague them. María tried desperately to recapture her husband's love and sexual interest and brought about her own death in the attempt. Pérez Galdós examines the couple's general psychological incompatibility rather than only their religious incompatability.

The work, however, has considerable importance for the anticlerical motif. María offers another study in the psychology of the *beata*. Unlike Perfecta she is more complicated and consequently less a monster. León has less religious conviction than either Pepe Rey or Daniel Morton and should be classed as an agnostic. María, however, accuses him of atheism: "If only I were not married to you, an atheist . . ."[23] Despite his agnosticism, however, he is able to pray in his own way for the recovery of Monina, the daughter of Pepa. In his calm and serene dedication to the intellectual life he seems to be a typical *ateneista,* whom the author might have met during hours spent at this center.

The anticlericalism of the novel is centered once again in a clash between religion and science, represented by the wife and the husband. María wishes León to be converted; he, reasonably, requests her to mitigate her ascetic practices and "beatific" observances. He proposes a *modus vivendi.* He promises to give up his studies and meetings with like-minded friends. He will wall up his library like Don Quijote's. There will be no conversation on science or history in his house and never a jocose or suspect word that might be taken with reference to the things of the spirit. For this concession León asks a similar one on María's part. "I am sacrificing what you stupidly call my atheism (although it is something quite different); you will have to sacrifice what you call your piety, a dubious piety I am sure. You will have to give up your unending daily devotions, as well as your habit of going to confession every week to the same priest . . . You will go to Mass on Sundays and feast days."[24] This bargain, was, of course, doomed to failure.

Closely associated with the theme of havoc engendered in family life through the abuse of religion is the thread of the confessor, Father Paoletti, who is presented in a striking uncomplimentary portrait. His familiarity with his penitent, María, disgusts León who is made to feel like an outsider in his own home. The baneful influence of Father Paoletti is augmented by María's brother, the tubercular seminarist, Luis Gonzaga, who, in his consuming fanaticism, appeals to his sister against her husband. Thus, though the theme of the novel is marital, the author introduces and bears heavily upon his anticlerical motif, insisting upon the harm that can be wrought in a home by an overinsistence upon the externals of religion.

3. *Other Novels and Dramatic Works*

In other of his vast array of novels the author redeveloped certain of the points which have appeared in the works we have examined in detail. The problem of the priest without sufficient education and with a vocation stimulated by family designs (as seen, for example, in Don Silvestre in *Gloria*) is developed at length in *El Doctor Centeno* (1883) and its sequel *Tormento* (1884). Don Pedro Polo y Cortés is just such a priest. He falls carnally in love with Amparo, a beautiful orphan, and spends his later years as a missionary in the Philippines. His "tamer," Padre Nones, is one of the author's most sympathetic clerical portraits. This old priest with his sincere love of God, and his life of zealous dedication to religion illustrates the author's sympathy with the religious spirit. In *El Abuelo* (1897), which appeared in a dramatic version in 1904, other moderate clerical types are to be found. This work is anticlerical only indirectly. The author is interested chiefly in stressing the basic, universally acceptable moral teaching that good character is not founded on inherited name or blood. Thus, through the Conde de Albrit, Pérez Galdós attacks the clerical "class messianism" associated with the mentality of the *cristiano viejo*.

The play *Mariucha* (1903) like *Tormento* is important in bringing into focus the author's full attitude toward clergymen. As in *El Abuelo* it analyzes some of the pretensions of effete aristocracy. Throughout the work the dynamic priest, Don Rafael, is "on the side of the angels." He supports María and León in their love and struggle toward eventual marriage; he contravenes the orders of María's brother, the imperious Cesareo. Don Rafael is as much a bearer of light in this thesis play as are the various scientists and engineers in the anticlerical works which we have examined.

One of the author's best known plays — hardly exceptional for its artistic merits — is *Electra* (1901). In it he returned largely to the theme of *Doña Perfecta,* in that the plot involves an attempt to stop the marriage of the heroine to a young man of science. The hero once again stands for the progressive spirit which is being throttled by the reactionaries, represented by the clerical party, who, through trickery, confine the girl to a convent. The staging of the play caused a furor, in the wake of which a cabinet resigned — the new one being dubbed "Electra." Political capital had been made of the play probably over and beyond the intentions of the author. There was a parallel between the plot and the forced retirement to a convent of a certain Señorita de Ubao. The case had caused bitter public controversy and partisanship was quick to note the similarity and exploit the implications.[25] In the play, Máximo (the lover and scientist) and Pantoja (who tried to thwart Electra's marriage) are on opposite sides of the ideological problem. Yet, they both can be numbered among the author's sympathetic representatives of the religious spirit. Pantoja is a sincere, deeply religious person whose weakness rather than malice led him to trickery. Pérez Galdós merely makes it clear that he believes Pantoja's piety is not of the best variety. Aside from these points of interpretation, however, the political and polemic significance which the play assumed pointed up the deep-seated nature of the conflict in Spanish society, which, approximately a quarter of a century before, the author had so clearly uncovered in the great cluster of anticlerical novels. The staging of *Electra* at the turn of the century coincided with a starker demarkation of the opposing sides and the entrance of the controversy into the active political arena. We have seen that the controversy emerged in ever increasing tempo in the decades leading up to 1931.

4. *Some Evaluations*

Pérez Galdós comes as close to representing the restricted meaning of anticlericalism as any other of the authors who will be treated. He is "opposed to clerical influences, especially in the realm of politics." We should, of course, understand by the term "politics" both its exact meaning and the extended sense of public policy in society. There is strong emphasis upon the effects of clericalism in educational and intellectual areas; problems of liberalism and the liberal outlook and conflicts predominate; the Monarchical and Republican controversies are mostly foreshadowed.

Like most Spaniards Pérez Galdós was a God-seeker and probably suffered several spiritual crises. Religion and religious preoccupations seem to press from the substructure of his subconscious mind to the forefront of his work. He seemed compelled to return again and again to the implications of religion (not only clericalism) in life. It is not essential that we probe his spiritual beliefs, but from knowledge of his own life and of the characters whom he permitted to represent him in his work, certain limited conclusions are rather evident. He believed in a supreme Deity; he reverenced Christ, but felt that His true image had been deformed by centuries-old formalisms and encrustations symbolized by Spanish reliquary art and outmoded religious customs. He was vigorously humanitarian (in the tradition of Kraus). His last brief play, *Santa Juana de Castilla* (1920), probably sheds very valuable light upon his deepest convictions. Here he depicts the later San Francisco de Borja as the comforter of Juana, whose *erasmista* tendencies were used as an excuse to consider her mad. Completely fictitious, the play none-the-less anticipates the modern re-evaluation of Erasmus. It also shows a longing toward the ecumenical spirit of Pope John XXIII and religious open-mindedness of the second half of the twentieth century. Certain it is, however, that the author, whatever his own beliefs might have been, is in no sense opposed to religion in general. He concentrates his fire on manifestations of any religious or denominational nature — or, indeed, of any social nature — which tended to separate rather than unite mankind. Because his own temperament was basically religious, he felt deformations of religion keenly — bitterly, at times. And his approach to clerical problems, strong as it is, is vastly different from that of certain other authors, who, it will be seen, have extended anticlericalism into an attempt to discredit all forms of religion.

At times some of the author's situations and characters may seem a bit extreme. At times some of the words and thoughts that Pérez Galdós puts into the mouths of his characters may seem, from our vantage point, to lie more in the realm of caricature. The de Lantigua brothers, for example — their ideas on church and state, the bishop's attitude toward people of other faiths. One has only to check back to the climate of opinion studied in the last chapter to see that this is not caricature or distortion. Serious people writing in respectable publications or in carrying out the exercise of important offices spoke very similar words and thoughts. The views that Pérez Galdós' attributes to the "clericals" are practically direct quotations from real Spanish life. It may also be hard to believe that a religiously-inclined woman could stage a murder. Yet Bernanos knew an ex-novice who figured in eight murders in Mallorca during the first days of the Civil War. It may be hard to believe that a bishop could call a Jew a God-murderer. Yet the Church in its official public worship on Good Friday has only recently stopped praying "for the wicked Jews." And the entire problem of the collective guilt of the Jews in the Crucifixion of Christ has not (as of this writing) been finally disposed of by the Second Vatican Council. Doña Perfecta's attitude toward science and the young scientist Pepe may seem extreme — hard to believe. Yet the confrontation of Perfecta and Pepe has all the tell-tale signs of the larger confrontation of clericalism and sincere liberalism that was taking place in Spain, and that was to culminate eventually in the murder and bloodshed of the Civil War.

VICENTE BLASCO IBÁÑEZ (1867-1928)

1. *Republican*

Anticlericalism in the novels of Blasco Ibáñez is much more intense and vehement than in the work of Pérez Galdós. This intensification is due in part to circumstances of time because the author's creative life spanned the aggravation of the conditions associated with the anticlerical spirit. The intensification is due in part also to the circumstances of the author's life, for, in his youth particularly, he lived close to the pattern of protest and shared in the aspirations of the downtrodden. These aspirations were summed up under the then rather loosely applied and nebulously understood term of "republican." At the age of eighteen he was arrested for writing an inflammatory sonnet and served six months in prison; in 1891, after his release, he emigrated to France. In 1892 he was back in Spain where he founded and edited *El Pueblo*, "one of the oldest radical newspapers of Spain."[26] The republican cause became the meaning of his life. He plunged into the labyrinth of socialism, anarchism and syndicalism and became noted for his oratorical abilities in addresses to large groups of workers and peasants. He served several times in the Cortes in the years immediately after the turn of the century. Pitollet accurately observes: "To be republican in the days of the regency of María Cristina meant in some way to be anticlerical . . . and to be in favor of social reform."[27]

2. *Anticlericalism in the Valencian Novels*

Critics have tried to divide Blasco Ibáñez' works into various periods. Consequently, there are almost as many divisions as critics. The subtleties of division need not be of concern here beyond the fact that the novels fall into three fairly definite general categories. The "Valencian novels" reveal Blasco Ibáñez, the young enthusiast and sensitive artist. The "Spanish novels" embrace the entire country and probe sociological problems (for example *Sangre y Arena* [1908], which is concerned with bull fighting). The "best sellers" exhibit the author's almost complete sacrifice of art in the interests of popularity. This latter tendency was first strongly manifested in *Los Cuatro Jinetes del Apocalipsis* (1916) in which the much travelled novelist and rather self-styled world citizen placed his talents at the service of propaganda. To the first group belong such famous works as *Arroz y Tartana* (1894), *Flor de Mayo* (1895), *Cañas y Barro* (1902), the *Cuentos Valencianos* (1893), and the masterpiece *La Barraca* (1898). These works are definitely "regional." Their intensity of plot and action and riot of keenly observed local color bring to life the *huerta*, or garden, of Spain, and, in *Flor de Mayo*, the life of the sea-faring folk of the region. In these works anticlericalism is usually incidental and not a main theme.

In *La Barraca* (*The Hut*), for example, the author was mainly concerned with his masterfully presented plot and the superb treatment of detail that evokes the plight of the simple people. He stresses their desperate need for education and liberation from prejudices, ignorance and the dead hand of an outmoded social system. The portrayal of "the Water Tribunal" shows the social system at its worst. An anticlerical thread is woven into the pattern of the scene. The Tribunal met to decide water disputes in front of the Cathedral of Valencia. The justice dispensed creaks with the abuses of age and the unrealistic traditionistic policy totally out of harmony with the reality of the peasants' struggle. The Door of the Apostles is described with the author's consummate skill, so frequently demonstrated in his treatment of Spanish monuments. But it seems as if the living judicial figures of the Tribunal merge with the stone apostolic figures in the tympanum. The scene, consequently, suggests the alliance of clerical power with the weight of thoroughgoing traditionalism.[28] If the living set of figures is outmoded, are not the stone representations also? Of what service can religion be in the social struggle of mankind? Blasco Ibáñez does not say this bluntly. But here and elsewhere he leaves his anticlerical symbols "open" in such wise that it is very easy to infer from the "clerical situation" to religion in general. The tendency to make such an inference is greater because of the vehemence and power of his prose.

Another important instance in *La Barraca* can be found in the death and funeral rites of the little boy, *Pascualet,* nicknamed *Obispillo.* The child's unhappy end had been caused by the equally unhappy confluence of prejudice, filth, and the lack of proper medical and sanitary knowledge. The vigil rites are described with a combination of brutal realism, the power of which is somewhat marred by typically Spanish repetition and over-emphasis. The general impression, however, remains true to the lives of these simple folk. Anguished cries of "Poor little Pascual! . . . Poor little Bishop!" are intermingled with the regionalized rites and pious ejaculations. The simple faith of the people emerges vividly amid the macabre ritual. Intermingled in the various episodes is a note subtlely suggesting that the comforts of religion — however much they may be believed by simple folk — are empty vain shows.[29]

Another Valencian novel, *Cañas y Barro* (*Reeds and Mud*), deals with the rice growing people in the swamp and lake district of Albufera. It is a tale of violence, jealousy, and illicit love. Immersed in the vivid projection of his plot and the thoughtfully wrought character studies, the author had little occasion to dwell on anticlericalism. From time to time, however, it does enter — largely through the character Sangonereta, who is a strange combination of drunkard, idealist, and vagrant. It was Sangonereta's habit to sit in the twilight and enjoy the beauty of the lake at sunset, seen through his alcoholic haze. At such times he would meditate upon Christian philosophy. Judging from what we know through other sources of Blasco Ibáñez' attitudes toward religion and clericalism, it is reasonable to assume that he considers the Christian solution to life to be as impractical as Sangonereta himself. In fact, the vagrant seems to personify the author's criticism of the elements of mysticism and impracticality found in certain segments of the Spanish character — qualities which lead people directly into the toils of the rapacious, symbolized by the hydropic inn-keeper, Cañamel. Sagonereta professed his philosophy of life "with a sort of mysticism that contrasted with his boozy breath." And he recalled "his readings in the Bible. The precepts that had clung in his memory. It was unnecessary to worry about food and drink because, as Jesus said, the birds neither sowed nor reaped . . . He wanted to be like the birds of the lake that throve in the reed-grass — vagrant, inactive, and without any resources except Divine Providence." Like the Spanish people, Sagonerata's religious philosophy does not exclude the possibility of being anticlerical. "He had fought with his pastor and left the rectory forever. It was repulsive for him to see in his old friends a spirit contrary to what he had read in his books. They were all the same. They lived tortured by the desire for the filthy *peseta,* thinking about food and clothing."[30] Other passages in the novel contain acrid criticism of poor taste in liturgical functions, particularly in music. "During the Mass the women melted when they heard the tenors sing Neopolitan barcarolles in honor of The Child Jesus; the men kept time with their heads as the orchestra played with the voluptuousness of a waltz."[31] Blasco Ibáñez continually alluded to liturgical bad taste, especially in *La Catedral* (1903).

3. *Anticlericalism in* La Catedral; El Intruso *and other non-Valencian Novels of Social Protest*

In 1903 Blasco Ibáñez entered the Cortes. The same year saw the publication of *La Catedral.* The author's participation in elected office in the national assembly symbolized an approach to his art on a national rather than a regional basis. This shift of interest, however, brought with it a perceptible decline in artistic achievement. In *La Catedral* the author's descriptive powers are unimpaired. His pictures of the Cathedral of Toledo and his many varied portraits of the people who live within the walls of the community continue to reveal the hand of a master. But in plot and action he slips from his previous heights. In this novel he adopts a technique that he was to follow in many other works. He creates a situation which provides a vehicle for description and conversational debate, the development of which conveys an extrinsic message. The novel form thus becomes a rather obvious instrument of propaganda. As time went on Blasco Ibáñez' plots became more and more threadbare.

In *La Catedral* the situation is the following: Gabriel returns to Toledo to spend his remaining days with his brother, a lay functionary of the Cathedral. Gabriel had been a seminarian who had changed his cassock for the garb of a *carlista* volunteer. Deflected from his vocation he spent some time in Paris where his religious convictions were displaced by revolutionary socialism. Upon his return to Toledo he is tubercular and almost at the point of death due to the many imprisonments and hardships suffered in the revolutionary cause. During his stay at the Cathedral Gabriel holds many conversations in which he alternately develops the tenets of his new creed to the laymen or defends his position against his brother and the other clerical supporters. Thus, he becomes the protagonist of a social theme which the author projects with heavy anticlerical coloring. Here it is difficult if not impossible to separate anticlericalism proper from antireligion. In Blasco Ibáñez' treatment the second seems to follow from the first. The symbolism of the Water Tribunal in *La Barraca* becomes the unambiguous theme of *La Catedral*. The Cathedral and its precincts are a sort of model-to-scale, a *microcosmus,* of Spain. Its beautiful galleries, residences, and porticos are peopled by powerful, predatory prelates and insignificant, quibbling canons. In the immediate shadow of the mouldering but magnificent walls and in the economic orbit of service to the Cathedral live the laymen (both the devout and the external conformists) whose children die of malnutrition and poverty. Gabriel, in his conversations, makes the people aware of their clerical oppression; his is the revolutionary voice amid the pattern of protest. "Who would have believed that he [Gabriel] was there. Who would have believed that that pile of stones seven centuries old, built by political power and a dying faith, would be his last refuge?"[32]

In his various conversations Gabriel tackles the multiple problems associated with clericalism. By indirection, Spanish fear of the free circulation of ideas — so frequently attended by policies of rigorous censorship — is attacked. Esteban, Gabriel's brother, exclaims in affectionate reproach: "Oh Brother . . . where has your avid reading of books and newspapers brought you? Why this desire to rearrange everything that is all right as it is, or if it's not all right, cannot be helped anyway."[33] Similarly, by indirection, Blasco Ibáñez attacks the Inquisition and the effects of the inquisitorial mentality upon Spain. In the description of Gabriel's deceased father, who was the Cathedral gardener, we learn that this worthy had been "indignant against the government of Fernando VII because it had not been sufficiently 'pure.' Out of fear of foreigners he had not dared to re-establish the salutory tribunal of the Inquisition."[34] By means of a retrospective description the author treats the unfortunate mixture of clericalism and carlism. The garden seems to symbolize the tenacious nature of the Spanish clerical point of view:

The garden, insensitive and deaf to the revolutionary tempests that were breaking over the Church, continued on her way amid the arcades of her gloomy beauty. The laurels grew straight up to the railings of the high cloister. The tops of the cypresses tossed as though they wanted to scale up the roofs. The twining ivy blended into the grill-work of the cloister . . . and tapestried the central gallery, ending at a black slate wall with a rusted iron cross. Inside the garden, after finishing choir, the clerics read. In the greeny brightness that filtered through the foliage they perused the newspapers of the *carlista* partisans or commented enthusiastically on the accomplishments of Cabrera.[35]

Catholic intolerance in history becomes the source of one of Gabriel's meditations. "After the pious tolerance of earlier bishops, accustomed to treat with Jews and Arabs within the broad liberty of the mozarabic practise, came the ferocious intransigeance of the Christian conquerer . . . Nothing was impossible for Don Gil de Albornoz. He was the sword of the apostle who had come back to the world to impose faith by

force."[36] Throughout the work Blasco Ibáñez' historical interpretations leave a pessimistic impression. His view of Spanish history seems as negative as the ideas later developed by Ortega y Gasset.

As the novel progresses these themes, all of which on face value can be classed as anticlerical in the strict interpretation of the word, become charged with a bias that seems to be directed first against Christianity and finally against religion in general. The attempts of French Catholicism to adjust its outlook in the scientific era is scorned. Gabriel while in Paris had noted that entire books had been written on scientific subjects by priests in a desperate effort to find tenuous sanctuary within the confines of new scientific directions. Gabriel describes the growth of Christianity as "the appearance of some obscure men in Judea who spread out through the world preaching a cosmopolite doctrine taken from the maxims of the oriental peoples and the teachings of Greek philosophy."[37] In contemporary times the Church is "a huge ruin, the petrified carcass of an animal that was powerful and strong in its own day; but it had died more than a century ago, its body breaking up, its soul evaporating until there was nothing left but this exterior shell."[38]

Like other authors (such as Pérez de Ayala and the writers of the Republican and Civil War Era) Blasco Ibáñez' priests are the antithesis of what would be desireable in servants of a religious cause. His fabulously wealthy, greedy, irascible, and vengeful Cardinal is grievously troubled because the people whisper uncharitable rumors about his "niece." She is his illegitimate daughter whom he dearly loves; rumor slanders her by suggesting that she is his mistress. One usurious priest is a monster of ugliness. He is described as possessing "the solid and saintly coarseness so esteemed in other centuries."[39] Dissatisfied with his salary he devised a money-making scheme which oppressed the poorer workers with exorbitant interest rates. The popular indignation against such types is expressed by Tomasa, Gabriel's aunt, who says she believes in the Virgin of the Ciborium and a little bit in God. She disdains clerics more for their pretense of virtue than their defects.[40] Don Martín is the one "good priest" in the novel. Like Padre Atienza in Pérez de Ayala's *A. M. D. G.,* he is continually victimized by his colleagues. His vocation was entirely the result of his mother's wishes. He devotes his energies to music in an attempt to raise the artistic level of liturgical ceremonies. He speaks his mind, in typical anticlerical fashion, on a variety of topics. He has a poor opinion of nuns in general. He has less hope for Christian democracy: "It's enough to make you die laughing when they speak of equality and of democratic spirit in the Church. It's a lie. No other institution is ruled by such a cruel despotism." He also takes quite a dim view of his own celibate state in life: "What a disillusion, Gabriel! To renounce love and the family, to flee from all the pleasures of the world — theatre, concerts, cafés."[41] It is not surprising therefore, when, upon the death of his mother, Don Martín abandons the priesthood.

Gabriel's indoctrinating conversations reach their peak and become more like revolutionary sermons in Chapter VII, when he preaches to a motley mixture of lay folk. He claims that the Church is dead and the battle is only with a lifeless form. He maintains that the people cannot understand their lot because they have been fed on rudimentary ideas of the universe propagated by rag-picking Jews. Catholic doctrine taught inside the Cathedral is nothing. So, too, the laws and governing conventions of society. God is humanity and the universe in their constant patterns of change. Man is god. When god was invented the earth had been in existence for a long time.[42] These sentiments succeed in unleashing the revolutionary beast. A group of the Cathedral workers, fired by Gabriel's words, enters to rob the altars of priceless treasures. Gabriel, who is serving as a guard, remonstrates and tries to convince them that their ends cannot be achieved by violence and plunder. He falls mortally wounded at their hands. Thus, Blasco Ibáñez, within the framework of his symbolism, predicted the social disorders and mob violence associated with the pattern of protest in the following decades. It comes as a shock when the author leads Gabriel's life to this lamentable end, because he seems suddenly to disengage himself from the revolutionary in order to stress the inherent social dangers of the people's struggle. He thus fails to identify completely with his protagonist. And he correctly shows that the force of revolution released into the hands of a mob will lead to tragedy.

One of the best descriptive passages in *La Catedral* is the portrayal of the Corpus Christi procession. Gabriel was one of ten bearers of the float on which the huge monstrance rested. He was delighted at this opportunity to see the streets of Toledo and to earn some money; the anomaly of his function caused him an ironic laugh. As in Pérez Galdós' description of a procession in *Gloria,* Blasco Ibáñez' picture vivifies the local color of the ritual amid satirical thrusts at the trappings of Spanish confessional unity. It was a theme which he frequently employed and which drew upon his descriptive skill. There is a similarly interpreted Corpus celebration in *Arroz y Tartana;*[43] *Flor de Mayo* contains a Good Friday procession which is full of local color and regional prejudices;[44] *Sangre y Arena* contains a Holy Saturday ritual.[45]

El Intruso followed hard upon the heels of *La Catedral* in 1904. Like most of the novels from the author's middle period, it projects a powerful theme of social protest. In this instance poverty and hunger, blighted life and sudden death are portrayed in the mining communities near Bilbao. Amid the cries and imprecations of the poor, the author skillfully weaves a specific and highly controversial motif: the influence of clerics (particularly the Jesuits) in family life — hence the title theme of "the intruder." The central figure of the story is Aresti, a young, highly talented, altruistic doctor who spends his time ministering to the poor. Endowed with an interior calm based upon confidence in the ultimate triumph of "Science and Social Justice" he is able to identify with the aspirations and sufferings of the poor and to stand apart and evaluate with a calculating eye what he conceives to be the causes of a suffering humanity. His disposition is less revolutionary than Gabriel's. His beliefs are basically the same but he realizes that time is not ripe; the masses are stupid and have no real leaders. Hence, he can only bind wounds and believe in the sure advent of a better day when science and social justice will have relegated the saints to the museum.

It would be redundant further to analyze Aresti's beliefs and anticlerical statements because of their underlying similarity with those of Gabriel. The specific theme of "the intruder," however, is most important and calls to mind Pérez Galdós' *La Familia de León Roch.* José Sánchez Morueta, Aresti's beloved cousin, is the most powerful magnate of the district. He is immensely wealthy and subscribes to no particular religion. Doña Cristina, his wife, has long been on the road to becoming a complete *beata* and has turned from the world to "the things of the spirit." Consequently, for some time Sánchez Morueta has been assuaging his sexual appetite with the delights of dalliance in Madrid, where he maintained a separate establishment and whither he went on frequent "business trips." It so happens, however, that the sudden collapse of this love affair was practically coincident with his wife's desire to recapture her husband's attention. Under the advice of her Jesuit confessor, Padre Paulí, Doña Cristina abandons her hair shirt and returns to her lingerie. Sánchez Morueta, broken in body and spirit by the loss of his love, is ripe for the change of heart in his wife and thus falls under her dominion. When Aresti visits his cousin he finds the latter reading a book of piety. The next meeting takes place at the Jesuit establishment which houses certain shrines hallowed by St. Ignatius. Aresti has stopped here out of antiquarian curiosity. About to leave after his conducted tour he is horrified to see his cousin as one of the retreatants. Aresti now realizes that the *intruso* is gaining ascendancy over Sánchez Morueta and is drawing him and his enormous influence toward the side of reaction. The third and final encounter with Sánchez Morueta takes place during the procession in honor of the *Virgen de Begoña.* As Aresti watches he sees the huge figure of his cousin loom up among the marchers. A riot breaks out between the faithful and the revolutionaries who have come to jeer. Aresti tries to remain aloof but gets swept along in the mêlée. Aresti and Sánchez Morueta come together in a terrible frenzied scene where Aresti realizes that the giant beating the rabble is his cousin. He spits in his face. The millionaire, enormously shocked to be so treated by his cousin whom he cherished like a brother, wiped the spittle of hate from his beard and was about to speak when "a black phantom that vibrated in a cloak furnished with funereal wings" pulled him away. It was Father Paulí, "urging Sánchez on toward Begoña as if the millionaire were the leading standard of the procession."[46]

As the novel comes to a close the rioting is still flaring spasmodically. Aresti wanders down to the river. He ponders his encounter with Sánchez Morueta and muses darkly:

Ah, the intruder; the god-damned intruder . . . who kills all affection and with a cold, deathly hand wipes out a past of fraternal love.[47]

A group of revolutionaries swarms down with the plundered statues, among them the "Virgen de Begoña," and casts them into the water. As the action moves toward the last paragraphs the focus maintained throughout upon Aresti's particular psychology becomes blurred and it is difficult to distinguish him from Blasco Ibáñez. The collaboration between clerical and wealthy elements in the new industrialism is resoundingly condemned:

The old Bilbao of the merchants and sailors, Bilbao ignorant of the value of iron had been happier. There was peace in its slow orderly work and in the fraternal gentleness of its customs. Not so in the modern town with its nouveau riche fortunes, its stupid ostentation and its rapid, erratic wealth which was soon to be swallowed, for the most part, into the dark gullet of the black intruder. The intruder appeared at the supreme moment of good fortune to take his place beside the favorites of Lady Luck, offering heaven to them in exchange for a share of the booty.[48]

With remarkable foresight, as at the conclusion of La Catedral, Blasco Ibáñez foretells the future course of the pattern of protest. A madman revolutionary, El Barbas, harangues the remnants of the crowd. The author puts into his mouth words whose vehemence can be paralleled only in the revolutionary writers of the Civil War. They are prophetic words:

"You haven't seen anything today," he shouted. "I don't think it's too bad if people have laid hands on the ones who have deceived them so long. But after this the bill will have to be settled by the ones who have done the robbing. Today was the battle over their lousy holy relics. Tomorow will be the battle for bread. Then they'll come down from the mountain — the ones whose labor has produced the robbers' riches. And they will demand their share. There will be no authorized petitions, or pay increases, or hand-outs. Out with blood-suckers. To each one his due. And to anyone who tries to stop it — dynamite! . . ."[49]

Thus, Blasco Ibáñez in *El Intruso* fordshadows the bitterness of the controversy over the Jesuits in the Republic and predicts the violence of the Civil War. *La Catedral* and *El Intruso* are his most powerful anticlerical novels. They also figure among the most violent anticlerical works in the Spanish tradition.

The year following *El Intruso* (i.e. 1905) saw the appearance of two additional powerful novels of protest. They were *La Bodega* and *La Horda*. The former takes place in Jerez in Andalucía and dwells upon the wine industry and — another side of the picture — drunkenness. Once again the claims of science and social justice are extolled by an idealist. In this instance it is Fernando Salvatierra, an active revolutionary, who raises the standard. The anticlericalism in the novel has the same basic tone. Most frequently it is leveled at the hypocrisy of the greedy and wealthy with whom the clergy frequently make common cause in the novel. For example, one of the wealthy wine merchants is described as follows:

[He]was capable of the greatest extravagances as a result of his religious exhaltation. For Dupont, every proprietor was so by divine right, like the kings of old. It was God's will that there be rich and poor. The underdogs had to obey the ones over them because this was dictated by the social order that had its origin in heaven. . . .
He made a great display of humility, to the point of becoming servile whenever some secular priest or one of the friars of the various religious orders with house in Jerez visited his office. He would try to kneel and kiss their hands, not succeeding only because they would restrain him with a benevolent smile. He was visibly satisfied when

these visitors would address him familiarly and call him Pablito as they used to when he was their student.

Let Jesus and His Holy Mother stand above all commercial enterprises. They would watch over the best interests of the house, while he in his turn, simple sinner that he was, would limit himself to receiving their inspiration.[50]

What little action there is in *La Horda* takes place in and around Madrid. The novel presents a motley picture of social outcasts — beggars, poachers on the royal preserves, derelicts, drunken women, prostitutes, etc. These persons wander in and out of the bleak and tragic life of Isidro Maltrana, an impoverished writer and idealist who found his hellenic quest most impractical. There is little anticlericalism in the powerful, dismal pages. Occasionally there is a flash of implication or insinuation when reference is made to the rich. The strongest passage of this sort is found in the final pages. Once again Blasco Ibáñez assumes the role of seer. He causes Maltrana to look out over the city and then writes:

It was beautiful and pitiless. It cast misery away, denying its existence. If from time to time it thought about the unfortunates it would be to build monasteries in the suburbs where the wooden statues were better cared for than the God's flesh-and-blood sons. They were the monstrously big monasteries whose bells tolled and tolled and nobody heard them. The poor, the desperate did not understand their language, but they noted the false timbre. Those bells tolled for others. They were not calls to love; they were snorts of vanity.[51]

4. *Best Sellers*

Blasco Ibáñez devoted the ten years following these novels of social protest to world travels, lectures, and adventurous agricultural experiments in South America. He began to pose as a seer, a sort of prototype of "Papa" Hemingway, whom he strongly resembles. Now his novels opened up to embrace the entire world. The tendency toward propaganda and all-inclusive condemnatory generalizations continued. The year 1916 saw the publication of *The Four Horsemen of the Apocalypse,* a work intended largely to stimulate sympathy for the allied cause in World War I.

Blasco Ibáñez' last decades show a steady decline in artistic merit. Many of his late works employ the "conversational frame" of *La Catedral* in ever increasing measure. The intentions of the people's champion become suspect as he developed a deepening affinity for the soft sophistications of life. Blasco Ibáñez the revolutionary had become a very old Riviera playboy.

In two related novels of the last years the author devoted himself once more to developing an anticlerical theme. By now, however, his anticlericalism has lost any immediate political significance; rather, the novels are simply vehicles for subjective antireligious and pro-Spanish bias. *El Papa del Mar* (1925) is built in the "conversational frame" of a sophisticated dalliance on the Riviera. Claudio Borja is in love with a wealthy Argentinian widow, Rosaura. The young gentleman has a Spanish antiquarian's interest in the story of Pedro de Luna, an anti-Pope at the time of the Great Western Schism. In the course of the lovers' travels to Avignon and other historic points of interest, the author sketches, through Claudio, part of the history of de Luna's medieval times. It is the various ecclesiastical recriminations, scandals, and conspiracies, however, which he portrays. A strong predilection for the Spanish claimant to the Papal throne is also evident. This extends even to saints when these were supporters of Pedro. Saint Vincent Ferrer, who supported the anti-Pope, is treated kindly. But the picture of St. Brigid of Sweden, who opposed, is hardly flattering:

St. Brigid enjoyed great popularity in Italy . . . She was rich and spent a lot of money on her trips and the people of that country liked their saints with money. She was a relative of the reigning dynasty in Sweden and they married her off to a great lord of the country who was equally mystical — a fact that didn't keep them from having nine children. . . .
Her books were considered heretical from the moment they appeared. Years later, when the Pope of Rome made her a saint, they were strangely considered free of such defects.[52]

The sequel to this novel, *A los Pies de Venus* (1926), continues the history of Claudio's love affair with Rosaura. There enters into the picture Don Baltasar, a *canónigo* who is

Claudio's uncle. The priest is a worthy cleric withall, only slightly addicted to over-eating and drinking. Although he looks with the indulgent eye of Latin Catholicism upon Claudio's youthful indiscretions, he wishes to extricate the young man from Rosaura's toils, because the *canónigo* is convinced that Claudio has a mission to perform in life, namely the writing of a history of the Borgia Popes, Claudio's remote ancestors. Don Baltasar had hoped to perform this historical service himself, but he explains: "I am a priest. And every time I take up my pen to write about them I have doubts, I am afraid. It seems to me that I am going to be derelict in the duties which Church discipline places upon me."[53] Don Baltasar explains further that he has no wish to clear these Popes of scandal. He merely wants to point out that they were no worse than other Renaissance prelates. Into this frame, Blasco Ibáñez weaves the historical pattern of the Borgias and their times. Once again the accent is continually upon scandal, sensation, intrigue, etc. Frequent Renaissance sexual excesses are treated with a lingering emphasis upon detail combined with a puritanical recoil of horror. As in *La Catedral* and *El Papa del Mar* there is a complete void when it comes to understanding of what people of religious sensibilities call the spiritual life. Although accurate in historical detail the author's treatment is tendencious and insensitive to subtlety or variations in shading. A random check reveals that he uses the same historical material as such Catholic writers as John Farrow in *Pageant of the Popes* and Ludwig von Pastor in his monumental *Geschichte der Päpste*.[54] But in Blasco Ibáñez' hands this history becomes a pastiche of excesses and a titillation of pruriency.

5. *Publisher*

Blasco Ibáñez' literary activity was not confined to editing the radical *El Pueblo* in his youth and writing novels in his maturity. Like Ortega y Gasset he controlled a publishing house, the *Editorial Prometeo,* the proceeds of which added substantially to his ever increasing wealth. As in the case of

Ortega y Gasset, Blasco Ibáñez ostensibly hoped to inculcate good Spanish reading habits and a receptivity in Spain for new or foreign ideas. A glance at a list of the *Prometeo's* "Popular Library" reveals such names as Guy de Maupassant, Pío Baroja, Ruskin and Altamira. The list also includes Bakunin, Engels, Marx, and Gorki. Mérimée is represented by *Los Hugonotes;* Nietzsche is favored by eleven titles; Renan is included as is Darwin; Gabriele D'Annunzio's *Epíscopo y Compañía* is advertised prominently. The violently radical anti-clerical Nakens and Blasco Ibáñez respectively treat the problems of monarchy in *Los Horrores del Absolutismo* and *Una Nación Encadenada.* It is obvious that in his publishing business as well as in his middle novels, the author maintained his revolutionary interests.

It is a tribute to the freedom of thought of the Spain of pre-Directorate days that this publishing activity, so inimical to a paternalistic confessional atmosphere, was allowed to continue. But if official sanctions were lacking, there was evidently no lack of private attempts of censorship. Arturo Barea writes in his *The Forging of a Rebel*:

We had to take care because of the Fathers at the school. If they caught us with a book of the "Illustrated Novel" series, they took it away and tore it to bits. We were only allowed a "Novel of Today." . . .

I had a funny experience because of this. Both series published one and the same book by Balzac, the "Illustrated Novel" under the title *Eugenie Grandet* and the "Novel of Today" under the title *Los Avaros de Provincias.* I showed them to Father Vegas, the most bigoted of all our teachers, and asked him whether I ought to tear up this "Illustrated Novel" edition as well, although it was the same book as the other one. He got as angry as a wild cat, punished me, and confiscated both books. After this he mounted the dais, banged his fist on the table and on the two books and explained:

". . . So as to make people confuse this edition of Calleja, as you all know, a Christian firm which would never lower itself to printing such filth as Blasco Ibáñez publishes in his dirty 'Illustrated Novel.' . . . No, gentlemen, it is not permitted to buy a single copy of the 'Illustrated Novel!!' "

At this the priest had a mad fit of rage; I believe he would have killed Blasco Ibáñez if he had been there.[55]

6. *Concluding Remarks*

It is evident that many of the topics that Pérez Galdós treated in his anticlerical works were reiterated by Blasco Ibáñez. Freedom in educational and intellectual areas is a theme which reappears constantly. The peculiar tendency of the Spanish religious spirit to turn in upon itself and dwell upon past glory, to the neglect of progress and adjustments with the modern spirit, is more vigorously and heavily underlined and anticipates Ortega y Gasset. The republican motif, however, only adumbrated by Pérez Galdós, emerges very strongly in Blasco Ibáñez. Protagonists such as Gabriel in *La Catedral* represent the *potpourri* of various radical philosophies grouped under the vague popular concept of "republican," to which the author himself adhered in his younger days. But Blasco Ibáñez differs even more strikingly from Pérez Galdós on one important point. As a professional champion of liberalism, he would be expected to avoid a doctrinaire viewpoint; yet the tone of his middle and late novels is as doctrinaire as the viewpoints which he condemns. He seems to extend his criticism of clericalism in a way that spread into a blanket condemnation of religion and the religious spirit. The fanatical clerical viewpoint which Barea records is hardly commendable. But many of Blasco Ibáñez' lesser novels and some of the work of his publishing house must in all fairness be classed as scurrilous. Of course, it is always possible — at times necessary — to ask the question: Where does Blasco Ibáñez end and where do his characters begin? For example, to what extent does the author identify with Gabriel? Is he not merely trying to project an adequate picture of a hard-bitten revolutionary type? Doesn't he disassociate himself from Gabriel at the end of *La Catedral* and grimly depict the awful result of revolutionary ideas in the minds of an illiterate mob? The answer is, of course, impossible, if we are looking for exact information, whether dealing with Blasco Ibáñez or Hemingway, or any other author. In this case, however, we must remember that Blasco Ibáñez was primarily a nineteenth century writer and nineteenth century literature is frequently didactic. Blasco Ibáñez was frequently didactic and openly propagandistic. In addition, he had long schooling in revolutionary thought and he was a rebel most of his life. Consequently it would be fair to say that he personally may not have espoused *all* the revolutionary, anticlerical, antireligious ideas that he puts in the mouths of his characters. And it is also fair to say that he probably espoused *most* of them. He remains one of Spain's most powerful, masterful writers.

Blasco Ibáñez became reconciled with the Church before his death.

MIGUEL DE UNAMUNO (1864-1936)

1. *Religion and Reason*

Vastly different from the tone of Blasco Ibáñez is the spirit of Unamuno. In fact, it can be said that Unamuno differs radically from all the authors treated in this study. He is quite unique. And yet in a very definite sense he typifies in his own life and in the interior of his consciousness some of the turmoil within the Spanish soul which produced the phenomenon of anticlericalism and its manifestations in men of letters. His life and thought were a continual struggle between "the old" and "the new" — vantage points which, we have seen and will continue to see, served also as points of departure for the various antagonists in the anticlerical controversy. In Unamuno, however, the struggle between the new and the old was centered in a clash between reason and religion. Reason clutched at his intellect, yet he would never accept any rationalist interpretation of man and the universe which reduced the solution of all problems to the application of science. The religious spirit was a very vital force of his life, yet he could not bring himself to accept the theological structure of Christianity.

As is well known, Unamuno examines these polarities and their resultant tension in his famous work, *Del Sentimiento Trágico de la Vida, en los Hombres y en los Pueblos* (1913) (*The Tragic Sense of Life in Men and Nations*). This work is an extended statement of the same all-absorbing thought which is central to practically all his significant production, whether it be novel, essay, or poetry. The "tragic sense" is the supporting pillar of his intellectual life and it casts its shadow upon his critical evaluations of esthetic, social, or economic endeavor. An understanding of Unamuno's position with relation to the Church and religion as well as an evaluation of what sense he can be called anticlerical can be gained only by considering the essence and implications of his tragic sense. But we should not forget that Unamuno contradicted himself freely, sometimes within the compass of a single sentence. Therefore I have tried to correlate, *pro* and *con,* as much of his significant work as possible within the limits of this study. My interpretation is only the sketch of a larger study yet to be written.

The fact that Unamuno's life was torn between the claims of reason and religion should never lead to the superficial conclusion that he was atheistic, irreligious, or even agnostic in the ordinary sense. Arturo Barea goes so far as to say that he "belonged [to the] Roman Catholic Church in which he had grown up, . . . irrevocably, heterodox or heretic though he was."[56] Preoccupation with religion and its problems can be seen in his first important work, *En Torno al Casticismo* (1895), in which, like his tragic contemporary, Ganivet, he propounded what he believed to be the formula for a common denominator of that which is basically Spanish and that which is "basically European." In the fourth essay of the series, "Mysticism and Humanism," he dwells at length upon the spiritual writers of the Golden Age. He speaks with guarded enthusiasm of the mystics' quest for God. He believes, however, that these writers should be re-interpreted with an eye to the Spain of the future and rejects them in so far as they are *"de El posesores"* — "possessors of Him."[57] This was a very important point in Unamuno's life and thought. He considered himself an "awakener of sleeping souls." Consequently he abhorred the thought of God wrapped up snugly in the supposedly irrefutable syllogisms of rational theology. Knowledge of God should be a constant struggle, since His essence is infinite and the fonts of Christ's mercy and love unfathomable. A tradition of *"de El posesores,"* he consequently felt, led to an unbearable stultification of the individual and of society. From the viewpoint of Catholic theological thought, Unamuno was of course one hundred percent correct on this point. Most fair minded theologians would admit with Unamuno that the moment a person believes to have God neatly tied up without any further search necessary, that person can be quite certain that God has already eluded him. St. John of the Cross, for one, in his *Spiritual Canticle* eloquently describes the soul's constant search. To the extent that God dwells within the soul in Grace, of course, He has "adopted" the person, as St. Paul says. But any spiritual life worthy of the name is a struggle to in some way experience the presence of God who is basically beyond our rational comprehension. Unamuno felt that there were a great many *"de El posesores"* in Spain and that they had poisoned the Spanish air with their smug attitudes.

Within the passage of a few years, Unamuno's thought had undergone a radical shift with regard to the problems of Spain. He once had said in effect, "We'll have to kill Don Quijote and resuscitate Alonso Quijano the Good" if we want to get Spain back on the track.[58] In 1905 he published his *Vida de Don Quijote y Sancho (Life of Don Quixote and Sancho)*. Now he recreates the Sorrowful Knight (in the teeth of any intended Cervantist meaning), into the eternal idealist, the mystic soul of Spain, the continual searcher for the unattainable. And this Don Quijote is none other than Miguel de Unamuno himself, for he identifies completely with his beloved Knight. He was known to have said frequently "I am Don Quijote." Once he told John A. Mackay that "Spain is not at home when Don Quijote is wandering abroad."[59] In connection with this attitude he modified his views on both the "europeanization" of Spain and modern scientific advances. Now he felt the world should be "hispanized," in so far as Don Quijote represents the best of Spain's essence.

Don Quijote also represents Unamuno in his own battle

against a superficial sense of material progress which he believed was ruining traditional Spanish values. The retelling of Cervantes' masterpiece is continually colored by a religious interpretation and religious analogies. In the episode of the Cave of Montesinos, for example, the Knight errant is likened to another Spanish seer, Iñigo de Loyola. Throughout the work the religious nature of the struggle is defined and redefined in terms of desire rather than fulfillment: "One must try, above all, to make oneself immortal. To this end Don Quijote incarnated Glory and called it Dulcinea del Toboso."[60]

Some critics have felt that Unamuno's preoccupation with immortality and glory, in this commentary, does not extend to these terms in their transcendental religious sense. Is he not talking about the immortality and glory that live on in the works and deeds of any great man? Perhaps the *Vida* does contain thoughts of this nature. There can be no doubt, however, that Unamuno is coming to grips with the most profound problems of religion — the existence of God and the survival of the human person — in his essay *Mi Religión* (*My Religion*), written in 1907:

And if I believe in God, or if at least I believe that I believe in Him, it is because first of all I want to believe that God exists; and secondly because He reveals Himself to me, by means of the heart, in the Gospel, through Christ, and through history. It is an affair of the Heart.

Which means to say that I am not as convinced of it in the way that I believe that two and two equal four.[61]

Concerning the constant struggle and movement of belief, he says: "My religion is to wrestle with God from dawn till dusk, like they say Jacob wrestled with Him. I can't put up with the Unknowable — or the Uncomprehensive about whom the pedants have written — nor with that other idea 'you won't get beyond here.' I reject the eternal *ignorabimus* (we will not know)."[62] With regard to the particular form of his "belief of the heart," he states: "Yes, in the movements of my heart and sentiments, I have a strong tendency toward Christianity." But he quickly adds, "without paying attention to the special dogmas of this or that Christian confession."[63] He amplifies this position by stating: "I sincerely declare that the supposed proofs for the existence of God — the ontological, the cosmological, the ethical, *et cetera* — prove nothing to me; any proofs that God exists seem to me to be paralogisms and beggings of the question."[64]

Can this "faith of the heart," from the Catholic point of view, be faith tortured but not extinguished by doubt? His problems with rational theology — though they tortured him — do not present an obstacle to basic orthodoxy, nor do his doubts, for the greatest believers have often been plagued with doubt. And although the Church ordinarily teaches that God's existence can be proved by reason, she does not say that anyone has proved it. Furthermore, although rational theology (particularly in its Thomistic expression) has for centuries been the ordinary norm of theology in the West, there are great segments of Catholicism — particularly in the Eastern Churches — and of Christianity in general that stress Unamuno's formula: "because He reveals Himself . . . in the Gospel, and through Christ and through history." Rational theology is merely the study, within limited areas, of what Catholic tradition believes reason can know about matters of faith. The formula for the baptism of a person converted to Catholicism *in extremis* does not demand more than belief in the existence of God and the revelation of Christ in time.

It is necessary to abandon this question after raising it. Catholic critics insist that in the last analysis these are private matters between the individual and God, and God alone has the final answer. On the other hand, it is necessary to raise them because Unamuno chose to make them public property, intimately connected with his attitude on practically everything. And in his case he seems, according to my interpretation, to have come to a point where it would be possible to say, "He claims to have believed." In other words I interpret him more as a believer than as a non-believer. Of course, this is the last thing that Unamuno would want. He didn't want to be "pinned down." To do so would violate his meaning of the tragic sense. It also violates his wish to project himself as a great symbol personifying the enigma of the modern world tortured by metaphysical doubts. Yet, can any man continually experience the polarities of faith and agnosticism, or experience them at the same moment? Unamuno always maintained his religious attitude in the ethical sense. This point should never be forgotten. Indeed, it needs to be emphasized strongly against the grey army of non-committed intellectuals who are too ready to see him as a champion of their own cause. It is possible, also, that his fluctuating attitude was due to a constant interchange of belief and doubt. His writings are a most intimate diary of his life. But if he must be "pinned down," I consider him to be more on the side of belief. Of course, there is a certain sense in which he is almost continually agnostic. But so is everyman. All thinking men would like to know more about God and His ways, but must confess that they know very little. Uamuno is also skeptical in the sense of one who "investigates and seeks in opposition to one who affirms and believes to have found." This, too, can be a healthy attitude when correctly understood.

The essay, "My Religion," states in fairly simple terms the idea which the author investigates more fully in *Del Sentimiento Trágico de la Vida*. In the latter work he examines carefully the motives for faith and the motives for disbelief amid a complexity of historical contexts and scholarly criticisms on both sides of the issue. In the fourth essay, entitled, "The Essence of Catholicism," he praises the Catholic tenacity of the doctrine of immortality and the organizational structure which protected this teaching in history through the Church councils. Once again he rejects the rational arguments supporting religious beliefs, for in his view reason is the enemy of faith: "Rationalism, and by this word I understand the doctrine that depends upon nothing but reason and on objective truth, is perforce materialistic. It is necessary to state it clearly: the truth is that what we call materialism has no other meaning for us than the denial of the immortality of the individual soul."[65] The consolation of despair, the victory in (not after) the struggle is examined in detail in the sixth essay which the author entitles "In the Bottom of the Pit." The tragic sense, the resultant of the tension, he claims, is "the very bottom of the consciousness both of individuals and of nations of our day . . ."

In many other works Unamuno repeats this perennial theme. Strong traces of it can be found in the novel *La Tía Tula* (*Aunt Tula*) published in 1920; it is the dominant chord of his delicately lyrical "The Song of the Eternal Waters." Arturo Barea refers to the brief *San Manuel Bueno, Mártir* (*The Good St. Manuel, Martyr*) also published in 1920 as "a more naked struggle . . . his tragic sense of human life made flesh."[66]

In his poetry Unamuno also expresses his tragic sense. "I have cried out in public," he says. "The psalms that appear in my volume of poetry are nothing more than the groanings of my heart."[67] His most famous poem, *El Cristo de Velázquez* (*The Christ of Velázquez*), gives full play to the religious impulse of his spirit directed toward the person of Christ, the Saviour. There is little of the tragic sense in this work and many critics consider it one of the most powerful and beautiful Catholic poems of the Twentieth Century. Unamuno, a great poet, brings the Spanish tradition of mystic poetry into our times. In other poems, also, such as the brief "Lord, Don't Despise Me," conservative critics would be hard pressed to find the slightest trace of heterodoxy. But the *gritos* associated specifically with the tragic sense emerge in his "Beauty," a poem of surpassing loveliness. He rises first to an ecstatic contemplation of the harmony of the universe as it comes from and rests in the hand of God:

> The towers point to the glory of God,
> The poplars raise their heads to His glory
> The heavens proclaim His glory
> And to that glory the waters rest.
> Time pauses;
> The eternal unfolds its inmost depths;
> Care and anxiety are washed away
> In the calm waters
> Amid the motionless poplars

Amid the towers painted in the heavens,
A sea of high worlds.
Repose rests in the beauty
Of God's heart who then shows us
The treasures of His glory

But clouds wash around the briefly glimpsed battlements. Tormenting doubt speedily returns.

Night falls, I awake,
My anxiety returns,
The lambent vision has faded,
I become a man once more.
And now tell me, Lord, tell me sincerely:
Will great beauty such as this
Destroy our death?[68]

2. *The Extent of Unamuno's Anticlericalism*

It is precisely at the point where reason fails Unamuno in his quest for faith (the point where his tragic sense is generated) that elements enter into his writings which in various senses can be classed as anticlerical. For example, in *Del Sentimiento Trágico de la Vida,* when evaluating the rational structure of Christian theology, and finding it inadequate, he expresses himself in strongly derogatory terms: "It was found necessary, for the benefit of the social order, to convert religion into a police force."[69] These words, used when discussing the nature of theological speculation, extend by implication to the hierarchy and clergy who are the traditional representatives of theological teaching. It would be useless to lengthen this essay by adducing more thoughts of the same nature. They can be found and interpreted similarly in individual passagess throughout the famous study and the other meditations on religion.

Although the rejection of rational theology does not necessarily always imply the rejection of faith, it does lead Unamuno to make statements which the most liberal Catholic criticism would unquestionably judge heterodox, if they are to be taken at face value. In his essay "Popular Materialism," he once again states his frank lack of concern for dogma. But he combines this with an ever growing preoccupation with the increase of materialism and abandonment of the religious spirit among the masses, such as Blasco Ibáñez seemed willing to stimulate in his *La Catedral.*

Unamuno not only proposes his critical attitudes as proper to himself but intends that they should disturb the minds of his readers. A thoughtful Catholic, consequently, can take a large segment of his provocative statements as a legitimate, stimulating challenge toward a creative meditation on the foundations of belief. It is an axiom of intelligent Catholicism that objections be not feared but rather faced and, where possible, answered. Unamuno's objections, however, were not constructed in a fashion designed to afford them a tolerant reception in a confessional atmosphere. Here was a man who claimed to be the incarnation of Don Quijote, yet he derogated rational theology in Spain, "the most Catholic country in the world," whose soul he also claimed to represent. As a result, as Arturo Barea writes, "the traditionalists . . . scented a heretic in him from the moment of the publication of his *En Torno al Casticismo.*"[70] Furthermore, Unamuno surrounds his objections to theology and his doubts on the existence of God and immortality with a battery of the most famous rational philosophers and naturalistic interpreters of Scripture. This daring freedom in a popular writer — which Unamuno was — was tantamount to the "indirect anticlericalism" of Ortega y Gasset whom we will study later.

Unamuno, however, did not unduly concern himself with approval or disapproval of what he said; he continued to write with an abiding sincerity springing from the depths of his convictions. His frequently sharp, satiric tone seldom descends to the level of tendencious or doctrinaire polemics. This statement can be applied to but few of the anticlerical writers. Like Pérez Galdós, he condemns intolerance wherever he finds it, and he finds it on both sides: "the freethinker in Spain is just as intolerant as the Catholic."[71] He also frequently lashed out against the inquisitorial mentality. In *En Torno al Casticismo* he writes: "Just let us scratch a little and very soon we'll find, in our contemporary Spanish society, the Inquisition, immanent and diffuse."[72] In *El Sentimento Trágico de la Vida* he takes care not to extend this criticism to such institutions as Catholic belief in papal infallibility in matters of theological concern. It is the spirit of intolerance rather than what people believe that concerns him. If he himself can drink only from the font of "cardiac" faith, he does not recommend that the teachings of theology be removed from those who can accept them. In fact, true to his contradictory spirit, he defends the Church, in the historical context, for its attitude in the famous Galileo controversy — a position which does not correspond at all with modern Catholic historical interpretation.

In the pursuit of the actualization of his ideals for the renovation of Spain, Unamuno became the foe of the Monarchy. This enmity was directed more toward Alfonso XIII personally (against whom he was continually directing barbs) than against the institution itself, for Unamuno was also a Spanish traditionalist and the Monarchy is a strong Spanish tradition. The author's ire reached a white heat during the Directorate; the union of throne and altar under absolutistic, intellectually confining auspices typified the very antithesis of his liberal tenets. His writings against Primo de Rivera, consequently, are indirectly "anticlerical" inasmuch as they are against a political expediency which was thoroughly "clerical" in tone. These writings won for the author an exile first at Fuerteventura and later at Paris. During this exile he wrote biting invectives against the dictator, many of which are recorded in *From Fuerteventura to Paris* (1925). The following passage illustrates this phase of the author's anticlericalism:

Well do I know that the stupid-headed beast referred to is the Marqués de Estella, Miguel Primo de Rivera. . . . In one way or another he has declared himself to be incompetent. . . . By stupid I mean that although he has tried to study since he was a boy . . . he never managed to know anything thoroughly. By stupid, I mean just plain stupid or, if you wish, defective in his mind. The talks, letters, writing and pompous pronouncements of the supposed dictator reveal the most tragic stupidity . . . He reveals a sensibility — not a mentality — of a bull, of a stud-horse, a jackass, a sheep or a billy goat — not of a man. [He] would reestablish the most vile form of the Inquisition.[73]

This bitter reaction, however, did not blind the author to the defects too frequently found among the liberals. "Liberals of Spain, you beggars. You say 'Reality obliges us.' But this reality, may God forgive you, is the sheepfold of which you are the billygoats . . . Liberals of Spain, courtiers not of the sword but of the porter's cap, I finally know that you are not my brothers."[74]

Thus, to sum up a complicated, often paradoxical intellectual position, Unamuno's anticlericalism (like the bulk of his significant thought) departs from the point where the tragic sense is generated. This anticlericalism is manifested in his at times cavalier, at times harsh views on theology and the proponents of the rational schema of Christianity who have become stultified in their beliefs. He thus believed it to be part of his mission to combat people who believe they have reached the static condition of being *de El posesores*. A certain related type of anticlericalism can be found in his use and popularization of writers inimical to Christianity — authors whom he quotes in his unending effort to stir up thought. Finally, anticlericalism is found in his struggle against intolerance and thought control, particularly in his battles with Alfonso XIII and Primo de Rivera and their regimes. It should always be remembered in evaluating these manifestations that Unamuno's entire thought is suffused with the idea that "God will not give you peace, but He will certainly give you glory!" *Del Sentimiento Trágico* closes significantly with the date-line, "Salamanca, in the year of grace, 1912."[75]

PÍO BAROJA NESSI (1872-1956)

1. *Baroja and Iconoclasm*

Obvious to even the casual reader of Pío Baroja is the fact that he is one of the most strongly anticlerical writers of the era under present consideration. It is difficult to find a novel or an extended essay in his prolific production in which this tendency does not abound. Yet, it is often difficult to measure his anticlericalism accurately. This difficulty, however, is a hallmark of Baroja in general, for in some ways he is similar to Unamuno, frequently taking strong positions which he freely contradicts. He is well aware of his own inconsistencies and alludes to them constantly. Like Unamuno, also (though vastly different in innumerable important areas), Baroja delights in stimulating reactions in his readers. He achieves this effect partly through an incurable iconoclasm. For example, his book *Juventud, Egolatría* (*Youth, Egoism*) exhibits his ability to pass negative judgements on a variety of subjects such as literature, art, religion, politics, ethnology, etc. — judgements which are usually out of step with opinion accepted by large segments of the human race. One is led to believe that he considered being in step with any majority opinion was the worst evil that could have befallen Baroja. Great figures of the past and present pass in review before his critical gaze; many he "damns with faint praise," others he dismisses with a cavalier comment or a terse sentence. A few figures he reveres: Tolstoy, Poe, Dostoiewski, Nietsche and whatever side of Baroja seemed to be in current favor with Baroja. His range is enormous. Groups of essays, such as *Divagaciones Apasionadas* (*Passionate Digressions*), span a variety of topics that stagger the imagination. Constantly he exhibits real breadth of knowledge and a capacity for broad generalizations that would frighten a specialist in a given field. There is usually an arrogant security in the projection of his particular point of view.

Another side of Baroja, which, like the above, has bearing on our study, is his interest in ugliness and in pathological types. This tendency is not surprising in a modern writer, particularly a Spaniard familiar with the Peninsula's long history of realism. But in Baroja the symptom is more acute than mere realism or naturalism. It is more than a preoccupation. It is a fascination with ugliness and the centrifugal forces of the universe which cause decomposition leading to ugliness. His inveterate iconoclasm is directly associated with this fascination and the combination results — on the intellectual plane — in a brand of anarchism, a quality of soul that seems to be indissolubly associated with certain segments of the Spanish spirit and mentality. In fact, the trilogy, *La Lucha por la Vida* (*The Struggle for Life*) published in 1904, illustrates the author's position on anarchism on the practical level. An examination of these works yields the deduction that Baroja admires the self-denying love of humanity found in certain of the branches of the movement. He believes that anarchy functions at least as a destructive criticism of the existing order and accepted values.

It should be noted that it is very difficult to achieve a thread of unity on Baroja's anticlericalism (or any other subject which he touched). Any writer's thought, when spread over a period as long as Baroja's life, is bound to shift. But the situation is further complicated in Baroja's case. As a prolific novelist he projected some characters who speak for him completely, while others do so in a more or less varying degree. Consequently, in this treatment I have studied his essays first and later turned to the novels where the main characters seem to speak Baroja's mind in the anticlerical area.

2. *Baroja's Anticlericalism, Strictly So-called*

The pattern of Baroja's anticlericalism can usually be found in the areas which I called "keys" in the second chapter. Baroja, for example speaks out bitterly on education: "If there are no schools and the people don't know how to read it is because the priest has convinced them that truth is found in prayer, not in reading."[76] Although, like Unamuno, he frequently had a bone to pick with technological progress, he accuses the Church of being intrinsically opposed to science: "It is logical for the convinced Catholic, for anyone who believes that the truth only comes from the pulpit, to consider all scientific efforts to implant new forms of social life perfectly useless."[77] Statements of this nature and stronger are not isolated in his works. For example he wrote in *Las Horas Solitarias* (*Solitary Hours*), "Science has worn away religion. If the theory of Copernicus, the theory of evolution and the parasitic theory were clearly explained in the towns and villages, half of the faithful would stop believing."[78]

Without entering into the intricacies of the monarchical problem or expounding any particular segment of Republicanism, the author criticizes the *cristiano viejo* attitude and his tendency to "dogmatize political energy." "On one side are those (and they will always be there) who believe that the Church is the truth and that truth should have force. On the other side we believe that truth is not obtainable. And we believe that even if truth were attainable it should not use force ever."[79] This criticism extends to the very fabric of the *ancien régime* and the clerical support of traditional temporalities. In *Red Dawn* Juan asks: "What would happen if these men should ever develop a conscience? A strike of hangmen would be unusual." The *Libertario* replies: "It would take the supporting pillar out of society. The hangman, like the priest, the soldier and the magistrate is one of the props of this capitalistic society." Then *"el Bolo" asked,* "How long will there be hangmen?" And the Libertario answered: "They will be around as long as the magistrates punish, as long as the soldiers kill, and as long as the priests deceive."[80] In *La Sensualidad Pervertida* (*Perverted Sensuality*) Baroja expresses similar thoughts:

We have to respect the rich man even if he is a usurer; the aristocrat even if he's a cretin; the soldier even though he is constantly making mistakes. This has been enjoined upon us by Mister Priest, who is God's representative on earth. Society should have a firm base and it does not matter if the foundations rest on living rock or on a dung heap. We must respect the work of our predecessors, even though it is a mixture of extravagance and absurdity.[81]

3. *Baroja's Reaction to Religion*

The examination of the more or less traditional anticlericalism cited already will not suffice for an author as complicated as Pío Baroja. Reactions to religion and multi-shaded portraits of clerics abound in his works. The roots of this preoccupation must be sought frequently in areas other than the political.

It must be stated that Baroja's general view of life is thoroughly agnostic. " 'Ignoramus, ignorabimus' (we do not know, we will not know) said the celebrated psychologist Duboys-Reymond in a famous lecture. This position is the most decent one a person can take . . . Who believes in the atom now? Who believes in the individuality of the soul? Who believes in the certitude of the senses? The atom, the unity of the soul and of the conscience, the certitude of knowledge — all are suspect today. Ignoramus, ignorabimus."[82] In another passage he says: "I have a point of view that could be called agnostic . . . Agnosticism affirms that man has not come to the world but rather that he is in the world, and he has not noticed that he has a determined object."[83] Consequently, defense of religion is la mentira. "Lying is one of man's most vital possessions. By lying societies live with their soldiers and their priests — one group as useless as the other."[84] According to Baroja, Catholics skilled in science provide a good illustration of mentira. "Today there are some little friars who, having abandoned their old tomes, read a popularizing scientific manual and then frighten the wits out of simpletons by giving lectures."[85] Combined with this profession of agnosticism is the author's candid admission that he is completely devoid of any religious sensibility. In this aspect he is, of course, the antithesis of Unamuno. "I do not feel, nor have I ever even remotely felt this mystical dependence on the divinity, nor this pleasure in calling oneself a slave, as the Christians do . . ."[86] in Las Veleidades de la Fortuna (Fortune's Inconsistencies) through the character of Larrañaga, he expresses similar thoughts: "I don't feel like a Christian because I don't feel like a sinner; I don't believe in sin. The thought never entered my head that I could be better or worse."[87] In the same work the author extends his personal sentiments into sweeping, questionable ethnological generalizations illustrating that his lack of religious conviction and sentiment is also fortified by a strong distaste for religion.

"The European, the good European, as you call him, is without doubt a skilled mechanic, a good scientist, an excellent watch maker . . . but in religious questions he cannot compete with the Semites. Luther, Calvin, General Booth are stupid fools. . . .

"Those minor prophets, Ariophiles, try to demonstrate that the Arian, the German, is a man of tempered intelligence and common sense. This may be possible, but this sort of person did not invent religion. Without doubt religions were created by the insane visionary, feverish, exalted types. Do you know what Hume thought about religions?"

"What did he think?"

"He said they were the fantastic hallucinations of half-human monkeys."[88]

4. *Priests*

Against this background it is impossible to restrain a chuckle when we read that Baroja had no real fight with the clergy and that he was not really a violent anticlerical. He leaves priests alone as long as they don't bother him. His outlook has nothing in common with the pungent extremism of the anticlericalism of the periodical *El Motín*. He does not believe that priests are vicious or effeminate — certainly he has not found them that way in the Basque Country. "They may be hypocritical, coarse, clowns, lackeys; but dissipated — no. Their defects are the defects of their country and the dogmas they defend."[89] Despite this disclaimer it is difficult to conceive of a more colorful rogues' gallery than the various portraits which he presents in, to mention only one work, the quasi-novel *César o Nada* (*Caesar or Nothing*). Here are a few of his odious types — not necessarily the most repulsive — whom he met in Rome: There was Father Herreros who lived in a monastery in Trastevere. He had a "huge, rough head, black bristly eyebrows, a short nose, an enormous mouth, yellow teeth, and a grey complexion. He wore a chocolate colored habit open from the neck to his waist. The expression around the good friar's mouth was that of a man who wanted to pass as understanding and clever. His cassock was dirty and . . . he had the habit of leaving burning cigarette butts on the table."[90] Father Miró was "a little bit of a man, with dark scaley skin. He had a threadbare cassock covered with dandruff and a large pointed dirty cap with an ample fringe."[91] "César got the impression that it was not very easy to find the crack through which to peer at what went on in the clerical world. It was evident that the Church gave these people an instrument of defense that served them. Basically they were an innocuous bunch. But they had a great organization and it would not be easy to put one's fingers inside the meshes of their net."[92] César also gives a group picture of clerical types and the diction Baroja puts in his mouth speaks for itself.

"What a variety of types you have here in Rome!" César went on saying. "What motley nostrils and facial appearances! Jesuits trying to appear wise and scheming. Carmelites that look like highwaymen; Dominicans — some with a sensual air, others with a doctoral air. Slyness, intrigue, brutality, intelligence, and mystical stupor. And the secular priests? What an exposition! Tall priests, trying to look like professors, with white manes and flowing cassocks; little dark greasy priests. Noses as sharp as a knife. Bulbous warty nose. Coarse types; distinguished types. Pale anaemic faces; red faces. What a fascinating collection!"[93]

Similar passages can be found in other novels. But it is not only the priests whom Baroja singles out for treatment with his racy vocabulary and the lash of Spanish pejorative suffixes. Nuns are managed in a similar fashion. Hurtado in *El Arbol de la Ciencia* (*The Tree of Science*) calls them poverty-stricken girls who entered religious life so they could eat.[94] In *Camino de Perfección* (*Path of Perfection*) they are described as bodily unclean and stupid.[95]

5. *Catholics, Protestants, Jews*

In keeping with his "anarchistic iconoclasm" and destructive criticism, Barja's view of society is always pessimistic and dismal. "The truth is that this civilization is an absurdity."[96] But the Church is frequently depicted as a major contributor to this sad state of affairs. In *El Mayorazgo de Labraz* (*The First-Born of Labraz*) the savagery of the town is described with morbid naturalism: bullfights, alcoholic abuses, bestial dances are all attributed to the influence of the Church. The clergy publicly denounces houses of prostitution but supports two whores.[97] In *Los Amores Tardíos* (*Late Loves*), the tendency of Catholics to ally themselves with the powerful and yield to the totalitarian temptation is roundly criticized. No attempt is made, however, to single out historical instances. The general impression is that the Catholic Church favors war. No mention is made of the Church's great work toward peace and the arts of peace. Priests are referred to as a branch of the *Guardia Civil,* ready to sanction anything in favor of the strong, even murder, "to preserve the digestion of the beloved owning class. And if there is a war they will be there to bless the machine guns, the poison gases and sing the *Te Deum.*" Their only achievement is that "the excrement is not stirred and for a passing moment there is less odor, but in the long run the whole thing stinks."[98] In *César, o Nada,* the author, like Blasco Ibáñez, sketches a few of the more unsavory scandals of the medieval and Renaissance Papacy. At times his flippancy extends even to the person of Christ.[99]

Like many anticlerical writers, Baroja claims to be scandalized by Catholics' ignorance of their own faith, as well as by their failure to try to live up to the ideals in which they believe. In *Las Horas Solitarias* he mentions overhearing two village women discuss the "fact" that God had revealed what days were to be observed as vigils by the faithful.[100] In *La Sensualidad Pervertida,* José Marí leads a free, vicious life, while proclaiming that man's natural procedure is to sin, repent, and be absolved.[101] In *Camino de Perfección,* Ossorio, vaguely seeking mystical comfort in Toledo, discovers that the priests have mistresses and waste time at cafés and with cards, that immorality and complete lack of interior faith are rampant.

It may be some small comfort to Catholics to learn that they are not the only religious body against which the author's destructive, devastating ire is aroused. Protestants and Jews fare no better. In *Las Veleidades de la Fortuna,* Larrañaga, a spokesman for Baroja, refers to the break in the unity of Christianity as a good thing as long as it served the historical function of battling against Catholic tyranny. Now that it is without an enemy, it is worth nothing or almost nothing. "I really have no sympathy at all for Protestants. When I am among

Protestants and Jews, I feel like a Catholic."[102] Protestant ministers are called "pathetic when not idiotic . . ." and "the Jew, like the German, is intelligent and ignoble."[103] Jewish literary critics direct public opinion and taste "to the advantage of money-making."[104] In another passage the author pens the following little descriptive note: "They were in Saint Moritz. The hotels were filled to capacity with Jews who had come in from everywhere . . . In all the charming places in the world you don't see anyone but Jews. The dark ones still have a certain charm; but the blond ones are very unpleasant. A lady said to me that they looked like red cockroaches."[105]

In *Las Horas Solitarias* Baroja comments satirically on contemporary Catholicism and disparages the Semitic monotheism which it embodies. In the same passage he speaks of "semitic nations or nations made semitic by Christianity."[106] In *César o Nada* he writes that "Catholicism is a Jewish meat with Roman gravy."[107] References of this nature lead to the conclusion that Baroja is as anti-Protestant and anti-Semitic as he is anti-Catholic and anticlerical. But racial and religious sensibilities need not be offended for they have considerable companionship in exile. For example, the Italians are laughed into exterior darkness: "Some Italians are stupid and the rest are Fascists. When they are together they all look like clowns."[108]

6. *Other Portraits; Jesuits*

Despite the torrents of unfavorable criticism and personal dislike of the clergy which Pío Baroja shows in so many of his works, it would be unfair to neglect his milder side. Through his character Larrañaga he implies that there are instances where religion can be viewed as a neutral area for a non-believer "which brings neither honor nor dishonor."[109] In *César o Nada*, so fruitful a source for devastating portraits, there are a few priests who appear to be attractive human beings. Cardinal Spada is portrayed as "basically liberal and friendly to the French." He was a strong man, frank and intelligent, in whose person could be noted "an underlying bitterness and desolation." When César explained his ideas to the Cardinal he understood that he was a man worthy of his entire respect.[110] In the same work the French priest Tardieu is described as "young, tall, thin, rosy-cheeked, with a long nose and a smile that went from ear to ear. He seemed to be a clever, jovial man" and he was "liveliness personified."[111] In *La Dama Errante* (*The Erring Lady*) Baroja admits that some clergymen are aware of the land problem. The jolly curate is proud that he is the son of a laborer and claims that life in Spain is impossible.[112]

The Jesuits in the author's work require a special formula. While they are the *bête noire* of most anticlerical writers, Baroja is never able to forget that their founder was a Basque and that the members of Loyola's Order share some of their founder's characteristics. Thus, in *Vitrina Pintoresca* (*Picturesque Showcase*) he shows guarded admiration for the original theologians and moralists, such as Escobar, Soto, Mariana, Súarez and Molina.[113] In *César o Nada* he expresses this admiration in a rather negative fashion by stating that without the Jesuits' support the Church would have (and should have) rotted away long ago.[114]

Pio Baroja's last years presented a paradox as striking as the paradoxes and contradictions in his writings. On the one hand was the fire-eating anticlerical, equal in violence to Blasco Ibáñez and exceeded only by the communists. On the other was the quiet elder man of letters sitting, enveloped in his overcoat, in the warm library of his Madrid apartment. During those last years he was keenly interested in literary news, especially when some mention of Baroja was expected. This was not unwarranted for the booklists frequently featured announcements of reprints and studies of his work, or, in some instances, new titles. How was it possible for such a vigorous supporter of leftist theories, such a lucid exponent of anarchistic, negativistic attitudes, such a thorough-going anticlerical to be accepted and at ease in the official latter-day Spanish atmosphere with its anti-liberalism, centripetal nationalism, and official Catholicism? The answer is not as difficult as it seems.

A perusal of the third section of *César o Nada*, particularly the last pages, indicates what many long suspected. On the practical level Baroja was not at all opposed to dictatorship. Furthermore, there is frequently apparent in his work an implicit distinction between the revolutionary ideas which he apparently revered, particularly in his youth, and the practical embodiment which he avoided. He had no confidence in human nature's ability to make any real progress. Consequently he was not ashamed to fall back on the most expedient solution to his problem and the problems of his nation. His occasional championship of liberal tendencies combined with his massive nihilism thus take on the contours of an academic *tour de force*. The author of *Zalacaín el Aventurero* was not a man who himself really lived dangerously. And the message of his writing — if it has any message — is about as meaningless as Zalacaín's life.

MANUEL LINARES RIVAS (1878-1938)

Manuel Linares Rivas is an important, though lesser known literary figure of the era under present consideration. He did not achieve the towering and enduring fame of men like Pérez Galdós and Unamuno. Nevertheless, he was a highly talented dramatist who achieved much popular acclaim. He was almost constantly preoccupied with the prejudices of social conventions and the rigidity of Spanish civil and canon law. Thus, he touched upon themes which are directly concerned with the main lines of this study. Stylistically, he is frequently linked to the school of Benavente.

1. *Aire de Fuera* (*Air from Outside*)

In this play, written in 1903, there is perhaps a line or two that could be called specifically anticlerical in the sense of a slurring remark made in reference to the clergy. Of much greater importance is the title theme which, of course, has reference to the idea, so often repeated by the anticlericals, that Spain needs fresh air from outside, from the other countries of Europe and of the world, to help find solutions to her stifling problems. The chief proponent of this particular stand in the play is Baltasar, a successful young mining engineer. He is accused of being a renegade because he was educated in Belgium and the United States. Baltasar, however, insists that he is proud to be a Spaniard but sad to see his country as backward in some matters as it was in the time of King Wamba. He scorns the idea that people in the more advanced countries do not believe in God. And he is completely convinced that a superior education can be obtained only outside of Spain.

This theme of "air from the outside" is given a more specific application by the plight of Magdalena, a young woman who had been most unhappily married and is now living in retirement in Baltasar's supposedly happy home. Her marriage had consisted of "a month or two of happiness; six years of fights and tears; one day of scandal and brutal beating."[115] Finally, after being dragged through the courts for a year and a half the girl and her husband were sentenced to five years of marital separation. Baltasar questions this procedure. "And in conscience should she really be eternally united to a brutal vicious gambler? Or would it be more blessed and logical if they could be really separated?"[116] The objection is then made that "God ratifies in heaven what religion has united on earth."[117] Baltasar, however, scornfully rejects the traditional interpretation of this statement. Without raising the problem of second marriages he maintains that the bond can be broken by the death of one of the parteners. How then can the eternity of the union be established? Whatever way the question is approached nobody can claim that poor Magdalena's plight is either just to her, or pleasing to heaven.

As the plot of the play develops, Magdalena's situation becomes worse. Her husband, Juan, comes to claim her that very day, after the five year separation has been completed. Baltasar stoutly defends Magdalena. On the grounds that the young woman is unwell, he manages to obtain for her a legal stay of two weeks. In the course of an argument with Juan, however, Baltasar is given a strong hint that his own wife's marital deportment has not been exactly exemplary, especially during his long absences at the mines in Bilbao. To prevent further disclosures, Magdalena goes home with her husband. Baltasar's misgivings are strengthened when he learns that his wife, Carlota, owns jewels which cost far more than the money he had given her. Thus, the stage is set for the final *dénouement* of the two interlocking marriage themes. Magdalena's problem is quickly settled — the "Spanish way," Linares Rivas seems to say. In rather melodramatic fashion some of the erstwhile "chatty" friends burst in and announce that Magdalena has been run over by a carriage. Baltasar mutters that it was, rather, the "carriage of the law" that caused her death.[118] Having once inhaled *aire de fuera,* he is unwilling to wait for any similar solution to his own problem. Magdalena's solution was that of the oppressed. For those who have confidence in the future the solution is to become an expatriate and petition for separation. And this he determines to do, as the play ends.

2. *La Garra (The Claw)*

La Garra was written in 1914 and contains an even stronger plea for the separation (or divorce) of incompatible couples. As in *Aire de Fuera* there are two intertwining themes of marital unhappiness. Once again the author's emphasis is more on the effect of law than upon the theological problem.

The action takes place in Campanela, a mythical city whose name suggests the region of Campostela, long associated with traditionally Spanish Catholicism. Santa has been unhappily married to a man, who, after mistreating her shamefully, finally abandoned her. Legally, she is unable to consider him dead until after a lapse of thirty years. Alvaro, however, declares to her his love — an emotion which she reciprocates but to which she cannot yield without, of course, breaking the laws of both Church and State. Alvaro is infuriated by this dilemma and voices much the same view as Baltasar in *Aire de Fuera.*

He considers the laws unjust, illogical, absurd, cowardly, futile. The Marquesa, Sol de San Payo, agrees with Alvaro. She is happily married to Antonio, but expresses extreme compassion for Santa and lashes out against "wicked men and their absurd laws." She goes so far as to say that she would never submit to such injustice, were she in Santa's place. She would appeal against all the laws, and if she got nowhere, she would go beyond and above them in defense of her life and happiness. When her mother, Esperanza, hears these rebellious sentiments she cries out in anguish: "How horrible! No, no!" And her father, the patriarch Tirso says: "Silence, silence! Sol de San Payo, the Marquesa de Montrove, the blood niece of his Eminence, the Cardinal of Campanela, cannot utter such blasphemy and remain in her right mind."[119] By a strange coincidence, however, it happens that Sol soon finds herself involved in precisely such a similar marital problem. A chance guest at the home inadvertantly reveals that Antonio had contacted a previous marriage in the United States and that this wife is still living. When confronted with this information Antonio readily admits the fact. He explains that the marriage had been in every way unsuccessful and that he had tried all means to obtain an ecclesiastical annulment. When these failed he contracted the second marriage and concealed from Sol the canonical impediment. He justifies his action by saying that he thinks it is stupid to maintain that something cannot be broken which is in fact already broken. "The bond is a spiritual link uniting two people. I am one person. And the other one? Who is the other one? There is no other one."[120] Antonio manages to convince Sol that it is unjust to disrupt their happy marriage. She consents to flee with him, according to the sentiments she had previously expressed to Santa. But "the claw" reaches in at the last moment and rips this plan asunder. Sol changes her mind when she realizes that her action will cut her off from the life of the Church. Her husband commits suicide.

3. *The Extent of Linares Rivas' Anticlericalism*

In both plays Linares Rivas is specifically anticlerical in that he is attacking juridical consequences that flow directly from a union of Church and State. Furthermore, in *La Garra* Linares Rivas surrounds his argumentation with many of the *clichés* of anticlericalism that by now have become commonplace in the authors whom we have examined. Like all anticlericals, he places considerable emphasis upon foreign ideas and customs, particularly those of non-Catholic countries as an antidote for the clerical outlook. It is also hardly complimentary to the clerical class to refer to the influence of its teaching as "the claw." Finally, *La Garra* is peopled by an array of *canonistas* and *civilistas* whose syllogistic casuistry and lack of human understanding make them most unattractive. The Cardinal is proud and inquisitorial. Although he promises to help Padre Muiños who is having difficulties with his superiors, he recoils in horror at the illicit union of Sol and Antonio. Don Tirso, surrounded by his clerical friends, is a simpleton, particularly in matters of piety, as is his wife, Esperanza. After Sol's first outburst of rebellion (before the revelation of her illicit marriage) we read:

Acisclo: This is a flare-up of nervous hysteria. She really doesn't believe that, I'm sure. She would never speak against the sanctity of the laws. Never.

Tirso: Yes, it's nerves, my friend. Evidently.

Esperanza: The devil is loose in this house, Tirso.

Tirso: Evidently.

Esperanza: Ask his Eminence for some relic so we can celebrate the most solemn rites of reparation.

Tirso: Very well. A good idea! The strange part about it, Antonio, is that you made no attempt to make her see reason.

The Marqués: I agree with her, Don Tirso.

Tirso: You, too? Tomorrow we'll have to go to confession, Esperanza. Evidently we're in mortal sin. Evidently![121]

Don Acisclo, *Presidente de la Audiencia,* is presented as a cold legal machine slavishly devoted to the letter of the law. Don

Antero (*Señor Doctoral*), his clerical counterpart, is equally zealous for the integrity of the ecclesiastical canons. Together they present a formidable front against Antonio and threaten him with heavy imprisonment, not realizing that the culprit had anticipated such an exigency. He took good care not to lose his *nacionalidad yankee*. As they spout canons and codexes from memory one thinks of Padre Paloma in Pérez de Ayala's *Los Trabajos de Urbano y Simona,* which will be treated later.

Padre Muiños is an interesting exception. We learn early in the play that he had spoken out against unjust laws; in short he was a maverick. Throughout the play he is compassionate toward the unfortunate couple. In the final scene, after Antonio had fired his fatal shot, Padre Muiños sprang forward to give him conditional absolution. *El Doctoral,* true to his narrow legal mind, was unwilling that the culprit be granted the Church's benefit of doubt. He shouted, "No!" and tried to restrain the priest's hand. Padre Muiños, however, calmly answered, "Yes," and completed the formula.

At this point a few considerations on the Catholic theological concept of Christian marriage are necessary. It is well known that a valid marriage between two baptized persons is absolutely indissoluble once it is consumated. It is not as well known that at times an annulment can be granted, provided some impediment to the marriage can be proven. An annulment (sometimes popularly confused in terminology with divorce) is merely a declaration that no marriage had in fact existed. Furthermore, it is not as well known that "the Church teaches . . . that there are many causes which justify the separation of husband and wife. The sin of adultery, as Christ teaches, gives the innocent party the right to complete and permanent separation."[122] This separation, when ratified by civil law, is indistinguishable, from the civil point of view, from divorce. No theological problem is created unless one party should seek a new marriage.

It is difficult to determine whether Linares Rivas extended his opposition to the rigorous Spanish civil law on separation (divorce) to an espousal of new marriages for separated couples. This point touches a sensitive theological nerve and here he seems to be, at most, ambivalent. In none of the instances do any of the characters permanently succeed in new marriages even though they may, like Baltasar, gain permanent separation by recourse to law outside of Spain. To be sure, the author allows his characters who are caught by "the claw" to present eloquent statements of their subjective states of mind and the human issues involved. But in the end they either have to put up with a bad situation or die. Their complaints do not constitute a sustained thesis condemning the Catholic position on the dissolubility of marriage. Rather, they probe in a literary medium the state of rebellion which human beings inevitably feel when faced with no favorable alternative that can be followed in conscience. The bulk of the persuasive argumentation is centered about the various civil aspects of the problem of a civil separation. It would appear, therefore, that he would leave the question of remarriage up to the conscience of the individual. In other words, he looks upon the problem of remarriage as a matter of the individual's private response to Catholic teaching and does not consider it to be in itself a matter of public policy. His basic adherence to Catholic teaching is evidenced by the final scene in *La Garra*, with the priest giving conditional absolution to a tortured soul who in the Church's opinion had erred. The scene also strongly suggests that clerics should deal charitably with people who have marital problems, rather than reject them with the narrow legality of *El Doctoral*.

4. *The Significance of Linares Riva's Anticlericalism*

The *Biblioteca Hispánica* edition of *La Garra* contains an interesting appendix entitled "Judgments of the Press" in which various reviews of the first performances are brought together. Practically all the newspapers quoted gave favorable notices to the dramatic excellences of the work and the fine performances which the actors rendered. However, lines are quite sharply drawn between liberal and conservative when it comes to a question of the play's ideological content. Thus in *El Liberal* the reviewer became almost ecstatic. The play was termed:

The best, the most profound, the most beautiful, and the most valid of all the many works of Don Manuel Linares Rivas. . . . It is the most valid because not since Galdós have such things been said — and said competently against the overlords of unhappy Spanish society! Under cover of the [civil] law and invoking Christian doctrines these people indeed commit crimes against persons and consciences. . . .

It is a work of combat. At the present time it could not be more opportune.[123]

El Imparcial was equally partial. *La Garra* was praised for its sincerity and called an example of "supreme art." The *Diario Universal* took a diametrically different view and hoped that the people who applauded would think it over. The reviewer, Alejandro Miquis, assumed that the author subscribed entirely to the rebellious views of his characters, and implies that the play was blasphemous to Christ and revolutionary. The *A.B.C.* adopted an enthusiastic but balanced opinion. The reviewer called the work "strongly formed, brave, generous" and unquestionably a source of much discussion on the *pros* and *cons* of divorce, because there always have been people in Spain of one or the other opinion. He praised Linares Rivas for not having proposed an ultimate solution but rather for isolating two cases which "he studied, constrasted, and held up for the consideration of the Church and the civil law, calling attention to this area . . . [and] invoking charitable feelings of love and justice."[124]

Thus, in the midpoint of this investigation, Linares Rivas' *La Garra* has a middle position in the anticlerical controversy. As seen in the reviews, opinion was for him or against him according to the view point of predilection. The author himself relies upon the attitudes of those who have gone before and utilizes the most moderate of their anticlerical techniques. He foreshadows the important anticlerical issues of the New Constitution under the Republic, especially Article 43. The clarity of his own anticlerical position avoids the extremes of anti-Catholicism or anti-religion. His concept of *aire de fuera* is reminiscent of Castelar and the *krausistas* and anticipates the first issues of Ortega y Gasset's *Revista de Occidente* (*Review of the West*), which will be treated in the next section.

JOSÉ ORTEGA Y GASSET (1883-1955)

1. *Intellectual and Republican*

In a sense Ortega y Gasset was not an anticlerical. He was basically a writer on philosophical topics with a strong affinity for the Germans — particularly the neo-Kantians. A large section of his work is devoted to historical speculation and the elucidation of problems in esthetics. One of his most important works, *La Rebelión de las Masas* (*The Rebellion of the Masses*), published in 1930, deals with the decline of human values attendant upon industrialization and the rapid spread of the bourgeois mentality. In his own prose he exhibited a classic excellence that secured his literary reputation.

The circumstances of his life at times brought him personally into the midst of practical affairs. Before the advent of the Republic he had written vigorously against the Monarchy. Long a member of the Ateneo, he, together with two other members (Dr. Gregorio Marañón and Ramón Pérez de Ayala) had formed the "League for the Service of the Republic," which called upon the liberal intellectuals and professional men (the heirs of Giner de los Ríos) to aid in the regeneration of Spain. Evidently Ortega y Gasset had some hopes for Spain in the practical order, even though his general evaluation of his country was very pesimistic in *España Invertebrada* (*Invertebrate Spain*), published in 1921.

In his political activity, as in his literary style, Ortega y Gasset was the soul of moderation. He has been quoted as being one of the first to utter the slogan of discontent with which the intellectuals greeted the illiberal measures of the New Constitution: *"No era eso"* ("That's not what we wanted").[125] He favored the Rough Draft of the New Constitution which had dealt moderately and fairly with the

Church and was quoted as saying: "One must act with a certain generosity on account of the forces which it represents."[126]

2. *Ortega y Gasset's "Implied Anticlericalism"*

In the author's large production it is rather difficult to isolate texts which can be properly termed anticlerical. Volumes of his philosophical and critical writings have no bearing at all on our subject, except, perhaps, by a most remote inference. His writings on the interpretation of Spanish history also do not bluntly criticize either the clergy or the Church. Occasionally one meets a phrase which may possibly convey a note of criticism, but the spirit of partisanship and acrimonious debate (frequently found in the anticlericals) is generally foreign to his serene philosophic disposition.

Why then, do I include him in this treatment of anticlerical writers? The answer lies in *the implications* of the philosopher's interpretations of Spanish history. Ortega y Gasset represented some of the characteristics of the so-called school of '98, particularly its pessimism. This spirit he shaped into Spenglerian formulas (once more exhibiting his Germanic philosophical parentage) in the famous group of essays entitled *España Invertebrada*. The work was viewed with horror by the traditionalists and served as a focus of the negative criticism of the liberal intellectuals in pre-Republican and Republican days. The major theme of the work stresses that from the very beginning not only the seed but the very flower of decay has been the product of Spain's cultural soil. The brief ascendancy of the Golden Age was only the momentary result of happy conjunctions of fate. There is little hope for Spain, which in the long pageant of history represents an explosion of will (*hazaña* or the German *Tathandlung*) which has been blind, diffusive, and brutal.

A shift from the extremes of this philosophic pessimism has been noted in some of the author's last works. Be that as it may, the theme of *España Invertebrada* supplies a frame wherein it is possible to find strong evidences of the author's "implied anticlericalism." For example, when discussing the evils of "particularism" he launches into a critical analysis of the function of the military class in Spanish life. He prefaces his remarks with the following comment: "To avoid dealing with general and abstract formulas, I intend to describe one summary, concrete example of water-tight compartments. It is the one offered by the professional military class. Almost everything that I say about this area can be applied, with slight changes, to the other groups and social structures."[127] Then, after reviewing the defects of the military tradition, he adds significantly for those who have eyes to read between the lines: "Thus we have a pattern which . . . has to be considered in all the organic splinters of Spain. Each one has reached the point where it believes that its mission consists in imposing its will directly. Faith in national organization has been lost and sensitivity for other similar groups has been blunted."[128]

Particularism is a basic point in Ortega y Gasset's criticism of Spanish history. It is a tendency found in the *patria chica* (regional fatherland), but the author considers this to be a less serious manifestation. Far more serious is the tendency of each important institution to cease to think of itself as a part and accordingly "cease to take into account the feelings of others. The hopes and needs of others are not important." The inevitable result is "direct action" and the "immediate imposition of solitary will."[129] The author insists that particularism in Spain can be found at the very fountain-head of national life: "When a society is consumed as a victim of particularism, it can always be affirmed that the first to show itself particularistic was the central power. And this is what happened in Spain. Castile made Spain and Castile broke her to pieces."[130] Into this pattern the author weaves the *leitmotiv* of Monarchy and Church: "Beginning with the Monarchy and continuing on with the Church, no national power has ever thought of anybody but itself . . . The Monarchy and Church have obstinately adopted their own destinies as the truly national ones."[131]

Such is the pattern of Ortega y Gasset's anticlericalism. He skirted the practical polemics of the controversy. But he probed the roots of tradition. The preoccupations of other writers are for him the mere surface manifestations of an immemorial failure in national orientations. Despite his lack of vehemence and polemic rhetoric, this anticlericalism is farreaching in its implications and pierces the very core of Spanish history. He writes: "When has the heart of a Spanish monarch or the Spanish Church — both foreign from top to bottom — ever beaten for the deep national destinies? Never, let it be known. It has done quite the reverse."[132]

3. *Ortega y Gasset and Religion*

It is difficult to speak about Ortega y Gasset and religion. Throughout the bulk of his writing he seems for the most part to be neither *pro* nor *con*. In contexts where religion could be considered, he more often than not avoids the opportunity. The over-all impression is that he was largely neutral in this area. However, there are passages which on examination reveal that when pressed he tended to minimize the function of religion in civilization. This can be seen in his brief analysis of the central thought of the very eminent English Catholic historian, Christopher Dawson. Dawson, like Toynbee, looks upon religion as a powerful formative influence in the growth of culture. In the Introduction to his 1947 Gifford Lectures at the University of Edinburg, Dawson re-stated his central thesis: "The terms of the Gifford foundation presuppose the existence of a science of Natural Theology which is competent to study the nature of the Divine Being and the relations of man and the universe to Him . . . This is a tremendous claim . . . The historian cannot fail to recognize what a great tradition this claim has behind it — a tradition which is closely related to the main stream of Western thought."[133] Dawson's famous *The Making of Europe* is built around this theme. Ortega y Gasset comments on the book: "There can be no doubt that Dawson's book is inadequate. It is written by an alert and agile mind, but a mind that has not completely freed itself from the battery of traditional concepts in historiography — concepts more or less melodramatic and mystical, which hide rather than reveal historical truth."[134]

A similar inference can be drawn from the theme of Ortega y Gasset's famous *Meditación del Escorial* (*Meditation on the Escorial*). He begins humorously recalling the dedication of the huge pile to Saint Lawrence: "I am the first to admire [San Lorenzo]. He found himself well toasted on one side and asked to be turned over. Without that gesture, humor would be unrepresented among the martyrs."[135] Then he proceeds to muse about the real inspiration of the building. "All temples, it is certain, are erected to the greater glory of God; but God is a general idea and no real temple has ever been erected to a general idea."[136] From here he continues on to indict the religious "messianism" of the era of Philip the Second:

It is unquestionable that when various plans were presented to Philip the Second and he chose this one, it was because he found that it expressed his idea of the Divine. . . .

The Monastery of the Escorial is a nameless force, without dedication, without transcendence. It is an enormous force that reflects its own image. Satanically this force adores itself and sings to itself alone. It is force consecrated to force.[137]

Ortega y Gasset believes that the philosophical explanation of this is a result of Spain having adopted the Renaissance shift from the *maniera gentile* (the "gentle" manner) to the *maniera grande* (the grand style). It was a shift from Leonardo da Vinci who said, "Whoever is unable to do what he wills, let him will what he can do"[138] to Michaelangelo, who wrote:

> Oh God, Oh God, Oh God
> Who hast enraptured my very being
> Who hast taken me ever a prisoner;
> Thou has wrought more by me, than I myself,
> Oh God, Oh God, Oh God.[139]

The adoption of this attitude, Ortega y Gasset feels, was fatal to the development of Spanish culture. The Escorial is monumental proof: "This monument of our ancestors exhibits a petrified soul made up of force and empty of ideas and sensitivity. This architecture is all possessive love, desire, drive. We will learn here better than anywhere else of what stuff the Spanish substance is made. We will come to know the subterranean spring from whence the most abnormal history of Europe has come boiling out."[149]

Thus, it is evident that Ortega y Gasset takes a dim view of the function of the religious spirit in Spanish history, and, it would appear from his cavalier treatment of the great Dawson, in civilization in general.

4. Publishing Activities: the "Revista de Occidente"

Like Blasco Ibáñez, Ortega y Gasset dedicated considerable energy to publishing activities directed toward the renovation of Spain. Unlike the Valencian author, Ortega y Gasset's work in this field was on a high intellectual level focused toward a minority of the reading public. For a time he headed the *Biblioteca de las Ideas del Siglo XX* (*The Library of Ideas of the Twentieth Century*). This house published excellent translations of works such as Spengler's *Decline of the West* and other philosophic, critical, and scientific studies. In 1923 he founded the *Revista de Occidente* (*Review of the West*). The *Biblioteca de la Revista de Occidente* published various of the author's own works and edited (in translation) certain of his favorite writers such as Simmel (upon whom he relies heavily in the development of *El Tema de Nuestro Tiempo* [*The Theme of Our Time*], as well as Landsberg, and Bertrand Russell.

The pages of the *Revista de Occidente* were devoted to Spain's contemporary writers — both the established figures and the younger aspirants — together with many exponents of modern European thought. Poets like Rafael Alberti, Vicente Aleixandre, Manuel Altolaguirre, Gerardo Diego, Pedro Salinas, García-Lorca are represented among such notables as Juan Ramón Jiménez, the Machados, Rainer Maria Rilke and Pirandello. Antonio Espina and Pío Baroja are found in the company of William Faulkner, Franz Kafka and Thomas Mann. Articles by R. N. Whitehead and the famous egyptologist J. H. Breasted alternate with critical essays on music, plastic arts and the cinema. Menéndez Pidal contributed learned articles. Subjects of a religious nature are not neglected, particularly historical, comparative, and archeological investigations. Catholic poets, such as Gerardo Diego, appeared frequently and the Catholic critic, Angel González Palencia, was allotted space for his famous study *La Divina Comedia y el Islam.* Even the peculiar thought of Ernesto Giménez Caballero was not neglected, for this author was a fairly regular contributor.

In what way can the review be said to have participated in the anticlerical tradition or in the particular type of anticlericalism which has been singled out in the author? Once again the answer is, indirectly. In the first issue a flat statement was made: "We turn our backs on politics, now that it never attempts real understanding. This *Review* will follow a policy designed to give its readers an essential panorama of European and American life."[141] True to this proposal the periodical adopted a broad, varied, and scholarly tone removed from direct polemics. Divergent opinions were freely expressed with a candor which had been longed for by earlier writers, such as Pérez Galdós. On the other hand considerable space is given over to non-Spanish authors noted at least for their disregard of, if not hostility toward, religion. Thus, amid Ortega y Gasset's attempts to familiarize Spaniards with European thought come such writers as Bertrand Russell—a favorite with the author— who in a long article discusses the advisability of eugenics to preserve the superiority of the white race. He wrote: "If a world government was established the convenience of making the subordinate races less prolific would be seen. And this would permit humanity to solve the population problem."[142] It was ideas and the free discussion thereof that motivated Ortega y Gasset in the *Revista.* But the flood of European ideas swept in many which were hostile, directly or by implication, to the Church and to religion, particularly in the protected atmosphere of a confessional state.

147

In this sense Ortega y Gasset's *Revista* participated in his "indirect anticlericalism."

It is evident that Ortega y Gasset's evaluation of particularism, his implied anticlericalism, and his negative interpretation of the function of religion in Spanish culture are closely interwined themes. Whether or not he really extends his criticism of religion in a blanket fashion to all history is an esoteric point and not a vital issue in this study. Some critics noted a more positive direction in his thought on religion in his last decade.

Ortega y Gasset was one of the intellectuals who returned to Spain after establishing some sort of an *entente* with the present regime. Today one of the main streets of Madrid bears his name. During his last years he travelled frequently between Spain and Portugal and engaged in various lecture programs and private school projects. In October, 1955, the provocative thinker died. It was reported in *A.B.C.* that he was attended in his last hours by the noted priest-scholar, Padre Félix García. The report read as follows: "In his Madrid residence, Montesquina 28, at eleven-twenty on Tuesday, Don José Ortega y Gasset died in a Christian fashion attended by Father Félix García."[143] It should be noted that this slightly ambiguous statement should not lead to the conclusion that he became reconciled to the Church. Most probably the notice was worded to convey the impression that another great intellectual rebel returned to the fold. Informed sources believe that Ortega y Gasset's wish was to die "in a Christian spirit" and that he did not recant any errors or receive the sacraments.[144]

RAMON PEREZ DE AYALA (1881-1962)

1. *Writer and Republican*

Pérez de Ayala is a native of Oviedo where he was educated by the Jesuits and where he cultivated the friendship of Clarín. He sprang into literary notice in 1903 when his poetic work *La Paz del Sendero* (*The Peace of the By-way*) was published. From that date he continued to add a number of well-written poetic collections and provocative novels to his name. He became a member of the Spanish Academy in 1928.

Politics and diplomacy have also occupied his talents. Long a member of the Ateneo, he cooperated with Ortega y Gasset and Dr. Gregorio Marañón in the "League for the Service of the Republic." In 1931 the Republic sent him as ambassador to London where he remained until 1936. While in London he arranged for the staging in Spain of his highly controversial novel, *A.M.D.C.* The production caused unfortunate violence and demonstrations at a time when the political scene was agitated by the status of the Jesuits under the New Constitution.

After the Civil War the author lived for about fifteen years in Buenos Aires. He returned to Spain and lives in Madrid.

Pérez de Ayala's anticlerical thought can be rather easily analyzed. Its key is found in the educational area in two basic works. The atmosphere created by his criticism reflects the Republic's left-wing climate of opinion in one of its extreme manifestations. The two-part novel *Luna de Miel, Luna de Hiel* (*Honey-Moon, Vinegar Moon*) and *Los Trabajos de Urbano y Simona* (*The Trials and Tribulations of Urbano and Simona*) was published in 1923. It deals with marital problems related to sex education. The novel *A.M.D.G.*, like James Joyce's *Portrait of an Artist*, deals with life in a school conducted by the Jesuit order.

2. *Luna de Miel, Luna de Hiel*

The basic construction of *Luna de Miel, Luna de Hiel* and its sequel is uncomplicated. Urbano and Simona marry, largely because of the social and economic aspirations of Urbano's mother, Micaela. The two young people are truly in love but they know nothing, to use a cliché, about "the facts of life." Urbano is strangely frightened and "returns to mother." Simona develops a religious conviction that, as a result of her status as a married woman and her mere proximity to Urbano, she is pregnant. The two are brought together again and for close to a week they live under the same roof. Although they learn more about love they fall far short of consummating the marriage. The sudden death of Simona's grandmother now makes the marriage as economically awkward as it had previously been desirable. Micaela, knowing her son's ignorance of sexual matters, rushes to take him away from Simona. The mother hopes that the marriage is still unconsummated and, consequently, her boy will be able to obtain a "Catholic divorce." The *trabajos* of the lovers, equal in intensity to those found in the old sentimental novels, now begin. Eventually the obstacles are surmounted and they begin their real wedded life.

The book is filled with passages where most unattractive portraits of priests are either drawn by the author or are the subjective reactions of some of his characters. Don Cástulo, Urbano's harried and pedantic mentor, refers to the priest who was in league with Simona's mother as a "filthy levite, an execrable priest."[145] When instructing Conchita, his wife-to-be, he delivers the following little sermon:

Don't trust priests, Conchita. . . . I warn you, Conchita, don't trust priests. A priest is a person beaten by life, a wasted man, because against his wishes he hates what he really wants — love and happiness. The poor man envies the rich, the fool envies the intellectual the ignorant envies the wise, the ugly envies the handsome, the sick envy the hearty, the eunuch envies the lover, and the priest envies the man. . . . I will never permit you to go to confession and thus put yourself and me in the hands of the clergy. By the confessional the priest makes himself the spiritual husband of the woman. *"Concuage* [sic] *mistique"* is what a French author called confession. Translated — mystical cuckoldry. I beg God, Conchita, that you never plague me with a priest.[146]

The theme of the passage is closely related to the moral of the book. Pérez de Ayala, however, writes his novels on various levels. Consequently, I do not believe that this passage represents the anticlericalism which should be associated with the author himself. Cástulo does not speak entirely for Pérez de Ayala. Rather, he is a coarse, almost picaresque character reflecting the popular irreligious reaction against the attitudes which inspired the novel. Pedantic and pompous with his "classical learning," Cástulo is actually closer to Sancho Panza

than he is to being an intellectual — a fact that is born out
in his choice of Conchita. He represents the peasant of popular
republican aspirations just beginning his up-hill road toward
education. As we have seen and will continue to see in later
references to the popular spirit, anticlericalism on this level
frequently becomes irreligious as the popular classes begin to
rise amid the pattern of protest. They almost always fail to
make a distinction between clericalism and religion. Don
Cástulo also exhibits the strong distaste for celibacy so often
found in Spanish literature, particularly on the popular level.

Celibacy is enough to make a monster out of a woman. The abuse of
religious practises can also make a monster out of a woman. Put
celibacy and pietism together and you have two agents of corporal and
psychological deformation that produce a monster much more grim
than what the ordinary imagination of simple men can conceive. The
most fabled monsters, the vampire, the harpy, the dragon of the Corpus
Christi procession, are like caged canaries or lap dogs compared to
the perversity of a pious single female.[147]

When Urbano meets Padre Paloma, the "theologian," we
encounter the anticlericalism associated with Pérez de Ayala's
main theme, although it is cast in baroque caricature. Padre
Paloma is not an attractive priest. When we meet him first,
he is rolling cigarettes from tobacco taken from the Archbishop's palace. The priest is determined to smoke as fine a
blend as "his Grace." He is crafty, coarse, and unable to open
his mouth without displaying his "latinity" or quoting canons
and theological tracts from memory. This priest, finally realizing that Urbano's sexual ignorance is real, decides to instruct
the boy. Urbano sums up his biology lesson in the following
meditation:

In substance Father Paloma said the following: "Why do we have to
conceal the truth, when we are alone talking face to face?" The fact is,
[God], that you amuse yourself making fun of your creatures, your
toys . . . your children. This cruelty could be borne if it were not
accompanied by deception. You are omnipotent; you could have
brought about the propagation of the human race by means of a
noble, beautiful act. . . . With this possibility within your power you
invented — YOU invented — a filthy procedure for which, as with
all dirty necessities, people hide. They do not want to bespoil their lips

by speaking of it — an act worse than dirty. Monstrous . . . The only pure love, they say, is in the one who consecrates himself to you. The only clean betrothals are those made in religious profession.[148]

This passage, it goes without saying, is a gross distortion of the Church's teaching on sex. It is caricature gone wild. If it were taken at face value as the author's statement it would be blasphemous. Representing Padre Paloma's warped mind and deliberate desire to mislead the boy, it is merely fictional pathology. On the other hand — caricature or no caricature — it should not be forgotten that overtones of this nature — strong overtones — can be found in certain conventual or pietistic atmospheres such as Jansenism, which contaminated Western spirituality for centuries. St. Augustine (who enjoyed a vigorous sex life before his conversion) tells us that marital copulation without the explicit intention of procreation is a venial sin. And (we need not document the point) Catholic laymen even today resent the subtle, jarring derogations of marriage still heard in some quarters (for example in girls' convent schools and colleges). Marriage, it is affirmed, is a good state in life; but religious life (and the concomitant celibacy) constitutes a "superior" way of life, the "highest state in life." The fact that people have different psychological structures, the fact that what is best for one is not necessarily best for the other, falls bloodied by the wayside. This attitude of some segments of the Church toward sex is unfortunate but to be expected. For years the moral theology text of Hieronymus Noldin has been used (and still is used) in seminaries in Europe and America. Moral theologian Noldin refers to the marital act as *res in se foeda,* "a disgusting thing in itself."[149]

At any rate — to return to our *carneros* — Urbano worsens in his despair when he associates these ideas with impressions heard previously in a series of spiritual exercises conducted by a Jesuit: "The only woman worthy of love is the Virgin Mary. This woman is our true mother. We should loose ourselves from the weakness of excessive love of our earthly mother here below. God's voice clearly warns us to abandon father

152

and mother, meaning that we should forget that we come from an impure man and an impure woman."[150]

Thus, we have Pérez de Ayala's basic anticlerical viewpoint found in this novel. Sexual ignorance is the result of improper education, especially education that debases man's procreative function in the name of religion. Does the author really maintain that these distorted notions are part and parcel of Catholicism or merely historical distortions of doctrine? It is reasonable to assume that the latter is the case. Urbano says:

> But who has shown me that religion really imposes these maniacal ideas; that the Heavenly Father willed this . . . Could it not rather be the stupidity and evil interpretations of the Lord's ministers who have been called to decipher the message of the divine Dove? I believe in God the Father, I believe in God the Son, I believe in God the Holy Spirit. But I also believe that between the Dove of the Blessed Trinity and "Father Dove" there is an immeasurable distance.[151]

Urbano's father, Don Leonicio, echoes this view. "I maintain that the viewpoint and manner of education on love which the Church as well as society obliges us to accept is bad, bad, bad. I don't know where it is bad or how it could be cured, but it's bad, bad, bad."[152]

In addition to the thematic problem of the novel, the author turns his analytic eye toward other related areas. Don Leonicio, for example, has lost all carnal desire for his wife, Micaela. He seeks compensation in his relations with "María Egipciaca." Micaela, as a result of her son's unhappy experiences, realizes her own long-standing conjugal shortcomings. Her pitiful efforts to recapture her charm lead to her equally pitiful insanity. Thus, without presenting (and perhaps not hoping to find) any solution, Pérez de Ayala probes this marital-social fester — the respectable, Catholic *paterfamilias* whose real sexual life is lived apart from the family in carefully shrouded dalliance. This situation, not uncommon in many societies, is evidently very prevalent in Spain. The author's development of his theme suggests that the poor beginnings made in many marriages are at least a partial factor in the evolution of this abuse. However, he neither suggests that society can rid itself of it nor does he necessarily condone marital infidelity.

Other related subjects to which Pérez de Ayala addresses himself are prostitution, syphilis, and the position of the prostitute in society. He feels that the social ill which creates prostitution should be castigated rather than the unfortunate women. He paints a very poor picture of a convent (to which Simona had been brought by her familial and clerical abductors). In this convent moral renovation of prostitutes was attempted by unending pious devotions alternating with menial labor.

3. *A. M. D. G.*

This novel is similar in many ways to *Luna de Miel,* but vastly more devastating. The initials stand for the Latin motto of the Jesuits, *"Ad Majorem Dei Gloriam,"* "To the Greater Glory of God." The story deals with life in a school conducted by this order. The picture is universally unattractive and condemnatory. There is little plot, the trials of the boy Bertuco being but the occasion for a series of episodes which become more fantastic and nightmarish as the story progresses.

The earlier pages of the book provide various character sketches of priests (like Padre Mur) who are coarse, evil-tempered, and evil-appearing. At the same time, there are some sympathetic types (like Padre Sequeros) who are victimized and misunderstood by the others. The composite picture, near the end of the book, of the fathers in procession for a community exercise could not be surpassed by Pío Baroja and recalls the massive baroque satire of Francisco de Quevedo. Much is lost in translation, but the passage runs in part:

The glow from the lamp was dim but the priests were silhouetted against it. All of them were swaddled in their long cloaks. And they passed by: There was the long, lanky . . . Estich, the frisky Ocaña, the Jesuit-hater Atienza; there was Mur of the enormous nose from which hung, as from a perch, winged accessories; there was the valetudinarian Avellaneda, panting and expectorating; there was Arestegui, bent over and solemn; then Olano, oblong and fleshy; then Landazábal with the bulging buttocks; then Numarte, vulgar and uncouth; Sequeros, rigid and calm — in short, the whole community.[153]

The earlier episodes of the book concentrate on the barenness of the students' lives, the backward educational methods, the order's pursuit of wealth through power over pious women. These evaluations are interspersed with details such as whippings, continual spying, and abuse of the role of counselor by attempting to unlock confidences. Considerable space is devoted to a retreat conducted for the students by Padre Olano. Long extracts from the priest's notes reveal, for the most part, nothing startling to a person familiar with the Spiritual Exercises of Saint Ignatius. A few deft touches on the author's part, however, produce a *reductio ad absurdum,* for example, Padre Olano's efforts at visualizing the Deity is about on the level of a Sunday school kindergarten class for the mentally retarded: "Just imagine God, full of His majesty and grandeur, seated on His throne. A long beard, down to the middle of His chest. Eyes that blind. The throne adorned in purple. Many precious stones. Richer than all the riches in the world."[154] The retreat master also had a tendency to rely on his own imagination and pious myths, rather than on archeology and Biblical history:

The Blessed Virgin sent him food which she herself had seasoned with her own pure hands: cabbage, soup, spinach, and sardines.
Jesus Christ's tunic was grey, . . . the Virgin herself had sewed it and as Christ grew the tunic grew with him and did not suffer any deterioration . . . .
During the scourging they gave Him six thousand lashes. Five thousand of these were on the body and one thousand on the head. The crown of thorns had one thousand spines.[155]

The theme of sex and Christianity again engages Pérez de Ayala's thought when he describes Bertuco's confession. The boy had indulged in a summer dalliance with a girl named Rosaura. Terrified and filled with a morbid sense of shame intensified by the retreat, he sought a confessor. *El valetudinario,* Avellaneda, was his choice because Bertuco believed that the priest's proximity to death would render him understanding. Bertuco was mistaken and underwent a harrowing experience: "When the old man heard the tale he became galvanized with rage. Driveling and stammering from his toothless mouth he hurled forth threatening phrases. 'You should die right now, without absolution, you wretch! I have a good mind not to absolve you, you wicked beast!' " Bertuco fell on the floor imploring, "Absolution! Absolution! In God's name have pity."[156]

The sex theme continues to occupy the author in the following episodes. A lovely English woman named Ruth came to the fathers to receive instructions in Catholicism. Padre Sequeros was assigned to her. Attracted by her beauty, he was tempted by sentiments of human love. Having uttered these thoughts aloud in an unguarded moment he was promptly denounced, and restricted in freedom. The baptism of Ruth was detailed to Padre Olano. Shortly after her conversion Ruth's husband died by his own hand. In anguish Ruth sought out her friend Padre Sequeros, whom the other Jesuits had repeatedly reported to be ill. Ruth was met by Padre Olano who took advantage of the lady's distress to divest himself of the piety of his sermons:

He took her by the hand and thus led her to his room, leaving her there while he disappeared behind the curtain at the entrance to the closet. Father Olano's mouth was dry, his heart beat rapidly and his hands were shaking with emotion. . . . Meanwhile he unfastened his sash and removed his soutane, for he was very careful not to incur any unnecessary infraction [of canon law], the violations of which he had at his finger tips. Thus, Olano was well aware that a religious who fails to wear his garb makes himself *ipso facto* victim of excommunication. But the same quitting of the habit is converted into a meritorious act when it is done in order not to profane holy garments while fornicating, or while going incognito to a whore house.

Ruth stood up and Olano did the same, imprisoning her in both hands. Up to that moment the unfortunate woman had not noticed the unusual preoccupation of the Jesuit — his plebeian face tortured with venereal fury; his bovine neck colored crimson; his course dirty shirt open at the neck, revealing a strong, knotty, hairy expanse of chest. . . .

[Ruth] as if in a dream realized that the lewd, heavy hand of the Jesuit was exploring her breasts. Then warm flabby lips were upon her mouth. Ruth was able to shake herself away from that bundle of lust. . . . She slowed him down with a fist in the eye. . . . And then she flew from that cursed room, and she fled from those gloomy halls . . . and she escaped from that black house.[157]

The succeeding pages become increasingly episodic, increasingly fantastic. A succession of nightmares foreshadow some of the novels of Ramón Sender (who will be studied in Chapter IV). Padre Olano recovers his sexual balance sufficiently to deliver, to a weird collection of village *putas,* a long, pompous, theological harangue on the evils of prostitution. There follows the episode of the boy Coste, a friend of Bertuco. Having been placed in solitary confinement for an indiscreet remark, Coste finally succeeded in making good his escape. For several days he wandered hopelessly, calling upon his religious beliefs ever more fervently as his plight worsened. Finally, he fell over a precipice and broke his head open on a rock, half way through a prayer to the Virgin for help.[158]

The novel concludes with Bertuco's departure from the school forever. He had been beaten to the doors of death by Padre Mur (a scene which the author described with well-seasoned gore). Don Alberto, the boy's uncle, arrives and is told that Bertuco had been taken ill in class — "a very violent attack, doubtless due to the coming exams and too much study."[159] But the uncle realizes the real reason and decides to take the boy away at once. In the plans for departure they are joined by Padre Atienza, who has determined to leave the order. This priest had spent his scholarly energy on a book about evolution. But "the board empowered to censor it has decided that it is not sufficiently good to be published by a son of the Company . . . so now long live Jossie!"[160] During the journey Don Alberto asks Padre Atienza, "Do you think the Company of Jesus should be eradicated?" Padre Atienza answers, "From the root!"[161]

Thus, Pérez de Ayala's anticlericalism is grounded in the educational controversy, but its implications reach much further. *Luna de Miel* and its sequel were foreshadowed by the works of Juan Valera and Armando Palacio Valdés, who had attacked "asceticism above all" — a concept nervously heightened on the Peninsula by sexual taboos grafted into Spanish life from Islam as well as from regional European pietistic outlooks. The heat of polemics, however, accounts for the fantastic nature of the plot, the vast overstatement of the case, the failure to outline the Church's true teaching on marriage. Similarly, *A. M. D. G.* must be classed as a violent polemic work. In the second chapter of this study I probed the major outlines of the Church's position on education. It had evolved in a favored position, hallowed in a confessional atmosphere of long-standing tradition. There is no significant evidence which I have found indicating that the Jesuit order made any effort to reverse the current of educational confessionalism. For example, the tenor of the articles in *Razón y Fe* over the decades reveals total commitment to the repressive confessional policy in Spain. As a result of this attitude — partially, at least — the order had long been a major target of the anticlericals. The tragic and lamentable culmination was Article 26 of the New Constitution. *A. M. D. G.* is nothing more than a reflection of the attitude that created the Article.

In the earnest pursuit of objectivity and fairness, however, it must again be strongly emphasized that Pérez de Ayala vastly overstated his case. And he did so with both the zeal of a pamphleteer and the centuries-old Spanish delight in picaresque verbiage and baroque distortion. Certainly there have been clerical school masters who have beaten recalcitrant youngsters to the point of death — even in the cherished English tradition. Certainly some priests have hung up their garb in favor of Venus. No sane person would deny it. But Pérez de Ayala does not leave a shred of human dignity to the straw men that he sets up to state his case. Certainly, there have been — there are today — clerics who carry on their labors under the heavy curial sanction of *ne publicet* (let him not publish). Most critics agree that Padre Atienza is a thinly disguised portrait of the brilliant Julio Cejador y Frauca, a former Jesuit whose monumental studies in Spanish Literature are basic tools of hispanists of the last half century. Cejador y Frauca left the Jesuit order when his clerical censors decided that his investigations should not be published. In *A. M. D. G.,* however, the propagandist's zeal ruined artistic creation. The intense bitterness eliminated the humor so frequently characteristic of Spanish realism. The novel is a fantasy peopled by monsters. Valbuena Prat writes: "Compared with other literary versions of Jesuit high schools and residences — Joyce, Gabriel Miró — Ayala's work is the most one-sided, tendentious, and passionate — not gainsaying its frankness and dramatic contrasts."[162] And Salvador Madariaga, hardly a critic who would be classed as "clerical," wrote concerning the Jesuits and the Republic: "Obsessed by its anticlericalism it [the Republic] . . . lightheartedly closed down the only type of school that for all its imperfections, bore a resemblance to a secondary school — the Jesuit college."[163]

Some students, after reading the quotations I have adduced from Pérez de Ayala, may be inclined to think that he was a convinced atheist with a dirty mind, to boot. This would be a false conclusion. The Spanish (and Latin) mind is casually capable of obscenity (and anticlericalism) quite shocking to Anglo-Saxon sensibility. In later life Pérez de Ayala proved this by writing scholarly articles in *La Nación* of Buenos Aires on great figures of the Jesuit order.

A. M. D. G., precisely because of its bitter excesses, provides an excellent point of departure for a consideration of the vitriolically polemic writers of the Civil War era who will be treated in the next chapter. Pérez de Ayala will be judged mild in comparison to some of them.

CHAPTER IV

ANTICLERICALISM IN "BELLES LETTRES" IN THE ERA 1931-1936

ARTURO BAREA (1897-1957)

Arturo Barea's greatest work was *The Forging of a Rebel* (1946). It is an autobiographical trilogy that tells the story of the author's tumultuous, varied life which reached a climax in 1936. In so doing the book also provides a vivid history of tortured Spain from the beginning of the reign of Alfonso XIII to the climactic period of the Civil War, which Barea terms "a war of two Cains."[1] The three subdivisions of the book are entitled *The Forge, The Track,* and *The Clash.* The book was composed by Barea in Spanish and rendered into English by Ilsa Barea, the author's Austrian wife, a gifted linguist.

Barea was born in humble circumstances in Badajoz. In relating the trials of his childhood he takes his readers to the very heart of Spanish life among the poorer classes where the pattern of protest was beginning to engage the forces of tradition. The conflicts in the three basic areas traced in Chapter II of this study shaped his life. In his boyhood he attended the Escuela Pía in Madrid. It was the time when educational problems and policy were beginning to cause volcanic rumblings beneath the surface of society. He personally experienced the conflict between the religious and secular drives in this area. In adolescence he was apprenticed in a bank and participated in the struggle between labor, associated with the parties rising on the left, and capital, long aligned with the predominantly rightist monarchical structure. Later, in early manhood, he witnessed monarchical policy in the military arena, during his service in Morocco. In his maturity he lived the culmination of this cycle of history during the Republic and the Civil War.

Like a person standing upon an elevation that reveals the contours and winding paths in a landscape, he writes in retrospect and presents his readers with a unified picture of the origin and development of the important tensions, whose misunderstandings and clash of interests caused the conflict. Barea's anticlericalism is three-pronged; that is, it extends chiefly to those areas which I have designated as the three keys, although he does not always speak specifically under these topics.

Like many Spanish liberals (as seen for example in the novels of Pérez Galdós) Barea was trained in the sciences. By virtue of his skills, he was at the point of passing into the wealthier class when he suddenly evoked his background — never really forgotten — and turned to the political scene at the time of the fateful elections of 1936. He remained in Madrid almost to the last, fighting for the Republic in various capacities in the Ministry of Information. After escaping to France he eventually went to England where he worked for the B.B.C. He also devoted himself to literature, lectured in South America and the United States, and wrote a number of brief, solid studies on Spanish Literature.

Barea's life story is written in a style which is blunt and bare — born of its time. It reads like a saga and is peopled with innumerable real figures representative of every possible type and status. Beginning with his youth in *The Forge* the author introduces his urchin companions bathing naked in the river. There pass in review child laborers, beggars, laundresses, *beatas,* laborers, farmers, poor relatives, wealthy relatives, relatives with true charity, relatives exuding avarice; the wealthy fail to pay his mother; the peasants struggle for the land; and Barea writes "I needed God . . . but I could not pray."[2] Upon the author's entrance into the bank, another view of society is opened up. It is a world peopled by unpaid apprentices, underprivileged clerks, overpaid directors, prostitutes, working girls, timorous socialists, political reactionaries. The forces of tension are beginning to be heard in shouts of "Maura — yes!" "Maura — no!" In *The Track,* during his army years, the procession of types reveals flea-bitten Moors, soldiers who deliberately contract venereal disease to escape combat; more down-trodden of the earth, more generous souls; Lieutenant Colonel Millán Astray who delivers panegyrics on Spanish courage; an officer who confiscates books by Anatole France, Blasco Ibáñez, and Victor Hugo; other officers who dally in the houses of prostitution. The power of the *juntas* grows amid an atmosphere that points toward dictatorial leadership. In *The Clash* we get a variegated view of the political maelstrom of the Republican years, which Gerald Brenan also evoked in his study, *The Spanish Labyrinth*. Anarchists, socialists, democrats, monarchists, syndicalists, communists, falangists, and their various subdivisions vie with each other to make their own particular ideology prevail. These pages are peopled by those who chose the Republic freely; those who chose it through fear; those who chose the Falange through conviction; those who chose it through ignorance; those who chose it through cowardice; those who chose it for the sake of having a cause. We meet Republican generals and Republican officials; officials with whom Barea could work and officials who sought to destroy him as the Republican movement crumbled under the Civil War. Staunch clerical supporters of Gil Robles are apparent. Sincere priests loyal to the Republic are not unknown even during the Civil War.

In presenting this picture the author in no sense accuses the Church of being the cause of the pattern of historical woe. He criticizes severely, however, when he feels that in given situations churchmen were aligned with or committed to the entrenched interests of the right; he castigates the political efforts to maintain these alignments and the prejudices which contributed to the failure of the clergy to appreciate the aspirations of the people, which, given more understanding, direction, and encouragement, need not have become antireligious. The book is, thus, anticlerical in the most generic understanding of the term. Barea, in other words, presents an intense personal reaction set in an historical matrix of the type which Conrad Bonacina has penetratingly analyzed.[3] Although Barea's feeling is strong and bitter, it is not basically antireligious. He summed up his position shortly before the elections of 1936, in a conversation with Don Lucas, the parish priest at Novés:

"You're pushing me into the personal sphere. It is possible that you yourself are one of those exceptional priests I've mentioned, and some of whom I have known and still know. But if you want to hear what I would do in your place if I were a priest, it's quite simple; I would drop the post of Chairman of Catholic Action — that's what you are, I think — so as to obey your Master's law, 'Render unto Caesar that which is Caesar's,' and that other word which says that his reign is not of this world. And then I would use the pulpit for teaching the Word of Christ, not for political propaganda, and I would try to convince all people to live together in peace, so that the poor need no longer perish, lined up along the stone wall of the road waiting for a piece of bread as for a miracle, while the rich let the soil lie waste and each night gamble away enough money to wipe out all the hunger in Novés."

It was now that the priest took offence. His lips went greyish white and quivered.

"I don't think you can claim the right to teach me my duties. In this place there are a good many of the rabble who need one thing and one only: the stick. I know you think our chief [Gil Robles] is a 'Church rat.' But whether or not it pleases your friends, the revolutionaries, who want to push Spain into the greatest misery — he is the man who will create a great Spain. I'm sorry to say that you and I can't be friends. You've come to disturb the tranquility of this place. We'll each fight for his own side."[4]

Barea expands his views on clergy and religion in the same conversation:

"The fact that I don't go to Church doesn't necessarily mean that I don't believe in God."

"Now don't tell me that you're one of those Protestant heretics — it would pain me greatly — but in that case I would not be able to tolerate your presence in this Sacred House for a single moment."

"In this Sacred House which is the House of God and therefore open to everyone, isn't it? Don't be afraid, I'm no heretic. It didn't occur to me to change the label. The trouble with me is that I've suffered too much from so-called religion all my life. You can rest assured I've been brought up in the lap of Holy Mother Church."

"But why don't you go to Church then?"

"If I tell you the truth, we shall probably quarrel."

"Just speak out. I prefer to be plain and to know where I am."

"Well then I don't go to Church because you clergy are in the Church and we don't get on together. I was taught a faith which by its doctrine was all love, forgiveness, and charity. Frankly, with very few exceptions the ministers of the faith I have met possess all sorts of human qualities but just not those divine qualities."

Don Lucas did not enter this field. He chose a tangent.[5]

These ideas need to be counter-balanced by the author's contact with Don Leocadio Lobo, a workers' priest who had remained loyal to both the Church and the Republic:

The deepest hurt to him [Father Lobo] was not the fury vented against churches and priests by maddened, hatefilled, brutalized people, but his knowledge of the guilt of his own caste, the clergy, in the existence of that brutality, and in the abject ignorance and misery at the root of it. It must have been infinitely hard on him to know that the princes of his Church were doing their level best to keep his people subjected, and they were blessing the arms of the generals and overlords and the guns that shelled Madrid.[6]

Barea's anticlerical reactions did not suddenly crystalize with these political considerations during the Republic. They began during his early contact with religion years before when his aunt, a *beata* and a good woman in many ways, forced him into almost monastic ritual of religious exercises. Initial distaste was heightened by his experience in school, particularly in the confessional, where he had the misfortune to encounter a priest who had a totally perverted notion of good and evil, especially in matters of sex. Personal dislike rises in pitch when he witnesses the position of the clergy with regard to the social order. Thus, his own humanly understandable emotional reactions color his anticlericalism and lead him to emphasize the darker side. He does not portray only reactionary priests, yet, the "good priests" are exceptions. The priests whom he does not like or with whom he has strong, well-reasoned ideological differences are either monstrously fat or otherwise ugly to look at. His picture of a certain Father Ayala will suffice to indicate this particular coloration:

I had found Father Ayala dirty and greasy. His habit slovenly, his huge, stiff-soled boots never cleaned, the nails of his splay fingers edged with black. I had no glimpse of his mind but I knew the strength of the man. At that time, the threads he held in his fingers led to the Royal Palace, to the Cortes, to the aristocratic salons, and to officers in important garrisons. But he never appeared in public. I knew that he now lived in civilian clothes in a Seville tenement house together with two other Jesuits. Why did he suddenly accompany his brother [the land holder and wine merchant] on this trip to Madrid, by air, unexpectedly? What new spider's web was he weaving?[7]

In other instances, Barea reacts almost puritanically to priests who use wine; none are drunkards but many are topers — a situation certainly not scandalous in a Latin land. In another sketch, the tortures of the flesh which a certain priest is probably undergoing redound to his discredit. On the other hand, the priests whom the author admires are almost invariably the victims of "beatific" mothers who forced their sons into the Church. This is implied even of Father Lobo. Thus, these clerics represent the impossible situation of apostolic dedication flowing from insincere motivation.

Another important insight into the anticlerical movement in Spain is offered by the circumstances of the author's life which placed him in proximity to popular sources of the phenomenon. Barea's grandmother, for example, is a hard-bitten old woman, not unlike Tomasa in Blasco Ibáñez' *La Catedral*. She frequently denounces religion and priests, and proclaims herself an atheist. The study of the inner reaction of such people in their *milieu* offers a psychological insight into the various violent outbreaks of anti-religious demonstrations and church burnings which in Spain have unfortunately been associated with the economic-political impetus of the uneducated working classes.

Further insights into Barea's anticlericalism can be gleaned from some of his subjective, youthful reactions. Circumstances had of course moved him externally to the left. But the author probes deeper and powerfully relates incidents and emotional reactions which suggest how certain tenets of communist ideology can germinate in the social conditions which he knew. For example, he analyses the subjective content of one of his own youthful outbursts. Angered during a family conversation and ever mindful of the poverty of his class, young Arturo had blurted out: "Parents have no rights. We children are here, because they brought us here for their own pleasure. And so they must put up with what had been their pleasure. I never asked my mother to bring me into the world, and so I can't allow her any right over me such as you claim over your son." Barea adds: "My mother said slowly, 'Yes. Having children is a pleasure for which you pay dearly.' " But a deeper subjective penetration was able to probe the weakness of his thorough-going, all-inclusive stand:

At that I saw tumbling visions of my uncle's house, of heaps of dirty linen, of her lye bitten hand and her meek silent forbearance, a smile forever on her lips. Kisses in the kitchen and behind the curtain of the Café Español. The struggle for centimos. Her falling into a chair utterly worn out. Her fingers in my rumpled hair, my head on her lap. It all surged up in me and it put me in the wrong, but not the outcries and protests of the others who disputed and shouted.[8]

Throughout his turbulent days during the Republic and the Civil War, Barea did not identify himself with any ideological group defined more specifically than by the rather general concepts of "leftist", "U. G. T.", "republican", and "strongly socialist." At one time he admitted to being almost a communist. During the last months in Madrid, as the communists gained greater ascendency in the government, he found himself surrounded with an increasing number of communist colleagues. He does not mention actually becoming a member of the communist party and stresses his role as a "loyalist" in the sense of remaining loyal to the Republic. He sympathized with the communists who he believed were honestly working for social justice. In fact, precisely at the moment that the hard-core communists reached their maximum power Barea faced another crisis. He felt his own power waning and realized that his life and Ilsa's were in danger. They both realized that their efforts in the social struggle were now fruitless and fled to France. Thus, Barea, whether or not he formally professed communism, certainly withnessed its genesis, passed through its intellectual *milieu* and transcended beyond its doctrinaire alignments. Strongly indicative of this transit are his reflections on the personality of "Poldi" (Leopold Kulcsar), Ilsa's first husband. Barea writes:

He had much the same proletarian childhood as I, he had hated the world as it was and became a rebel as I. But his hatred of power and possession made him obsessed with it . . .
 The terrible thing was that his power over others gave him pleasure . . . there was a streak of madness in him. There was in me. But mine was born of the fear and hatred of violence, while his seemed to push toward a fantastic dream of power.[9]

It was this fanatical power that drove Ilsa from Kulcsar to Barea, with whom she shared a belief in "the human individual" as "the final value" in the social struggle.[10]

The Forging of a Rebel is a shocking book. Its clear crisp prose, rapid action, concise character portrayals, and accurate historical recall make it easy to read. It is a book that is "hard to put down." On the other hand, the bare realistic narration of terrible but real history combined with the bitter rebellious and revolutionary reaction to that same reality could well cause a person to put the book down quickly — unfinished. Within that paradox lies its value. Beneath the vinegar, there is a warmth and a value structure that is bedrock in the ideology of Catholicism or any western religion, for that matter. The frequently tragic turns in Barea's life symbolize the tragedy of many other Spanish liberals who became embittered lapsed Catholics.

RAMON SENDER (1902-)

Ramón Sender is somewhat similar to but vastly more complex than Arturo Barea. Most of the works in which his anticlericalism can be found span the same historical period and are projected with a similar bitter force. Like Barea, too, Sender is a rebel and he was forged on the same historical anvil. Barea, however, is a philosophic historian and as such he gives a more analytic, detailed and kaleidoscopic picture of the reality of his times. Sender is a novelist with philosophical inclinations. As such he is interested in seeking explanations behind reality — not only the reality of Spain of his day, but of human existence, as well.

Sender had come to Madrid at the age of eighteen and took up the study of law. He worked to support himself as an assistant in a drug store. The city in 1919 was revelling in the turbulent gaiety that heralded the conclusion of World War I and was soon to enjoy the post-war boom under Primo de Rivera. Lurking behind the gaiety, however, was society's grim recollections of the first full-scale clashes between labor organizations and the employer class. The young Sender was strongly attracted to these movements and soon abandoned the legal profession. He was arrested and sent back to his home in Aragón, where he edited a small newspaper. Like Barea he served in the Moroccan campaign. A sensitive young intellectual, he became obsessed with the pattern of brutality, death, misery, filth, and "slaughter for prestige" which he witnessed there. This reaction is found in his first novel, *Imán* (1929), which deals with the Aragonese in the Moroccan campaign and the destruction of the Spanish army.

The young author did not completely despair of life as a result of Morocco, however. If he had, it seems reasonable to assume that his obsessions with the centrifugal tendencies in the universe would have led him to suicide, as it did Ganivet and Larra. An examination of Sender's first novel reveals, under literary symbols, that he discovered in the worst of situations and people a small light shining in the midst of the surrounding darkness of chaos and cruelty. This note is his saving grace; it pervades and becomes the touchstone of all of his major works; it is also the starting point for the philosophical system which he develops and continually reelaborates in succeeding editions of *La Esfera* (1947). Concerning this novel Sender writes: "I continue modifying this book in each new edition and it will not be in its definitive state until I go back to Spain and publish my complete works."[11] Other authors have acted similarly with some of their works. Above all the striking example of Goethe stands out, for he was always enlarging and changing his *Faust* up until the final version.

Sender's "formation as a rebel" continued upon his return from Morocco when he found himself imprisoned for activities against Primo de Rivera. During the first months of the Civil War he was bereaved of practically his entire family. He describes the death of his brother:

In the winter of 1936 my brother Manuel and I were hunting wild boars in the Sierra de Guara (Aragón). We were on horseback and talking politics.
"If the Fascists rise in rebellion and triumph," he said, "they'll shoot me before they shoot you."
He said so smilingly, as too serious things are likely to be said. Shortly afterwards the Civil War began and the Fascists triumphed in the provincial capital where he was mayor. Two policemen went to his house and said to him:
"We have orders to arrest you. Go away and we will say we have not found you." My brother Manuel answered:
"There is no reason for me to run away, and I won't go. Arrest me if you like."
He had a car full of gasoline in the garage, the French border fifty miles away, and on the other side of the border a comfortable home where Francis Jammes, the old poet, frequently spoke to him and his young wife of Christian peace. My brother found it nobler to remain and face the danger with his honest man's quiet smile. He was shot without trial one week later. To him I dedicate the narrative humbly and devotedly.[12]

In *Contraataque* (1936) Sender also tells us about the death of his wife, Amparo Barajón, who had borne him a son and a daughter. She had gone to Zamora to get safe conduct to France. At that city she learned that one of her brothers had been shot; three days later she learned that another brother had met a similar end. Señora Sender was arrested in the office of the Civil Governor while asking for a passport for herself and her children:

One month after her arrest they brought her a priest to hear her confession. Then they took her to a cemetery where they murdered her.[13]

Sender, revolutionary in temperament from youth, quite naturally assimilated the anticlerical spirit of the leftist groups which he joined. There also can be no doubt that his great personal tragedies — in the shadow of official Catholic alliance with the insurgents — intensified his anticlericalism. A man who would not be embittered by Sender's experience would be a monster. The great French Catholic writer, Georges Bernanos, in his terrifying book *Les Grands Cimetières sous la Lune* (1938) presents an eye-witness account of the general atmosphere in which Sender lost his family. In the interest of the balanced perspective which I am trying to achieve in this study, I intend to quote some of Bernanos' descriptions of what took place in Mallorca during the same period of Sender's multiple bereavement:

> Two days before, two hundred inhabitants of the small town near Manacor were judged suspect by the Italians. They were dragged out of their beds in the middle of the night, brought to the cemetery, had a bullet put in their heads and then were burned in pitch a little further off. Certain personages whom propriety obliges me to refer to as bishop and archbishop delegated one of their priests down there. His hobnailed boots in blood, he distributed absolutions between the shots.[14]

Another passage is even more compelling in its grim horror:

> Every night [the] gangs operated in the hamlets and even as far as the suburbs of Palma. Wherever these gentlemen exercised their zeal the scene did not change. It was the same discreet knocking at the door of the comfortable apartment or of the thatched hut; the same shuffling of feet in the full shadow in the garden or on the landing; the same funereal whispering that a miserable soul would hear on the other side of the wall, his ear pressed to the lock, his heart shrivelled up by fear. "Follow me!" The same words to the woman crazy with fear whose shaking hands gathered up the family clothing taken off a few hours earlier. And the rumbling of the motor continued out in the street. "Don't wake up the little ones, will you. You'll take me to prison, won't you, Señor?" "Absolutely," replied the slayer who sometimes was not twenty years old. Then, the climbing into the truck where he would find two or three comrades equally sombre, equally resigned, their expression vague. . . . The truck would grind its teeth and shake into motion. Another moment of hope — as long as the truck remained on the highway! But it was already slowing down; it started to bounce along the ruts of a dirt road. "Get out!" They got out, lined up, kissed a medal or somebody's thumb nail. *Pan! Pan! Pan!*[15]

During part of the Civil War Sender fought in the Republican front line. Like Barea he was attracted to the communists. In fact, in *Contraataque* he freely states that he was a communist.[16] As with Barea, his association with communism was the occasion for his passing beyond it. Barea himself writes of Sender: "When he found that he would have to surrender his heretical humanism and his spiritual independence as a man and artist, if he wanted to remain within the fold, he renounced his last attempt at belonging to a political group and went into the wilderness, true to his stubborn self and true to a living humanity."[17]

In 1938 Sender was in Mexico and the United States. In 1942 he again came to the United States. He married again and became a citizen and taught Spanish Literature for many years at the University of New Mexico. He is now teaching at the University of California. In addition to his work as a professor, he has found time to become one of the major creative writers of our epoch.

Sender's works tend to fall into two general classifications: works before and during the Civil War, and works after. The earlier group evokes the fights, illusions and hardships of his fellow Spaniards before and during the Republic. *Contraataque* reflects the agonizing pain of that war. His later works reveal a continual philosophic evolution and search for values in the twentieth century world of turmoil. As would be expected, anticlericalism is found, particularly in his earlier period, although it is not entirely absent — at least by indirection —in his later work. Consequently, I have divided the treatment of Sender's anticlericalism into three considerations (which occasionally overlap):

1. Sender's anticlericalism in the strict sense of the word.
2. Sender's portrayal of the anti-religious anticlericalism of Spanish radicalism.
3. Thoughts on the religious problem in Sender's search for meaning in life.

1. *Sender's Anticlericalism, Strictly So-called*

Under this heading Sender is quite similar to Barea. That is, he criticizes the clergy in the historical and political contexts that have by now become commonplace in our study.

Contraataque, his personal history of the Civil War, contains the strongest statements. The book was composed in the trenches and in the shadow of Sender's personal tragedies. Yet, the author is clear-minded enough to distinguish between clericalism and religion. "We had the Church to face," he writes. "But that does not mean that people of religious spirit were our enemies."[18] But Sender goes father than Barea, who gives the impression, despite his bitterness, that the clergy's greatest fault was their failure to understand and adapt to changing times. In other passages in *Contraataque* Sender makes a closer cause-and-effect relationship between the intrinsic nature of the Church in Spanish history and the present social woe. He speaks of "the contribution of religious education to class cynicism, which is the major bulwark of fascism."[19] He mentions the "necessity to guarantee political liberties and unwind the tentacles of the Church from the popular organs of power."[20] With regard to the land reforms he speaks of "reducing the feudal land-owning class to obedience, for it had always considered itself beyond or above the State and, after the coming of the Republic, wished to continue with the same privileges."[21] Thus, he speaks of "demolishing feudalism and the Church as an organ of the feudal caste."[22]

In *El Rey y la Reina* (*The King and the Queen*), published in 1947, a conversation between Rómulo and the Duchess highlights the employer class in their relationships with the workers. The Duchess tells Rómulo that he may belong only to Catholic unions, no matter what more liberal views the clergy may espouse. In *El Epitalamio del Prieto Trinidad* (*Dark Wedding*) published in 1942 there are various passages which, if taken at face value, cast the clergy in an unfavorable light. In general, however, there is not as much strict treatment of anticlericalism as can be found, for example, in Pérez Galdós, Blasco Ibáñez, or Pío Baroja. Sender, rather, accepts the anticlerical standpoint of the older authors and devotes more time to his psychological evaluation of himself or his characters and his philosophic preoccupations with the world of experience.

In the works of the Republican era, Sender's treatment of priests is very harsh. The young boy, Pepe, in *Crónica del Alba* (*Chronicle of Early Youth,* 1942), who largely represents Sender himself, shys away in horror from the repulsive priest who sought to proselytize him.[23] The priest taken prisoner in *Contraataque* is a gibbering idiot.[24] Another priest taken prisoner and released to fight with the Loyalists is commended as he begins to shed the deportment of his calling and seek secular freedom and the company of women.[25]

One of Sender's early works was written on the Guadarrama front in 1936. It was also published in 1936 and entitled *Crónica del Pueblo en Armas, Historia para Niños* (*Chronicle of the People in Arms, A History for Children*). It is a boiled-down sketch of the people's struggle. In his treatment of the Spanish Church the author makes a blanket condemnation of the contribution of all aspects of religion on the Peninsula from the beginning to the present. The tone of the brief work is not very elevating. Sender, for example, informs his young readers that the husband of Isabel II had to "urinate in a squatting position like a girl."[26] This "Chronicle" is not read frequently today — nor can it be easily found.

2. *Anti-religious Anticlericalism Portrayed in Sender's Work*

The author's distinction between anti-religion and anti-clericalism has been noted. Nevertheless, anti-religious passages of an ultimate blasphemous nature can be found in certain of his works, particularly in the important novel *Siete Domingos Rojos* (*Seven Red Sundays*), which was published in 1932. The book is the extreme expression of anticlericalism in its most virulent form. It is also difficult to conceive of anything more blasphemous. In creating this novel Sender draws heavily upon the Spanish revolutionary *milieu,* which he knew so well. He has an Espronceda-like sympathy for the downtrodden types, who, in our time gravitated to the extreme leftist movements. But Sender's sympathy is based on more than an emotional foundation. He believes that the extremist and revolutionary tendencies found in certain strata of Spanish life represent forces that never can be forgotten or ignored. They are a fact of Spanish experience. "If anyone should ask me, 'Do you believe in the existence of the anarcho-syndicalist phenomenon as a transcendental fact of Spanish politics?' I would answer in the affirmative and that no one can ignore it today or ever."[27] Any thoughtful study of the Spanish people, Spain, and her literature forces one to say unequivocally that Sender is right.

Sender of course states quite clearly that he does not necessarily agree with either the ideology or the methodology of the protagonists of *Siete Domingos Rojos*. He realizes, in fact, that their socio-economic aspirations are doomed to failure, for their basic centrifugal individualism cancels out any hope for effective action. He writes in the Introduction:

I myself speak seldom through these pages; the characters almost always speak. From the political or social point of view the book will satisfy no one. Well do I know that. But it is not a question of espousing a political cause or of pinpointing aspects of the social struggle. Much less is there a question of pointing out errors or virtues. I am not seking a functional truth — nor a social, moral or political truth; I am not even . . . seeking an esthetic truth. . . . The only truth — the only reality — that I seek across these pages is the human truth living through the convulsions of a revolutionary Spanish sector. I seek this truth in the voices and passions of the characters; I seek it in the light and air that surrounds them and in which they identified, forming a moral atmosphere which is muddy or diaphanous, logical or incongruent. . . . It is a reality which is simply human, the stupid mixed with the sublime.[28]

In the tumultuous pages of the novel Sender's characters run the gamut of revolutionary types: communists, socialists, syndicalists, anarchists, and their various subdivisions. Their common denominator is their anarchical drive and it is here that the author probes most deeply. Within this drive also is found the anticlericalism — if such is still the word. Here can be seen also the historical truth of the words of Leo XIII and other modern Popes who admitted that the social outcasts and certain segments of the working class had been completely, hopelessly lost to religion (and its civilizing influences). In *Siete Domingos Rojos* the Church, in the mind of the Revolutionaries, is identified completely with the worst and most ruthless elements of reaction. The book is peppered with anti-religious refrains on the folkloric level in the age-old ballad line. The priesthood and everything religious are treated with a cavalier picaresque vulgarity. But the climax is reached in a frenzied "anti-litany" of blasphemy. A machine gun has been smuggled into the group. It is a Hotchkiss. The characters play with the phonetics of the name and call it the "Virgen Joquis" (The Virgin "Hokiss") thus also evoking the first two words of the Latin formula for the consecration at Mass: *"Hoc est enim corpus meum."* Then, as if at a solemn service a ritual begins around the newly mounted gun. The solemn invocation is said:

> Thanks, Oh my God, that you have permitted a machine
> like this to come to our side. Thanks, my God, that
> you gave us the intelligence to put it together.

Then, the "prayer and responses" before the anti-litany are said:

> "The Virgin Hokiss," they all answered,
> "is our daughter."
> Graco raised himself up high
> with the gun in his hand.
> "Let's put our faith and
> our hope in the
> instrument of the revolution."
> "The Virgin Hokiss is our spirit.
> Hurrah, hurrah."

The anti-litany proper begins: Graco began to pray:

> "Government ministers,
> directors general, whory duchesses!"
> "You will die at our hands!"
> "Elegant intellectuals,
> servile politicians,
> pederasts in luxurious careers
> "You will die at our hands!"
> "Deputies, governors, priests!"
> "You will work the soil
> yoked to our ploughs!"
> "Nuns!"
> "For the first time they

will smile when they
press milk from their young breasts!"
"The saints of the Church!"
"They will make good kindling
wood to warm soup for our shock troops!"
"The sacred monstrances and chalices!"
"With them we will
make gay the day of
great and final blasphemy!"
"Debt titles, letters patent
of nobility, wills and
heraldic coats of arms!"
"We'll set them on fire
and our children will
singe their feet jumping
up and down on them!"
"The Virgin!"
"She will give birth in pain!"
"Jesus! God's son!"
"We'll send him to a school for the abnormal!"
"God one and three, all powerful!"
"There is no god! God's finished.
"We'll wipe the behinds
of our happy, newborn children
with the sacred cloths of his ritual!"
"Is there anything more than the revolution?"
"Nothing but the revolution!"
"Nothing more?"
"Nothing! And we adopt this machine as its emblem:
The Virgin Hokiss!"[29]

Anticlericalism and the blasphemous spirit of anti-religion can
go no further.

3. *Thoughts on the Religious Problem in Sender's Continuing Search*

While we have seen that Sender's personal anticlericalism
differs considerably from that of his revolutionary characters,
I believe there has been some deep connection between the
origin of the anti-religious spirit and Sender's own religio-
philosophic searching. In the minds of the anarchists, religion
and the forces of oppression, repression, and reaction are completely identified. In Sender's mind religion and the Church
are continually probed and tested as vehicles of truth and an-

swers to the deeper needs of humanity. Sender's most frequent answer is at most further doubt.

This probing can be seen, fo rexample, in *The King and the Queen* where both Rómulo and the Duchess speak to some extent for Sender. At the beginning of the tale both accept the Church. The Duchess is hardly an ascetic; she does not object to occasional dalliance and confesses regularly. Later, however, chaos has broken loose and the supposedly Church-centered civilization is shaken to its foundation. The function of religion becomes a source of meditation to her in her long hours of seclusion. The confusion in her mind is a microcosmic reflection of the larger contemporary picture — man wandering in desperate search of values in a landscape shattered by violent clashes: "Who could make me take anything that we're seeing and hearing seriously? God? God who made the world what it is, God who tolerates all the horror we know about, and then after tolerating it exacts not only admiration for what he's made but adoration, too? How can you yield to a divinity like that?"[30]

Earlier evidences of this doubt can be found in the semi-autobiographical *Crónica del Alba*. The most important passage covers the symbolic experiences which Pepe undergoes in the medieval chambers which his family discover in an old castle where the family is vacationing. A manuscript had been found which, in succinct medieval terminology, summed up the ordinances of life at the castle. Everyone was either a "saint," "hero," or "poet," and Christianity was the basic fabric of the society. Experiences with the ghosts of these people, however, reveal an ugly pattern of deceit, treachery, and horrible violence with the saints, heroes, and poets forever at each other's throats and all (with the exception of the drunken lay-brother) meeting a violent end. One is reminded of the medieval novels of Zoe Oldenbourg, where the adequacy of Christianity as a viable medium of civilization and culture is weighed in the balance and usually found wanting. Pepe can find consolation and security only in the arms of his sweet-heart, who symbolizes the creative, protecting aspect of life.

In 1942 Sender published his powerful *Epitalamio del Prieto Trinidad* which appeared in English in 1943 as *Dark Wedding*. The story — if it can be called that — is located in a penal colony in the Carribean and is peopled with types that would be labeled "picaresque," had they not been forced even further down the scale of existence. Thus, they are symbolic monsters all struggling in some way to find meaning and fulfillment. The novel moves episodically through a succession of night-marish scenes in which the author explores "the world of the ganglia." Sender here demonstrates his competence in the dark sub-currents of the human mind as well as his assimilation of some of the attitudes of James Joyce. (In his *Ensayos Críticos* [*Critical Essays*] published in 1955 Sender warmly praised the Irish author.) *The Epitalamio* closes with *Niña* Lucha and Darío electing to remain on the island. The Niña is another, more elaborate symbol of civilizing, feminine elements in life; Darío represents man who has attained the use of reason and its application to science. The use of the feminine symbol is as old as human recorded expression. In his manipulation of it, however, Sender shows his strong affinity for James Joyce.[31]

Sender's religio-philosophic questionings have continued in many recent novels. Successive revisions of *La Esfera* show a pantheistic monism of a self-sufficient universe. Personal immortality is replaced by the immortality of mankind of which the individual is but a part. The woman symbolizing the light shining in the midst of darkness is Sender's convic-tion of humanity's ability, within this framework, to realize its own potentialities. Frankly ecclectic, this philosophy offers nothing new beyond the author's enthusiastic experience of its evolution within him. In 1953 Charles L. King wrote: "Dare we hope that Don Ramón will achieve a more satisfactory synthesis of the claims of reason and ganglia in future ver-sions of *La Esfera?* . . . The word 'perhaps' is conspicuously present throughout the novel. Salia's meditations frequently end, as does the story itself (in a symbolic sense), with a question."[32]

In 1953 Sender published a brief novel entitled *Mosén Millán*. As the story opens, Mosén Millán is waiting in the sacristy of his church to say an anniversary Mass for "Paco of the Mill." In a series of dream-like flashbacks the priest recalls various scenes in Paco's life. Mosén Millán had baptized him, had given him his first communion, had instructed him for confirmation, had officiated at his marriage, and finally had given him extreme unction. In addition, Paco had served the priest's Mass and had accompanied him on sick calls to the "down and out" of the village. After his marriage Paco had become a village official; it was the time which Sender vaguely designates by reference to "the election" and the fact that "the King had departed with the sound of music to other parts and *bon voyage* to him."[33] Paco took a position in favor of land reform and this proved to be his undoing. Violence breaks out between the farmers and those whom the author identifies as "young gentlemen with pistols" and "foreigners."[34] Paco is forced to flee. Mosén Millán knows where he is hiding, however, and is intimidated and hoodwinked into revealing the information. In good faith he accompanies the militia to the hiding place and persuades Paco to give himself up. Paco surrenders; he is taken without trial to a cemetery where he is executed by a firing squad. The tone of the book is moral rather than violently polemic. The characters are drawn less as individuals than as universal types. The portrayal of Mosén Millán himself is one of Sender's most sympathetic and sensitive. Yet, there is no essential change in the "message" or theme of the book. Mosén Millán represents the clerical class and/or the classes associated with the old order — any old order, for the author in this work is not overly specific about time and place. Paco represents mankind, especially the hard-working poor. Mosén had willingly devoted his long life to hard service in caring for the spiritual needs of people like Paco. Paco, for his part, had helped Mosén Millán and had been on very good terms with him. But in the end Mosén betrays Paco. He does it half unwittingly, but he does it. The betrayal stems from the weakness of the class he represents rather than from his own character. Sender implies that it was inevitable that he would betray Paco. The reason seems to lie in the fact that the priest seeks God in the abstract rather than in the hearts of his flesh and blood brothers:

He loved Paco. He loved him a lot, but his affections were not for the man in himself but rather because of his relationship to God. His was a love above life and death. And he could not lie.
"Do you know where he is hiding?" the four asked simultaneously.
Mosén Millán answered by lowering his head. It was an affirmation. When he realized what had happened it was already too late. Then he asked that they promise not to kill him. They could try him, and if they found him guilty, put him in prison, but not commit another crime. The centurion with the generous face promised. And then Mosén Millán revealed Paco's hiding place.[35]

Mosén Millán is a modern morality piece.

In 1954 Sender published *Hipogrifo Violento* (*Wild Hippogriff*), a continuation of *Crónica del Alba*. The plot is devoted to the school experiences of the protagonist, José Garcés, in a boarding school run by a religious order in Reus. There is practically no external action, the entirety of the work being devoted to José's efforts to grasp reality. Sender says of the semi-autobiographical Pepe: "In these pages the author is seen trying in vain to draw the veil from an absolute reality attainable only to religion or to poetry."[36] As can be expected, the clichés of anticlericalism crop out from time to time. The various priests do not appeal very much to the brash youth and we are not surprised to learn that they made war on Voltaire and Rousseau. In general, however, Sender's picture of boarding school life in no way approaches the extreme caricature of Pérez de Ayala. The theme of the book is found in the *hermano lego*, the lay brother. Of him Sender writes: "The principal person of this small work is a lay brother. Pepe Garcés shows us, without saying so explicitly, that he could assimilate the lesson of this brother, who had no teaching post, and that . . . he was the only one from whom the boy

181

learned anything."[37] Throughout the novel Pepe visits the brother in his workshop and discusses such diverse topics as the statues which the *lego* manufactures and Calderon's *La Vida es Sueño* (*Life is a Dream*) in which play the boy took a leading part and from whose first two words the name "Wild Hippogriff" was taken. The *lego's* influence has a calming effect upon Pepe's youthful arrogance and helps him to gain a more balanced perspective. In an important episode Pepe tampered with the school's electrical system. Violence had broken out in the streets and the boy was convinced that the priests had wired the windows so that the workers would be electrocuted when they stormed the monastery. The net result of Pepe's action was that he turned on all the lights in the courtyard and extinguished those in the corridors. The *lego* helped him realize the futility of such impetuous action.

The brother is portrayed as a man of exquisite, yet simple religious sensibilities. Page after page is devoted to his statements of firm, and deeply charitable faith. He and Pepe discuss at length Saint Benedict Joseph Labré. They share their tremendous admiration of this "dirty, ragged . . . saint with his sack on his shoulder and a halo around his head."[38] Despite such new departures, however, it should not be too hastily concluded that Sender is abandoning "ganglionic monism" and possibly returning to the faith of his boyhood. There is abundant evidence to the contrary. For example, the *lego* is nameless. He is quixotic and there is something about him that unquestionably stands for humanity. Thus, considering the author's philosophical history, the brother can easily be interpreted as a symbol of the author's pantheistic humanity of which the individual is a passing expression. And Pepe's contact with the brother can be taken as symbolic of the boy's penetration into the core of living human reality. Furthermore, the *lego* fashions holy images and then prays fervently to them. His faith is indeed convincing. But, once again, given the spectrum of Sender's tendencies, the faith seems to symbolize humanity wandering in the wilderness of the universe and erecting images to a personal god who is needed but who does not exist. Or, possibly, Sender simply feels God's absence more than his presence?

It is evident that Sender cannot escape from the claims that Christianity and religion make upon his whole being. They pursue him; they lurk in every corner of his superb imagination. The liturgy of the Church emerges in inverted form as blasphemy when he describes an anarchistic *milieu*. The attitudes of Christian charity and the interior life flow from his pen with the ease of long familiarity, whatever their intended symbolism. Like so many Spaniards he appears to be a God-seeker. Or again, he could be included among the thinkers whom the German Catholic critic, Karl Pfleger, called "Wrestlers with Christ" (*Geister die um Christus Ringen*).[39] Violence and polemic in Sender's later work have mellowed into a sort of galdosian humanism. But the last lines of the surpassingly beautiful poem concluding *Hipogrifo* read ambiguously as follows:

> Oh God, great shadow of name,
> At times propitious or adverse,
> See how your absence illumines
> The cornice of the universe.[40]

RAFAEL ALBERTI (1902-   )

Rafael Alberti is another writer equally important for the anticlerical tradition in the era under discussion in this chapter. He is a native of the province of Cádiz, fought briefly on the side of the Republic, then fled to France and eventually South America. He has lived for years in Argentina and has been connected with the *Losada* publishing house.

Alberti's poetic powers developed rapidly and in 1925 he shared with Gerardo Diego the National Prize for literature for his beautiful *Marinero en Tierra* (*Sailor on Land*). The work is tender, poignant, and restless and reveals a yearning for the far off, a sort of dreamlike nostalgia for the unattainable. Critics were quick to note the music of Gil Vicente and some of the image-fashioning of Gongora. Throughout his life Alberti has continued to publish volumes of poetry, mostly of a very high order. Like Lorca, whom he at times strongly resembles, he belonged to the group of younger poets who are sometimes known as "the school of 1920-27," some of whose members we will have occasion to mention in the next chapter. Alberti is tremendously versatile and his poetry puts on many moods. It has undergone experimentation with practically all of the styles of modernity, such as surrealism, ultraism, neo-Gongorism. Today the poet remains (with Vicente Aleixandre) one of the greatest exponents of Spanish poetry of the epoch of García Lorca.

Alberti's poetry is at times abstruse and difficult to understand. Not so his verse in the anticlerical vein! Unlike Barea or Sender, his anticlerical position is not at all subtle or complex, for it is undisguised communist propaganda. I will treat the poet's work under three headings:

1. Alberti's anticlericalism.
2. Alberti's insights and contact with anticlericalism on the folkloric level.
3. Alberti's *Romancero*.

1. *Alberti's Anticlericalism*

In the prologue to *Poesía 1924-1930,* the poet states that since 1931 his life and work were placed "at the service of the Spanish revolution and of the universal proletariat."[41] The era 1924-30 thus represented what he considered an irremedial contribution to bourgeois poetry. Beginning in 1931 he became, in the words of Angel Flores, "the bourgeois poet evoking his bourgeois background and exposing its deadly corruption."[42] Valbuena Prat has said that Alberti's revolutionary poetry is inferior in quality and lacking in poetic roots. Factual evidence causes one to subscribe to the judgment in most instances. Yet no one can deny the power of his "Una Fantasma Recorre Europa" ("A Phantom is Crossing Europe"), a fairly early attempt in the revolutionary vein in which the onslaught of communism is announced. The imagery is all the more powerful when one recalls the historical elements and real grievances that fueled the revolutionary spirit:

> The old families close their windows
> And bolt the doors,
> And the father runs in the shadow to the banks
> And his pulse stops in the Stock Exchange.

The final lines are chilling:

> A phantom is crossing Europe,
> the world.
> We call him comrade.[43]

Alberti's dedication to the Marxist concept of life and history is complete during this era. Another poem strikes the Spanish chord for Russian communism, and the communist ideology is prescribed as a panacea for all the problems that plagued the era we have been treating. The anticlericalism is of course openly anti-religious. The polished, cerebral poet tries to identify with the spirit of the revolutionary rabble that Sender evoked in his *Siete Domingos Rojos*. I quote the poem at length to illustrate the anticlericalism embodied in his ideology:

> Comrades!
> The dawn of the day of uplifted hands
> draws near,
> behold it,
> the dawn of fear in the jaundiced eye of the usurer,
> the dawn of precipitate flight from beds,
> the dawn of the seizure of the banks,
> the dawn of the assault on mines and on factories,
> the dawn of the conquest of the land,
> the dawn of the defeat and expulsion of the angels,
> the dawn of the annihilation of the
> celestial monarchy.
>
> Until yesterday no one knew the hatred of these
> bricks and stones for the nuns,
> for the bald heads of syphilitic priests,
> for the traders in faith and exploiters of the
> illiteracy in which the villages wallow,
> Arise!
> Scythes aloft,
> reapers,
> sickles raised to the fever height of the blood.

185

Arise!
Hammers aloft,
workers,
toilers from factories that degrade and
      demolish you for the vultures' profit.

Arise!
pickaxes aloft,
obscure men who plunge lungs and eyes
      into the black dungeon of the mines.

Arise!
Guns aloft,
soldiers ignorant of treacherous pacts against
      the Soviet Union.

Arise!
UNITED FRONT
The clocks of the Kremlin salute you singing
      the Internationale
the radios of the U.S.S.R. speed you the
      cheers of the Red Army,
from Madrid to Lisbon a star grows
      till it covers all the sky,
and the whistle sounds from the first train
      that does not know the old frontiers
Arise, comrades!
Long live the Union of Iberian Soviet Republics![44]

Alberti's anti-religious anticlericalism becomes most violent when he turns his ire on the Jesuits. Strong elements of childhood frustration are evident:

HIGH SCHOOL (S.J.)

I

We were the outsiders
The high school students of bourgeois families now in decline.
Christian charity gave us culture without having to pay.
Piety opened our books and the classroom doors.
We were already the type who someday
      will be buried quickly.
We did not clearly understand why gold braid did not go round
      our caps,
Nor for what reason we didn't have it on the side of
      our pants.

We never saw our names printed
        Rather written on a typewriter,
Blue
Almost rubbed out.

We were the outsiders.

II

Such rage
Such hate
Ending in futile biting of nails,
While the blackboards became white with numbers
Or the book margins filled with stains.
Such rage pent up without outcry
Brought us to the sea where there is no bother
        about quadratic equations,
To the heavens free of theorems,
Without any teachers,
To the warm dunes
Where we urinated in a line looking toward
        the school.

We were the outsiders . . .
  .   .   .   .

I see the years,
The same ones that I hear returning this
        afternoon, loaded down with soutanes,
Obscure scarecrows,
Stuffed like dead pig-fish that had
        been wiggling along,
Leaving behind a trail of ink
        spotted with unclean sperm and vomit.

I hear the crucifixes invade upon me, and
Pitiless black shadows coughing with rosaries,
        and stations of the cross,
And a smell of coffee,
A half swoon,
Decomposition in lukewarm mouths of
        the confessional.
It is not possible that this landscape
        should return,
That it should recapture for a moment the
        irrational dreams of flies
Disinfectant and smoke.
This sordid toilet cannot come into
        being again with belches and tapioca soup.

It is impossible
I don't wish it,
It is not possible to wish for you, the
    same death of youth.[45]

In addition to poetry of this type, Alberti also wrote several
more extended works which contain the same sort of anticlericalism. Among these is the *Cantata de los Heroes* (*Heroes'
Cantata*), which was presented in November, 1938, in Madrid
and the *Romancero de Fermín Gallán* (*Ballades on Fermín
Galán*). In the latter work the poet tries to recapture, within
the ageless, popular ballad line, the spirit of the officers Galán
and Hernández who rose prematurely at Jaca for the Republic.
The following is a typical selection, which illustrates the anticlerical theme as well:

> His majesty goes hunting:
> He catches lice and fleas
> And mounts mares that soon
> Won't even be she-asses.
>
> Through the Palace salons
> Dance cuckholds and whores.
> Our sweet Queen
> Sips cognac with olives,
> And languidly . . .
> Swoons . . .
> On top of Monseñor Segura.[46]

2. *Alberti's Insight into and Contact with Anticlericalism
    on the Folkloric Level*

Like Barea and Sender, the poet was close to the font of
popular republican sentiment which frequently manifests a
concomitant anticlerical and anti-religious spirit. Valuable insights into this field are found in his essay *El Poeta en la
España del 1931* (*The Poet in Spain of 1931*). He quotes from
memory the refrain handed down in the folklore of Seville
from the time of the Republic of 1873:

> How lovely is Triana
> When on the bridge
> Appear republican banners[47]

He recalls student riots in which he himself took part. He mentions a revolutionary meeting in the Ateneo in Cádiz for the reading of his *Romancero de Fermín Galán*. The reading was preceded by the expulsion from the hall of the poet José María Pemán, who has figured prominently in the literature of the post Civil War period. Reminiscent of topics treated in our second chapter, Alberti writes the following:

What opinion about liberalism and other infernal doctrines was inculcated into the boys who studied in Jesuit high schools? Horror. They lumped into one package the democratic ambitions of a bourgeoisie that was beginning to become industrialized and confused them with the logical needs of the proletariat that this same industrialism was in the process of creating, together with the understandable shouts of the peasant who demanded his share of the land.[48]

He describes the extremist reaction of certain popular sentiment on the Monarchy:

> "Where are you going Alfonso XIII,
> Where are you going, my sad one?"
> "I'm not exactly going; four pimps are dragging
> Me through the streets of Madrid,
> Through the mud, senseless,
> In my general's sash."[49]

He describes the reemergence and growth of the old, popular republican sentiment. "Now it was not only the drunks who shouted 'Long live the Republic!' Though the tone was still muted it could be heard in the Ateneo of Madrid, in the literary gatherings, in the houses of conspirators."[50] He witnessed the emergence of this spirit in his native region: "The folklore of the second Republic, in hideaways devoted to flamenco 'deep song' and in inconspicuous taverns, dared to stir their guitars:

> The moon is republican
> The sun is republican,
> And so am I."[51]

Concomitant with these popular sentiments is the ever-present "picaresque" anticlericalism of the lower classes, which, we have seen frequently, became anti-religious in the twentieth century. Alberti describes the bold emergence of this spirit during his youth.

The very picturesque anticlerical spirit of the nineteenth century went on into the twentieth It could be seen in the streets of Madrid and was a source of terror to the boys and girls of the religious centers of education. It was personified by a man selling newspapers. He had a long black beard and used to cry out: *"El Motín* (Mutiny) is now out; *El Cencerro* (The Warning Bell) is now out! On with rebellion!" And ringing a big bell of the type used to hang on cows, he would break out into an *alelulia*:

> A Beata in Arganda
> Caught carousing with a friar.
> A nun in Almería
> Has become a wet nurse.[52]

Alberti further describes the content of these inflammatory newspapers. It will be seen in the following passages that a whole body of reactions — expressed in one way or another from the days of Blasco Ibáñez, down through the intellectual mill of Ortega y Gasset — had now become the property of any Spaniard who could understand a cartoon:

Considerably later, when I had grown up, I saw some of those terrible issues, the innocent pleasure of the provincial "priest-eater." Old Nakens in his review would alternate this smear-type anticlericalism with violent protests against the regime. And he did it in pictures as expressive as Goya's and as strong as Francisco de Quevedo in his "Memorial" against Philip IV. One of those sketches I could never forget. It showed a man, symbolizing the people, taking off his skin so there was nothing left but his skeleton. He was handing it over to three representatives of the state — a bishop, a government minister, and a general. At the bottom the caption read: "The people hand over the last thing left to them."[53]

Alberti draws the following accurate observation: "This sort of feeling came of age. No longer did it go about defending itself by sketches and bells, but rather with the explosions of the great strikes of 1917."[54]

3. *Alberti's* Romancero

When the national issues changed from Republic to Civil War, Alberti continued to foment and record the sentiment of the revolutionary *milieu*. In a work entitled *Romancero General de la Guerra Española* (*General Collection of Civil War Ballads*), published in Buenos Aires in 1944, he gathered together a considerable body of poetry and verse collected from the younger poets who chose the leftist side, at least for a while. Practically all the selections, as the title suggests, are in the venerable eight syllable line. Most of the poets were of the "School of 1920-27" and we note such names as Manuel Altologuirre, José Moreno Villa, Rafael Dieste, and José Bergamín.

The general warlike nature of the collections can be gleaned from the titles of the groups into which Alberti divides the ballads. Thus, we find such listings as "Ballads of the Southern Front," etc. Not infrequently, as with Alberti himself, the sentiments endorse communism without any reservation. There is very little anticlericalism as such. The symbols with which anticlericalism had long been associated are usually the mere object of radical, doctrinaire attack. At times a specific anti-clerical or anti-religious statement crops out. Thus, José Herrera Petere in a ballad called "Four Batallions" calls upon his "comrades:"

> Men of Madrid: hear me
> You men with the stake at your chest
> Masons, tram drivers,
> Metal workers, stonecutters
> Merchants and employees . . .
> The Fifth Column is speaking

The ideology is obvious:

> We have organized
> Four red batallions.
> One is called the Leningrad
> In memory of that people
> That wiped out the cossacks
> Of Yudenicht, like dogs.
> Today they live happy and free
> Rid of their bourgeoisie and usurers.

191

His anticlericalism is found in such lines as the following:

> The Fifth Column speaks
> And says . . .
> That the parasitical little gentlemen
> And the priests and the bankers
> Will not get into Madrid
> To tyrannize the people.[55]

The issue now is not so much anticlericalism as pro-communism.

From today's perspective and in the light of Alberti's many superior contributions to poetry in the last two decades, it is hard to believe that he lent his great talents to such propaganda. After leaving Spain he went to France. There he got into trouble with the Vichy government. Finally he left for Argentina. But while in Paris he was still reacting rather strongly to the bourgeois world:

> Piss.
> I'm continuing on in Paris.
>
> . . . .
>
> The dog pisses,
> The dogs piss,
> All the dogs do their piss.
> On your two shoes, fine sir.
> All over your nice stockings, madame.
> Little pisser.
> Piss at the Printemps gate,
> Piss at the base of Danton's statue,
> Piss on the revolution.
>
> . . . .
>
> Reactionary piss,
> Bourgeois piss.
> Piss.[56]

192

CHAPTER V

THE AFTERMATH

1. *Church and State and Freedom of Expression*

Bruce Marshall, the contemporary British Catholic writer, has presented an excellent fictional account of the causes and course of the Spanish Civil War in his novel *The Fair Bride.*[1] In the opening pages, hours before the onset of the conflict, the young priest and protagonist, Don Arturo, is in conference with his bishop. The bishop, as Marshall portrays him, is not out of touch with spiritual values, but he is blind to the problems of social justice and deaf to the clamor for reform. The young priest tries to convince his superior that the times demand the practical application of charity and that spiritual values cannot be sought exclusively apart from material necessities. The bishop, however, hands Don Arturo a notice which he is to translate into English so that it can be posted in a conspicuous place at the entrance to the Cathedral. The notice reads as follows:

Entrance into the House of God is forbidden to women clothed immodestly or whose dresses do not reach the elbows and knees.[2]

Don Arturo manages to object:

"I don't wish to be impertinent, Monseñor, but it seems to be rather like fiddling while Rome's burning." The priest tried to keep the emotion out of his voice because he knew that fanatics are rarely persuaded.

"And what makes you think that?" As usual, the Bishop's expression was as benign as that of any other perplexed old man.

"The times, Monseñor. The whole country's falling to pieces because Christians have failed to practice charity, and not a little because we haven't shown the way . . . After all, God made the human body," he concluded. "Even the bits Bishops don't like."[3]

Needless to say, the bishop remains unconvinced. The storm breaks overhead that same day. Tormented by religious doubts

193

engendered chiefly by the failure of Christians in the social order, the priest wanders from adventure to adventure in the maze of the Civil War. At the end of the conflict his disillusionment is heightened but he retains his faith; he feels that he must return to his work as a priest. For his first task at the conclusion of hostilities the new bishop hands him a notice. He is to translate this notice into English so that it can be posted in a conspicuous place at the entrance to the Cathedral. Don Arturo is dumbfounded and bewildered as he reads:

Women shall not enter the House of God in low necked dresses, with arms uncovered or without stockings.[4]

After translating the order Don Arturo retired to his quarters where he "prayed desperately for Christ's unexcited congregation."[5]

Marshall, within the framework of his particularly British approach, pictures Spanish clerical inadequacies with a force equal to that of some of the anticlerical writers. He seems to know Spanish literature well and some of his passages call to mind certain of the anticlerical authors. For example, his picture of the canons reminds one of Blasco Ibáñez' descriptions in *La Catedral*.

The symbolism of *The Fair Bride* (highlighted by the posting of the notices, with which the work opens and closes) indicates the author's estimation of dominant policy at the conclusion of the war. The establishment of the "new regime," he says in effect, actually is a return to the mental *status quo* before the Republic. The conordat established between the Spanish Church and the new government concretized this tendency. A commentator writing in an edited analysis of this concordat (which bears an ecclesiastical *imprimatur*) announces a return to thorough-going traditionalism. There is no attempt at accommodation. The dangers of this uncompromising attitude — dangers which writers from Pérez Galdós to Ortega y Gasset had hammered out in detail — are blithely ignored. Spain is called upon to march back into the past. "With the triumph of the Glorious National Uprising, Spanish legislation has recovered the stamp of her catholicity. Not the catholicity of the nineteenth century, but the catholicity of those who knew how to impose upon it the sign of their greatness — the Catholic Kings and the Imperial Austrian Monarchy."[6] The concept of republicanism, the vehicle of so many aspirations, is condemned *in toto;* the commentator evidently discounts the fact that many loyal Catholics voted for the actual Republic, championed it, and served it with distinction: "The Republic, in Spain at least, is the specific form of the revolution."[7] The concept of liberty in religious belief — so bravely championed years before — is now "out." "The Republic . . . with base desire began its destructive work. First there was the Decree signed the fourteenth of April, 1931, which announced freedom of belief and religion — a ridiculous attitude, an absurd thing since there is no plurality of religions in Spain. There is only one, profoundly rooted in the Spanish heart and that heart is Catholic."[8] The old dilemma of "Catholicism or atheism" was also reannounced. It will be recalled that this dilemma was discussed in Spanish periodicals and that Pérez Galdós frequently used it as a point of argument between his characters, particularly in *Doña Perfecta* and *La Familia de León Roch.* The text of the concordat reads: "The Spaniard is either a Catholic or an atheist. Here as in many other affairs, there is no middle term."[9] In the preliminary consideration to the section entitled "The Catholic Church and the New Spanish State," the editor says that the new regime is frankly traditional, Catholic, and totalitarian: "The New State was born beneath the flag of Unity and in a totalitarian regime. From the beginning it was the true depository of Spanish tradition, which . . . is one of indisputable Catholicism."[10] This revived "confessionalism" is further specified into regulations covering a number of areas. Of particular interest here is the policy on freedom of expression. To indicate its all-embracing nature and far-reaching implications, this section is quoted at length:

The prevention of pornographic or harmful literature is another of the vital needs of the New State, especially since this class of literature is opposed to the concepts of religion, civilization, and family upon which Society rests. For this reason it is decreed:

1. It is illicit to sell, deal in, and circulate books, newspapers, pamphlets and all kinds of printed or illustrated pornography and socialist, communist, or in general harmful literature. And it is decreed that Civil Governors, Mayors, and Governmental Officers proceed urgently and rigorously toward the seizure and destruction of any works of communist or socialist shading which may be found in mobile library units and schools. Similarly, the Inspectors of Education assigned to the authorized Directorships [will provide] that there be used in schools only works whose content corresponds to the same principles of Religion and of Christian morality and which inspire youth with their examples of patriotism.[11]

With this spirit abroad, it was obvious that the press could not be ignored. Accordingly, the Grand Council of the Spanish traditionalist *Falange,* which, together with the National Syndicalist committees, substituted for the discredited Cortes, established the Press Law of April 22, 1938. This law provided that control of the press by the Chief of State was insured by the establishment of a National Press Service with departments in each province. The Service was designed to control the number and content of news and periodical publications and supervises press censorship. Actual censorship is effected by the provincial departments which also regulate a roster of writers, who alone are allowed to function. Reports are submitted from the provincial departments to the National Service.[12] This censorship, practically unknown under the Monarchy before the era of Primo de Rivera exerts a greater control than that exercised under the Directorate or the Republic. In the words of E. A. Peers, this press policy of the Chief of State envisioned "freeing journalism (as he put it) from the 'servitude' both of capitalism and 'Marxism' and setting up (as he did not put it) a new servitude in their place."[13]

Despite the approval resounding in the traditionalist comments upon the restrictive measures of the concordat, certain developments in Spain indicate that some of the Spanish clergy have tried to adopt a more liberal policy in these vital areas. In 1951 the publication *Ecclesia,* at that time the only uncensored periodical in Spain, sponsored a proposal made by Bishop Angel Herrera Oria which envisioned the establishment of a law guaranteeing freedom of the press. In May 1954, in the same publication, the editor-in-chief, Father Jesús Iribarren, stated in an editorial that he regretted the lack of press freedom in Spain as compared with the situation in other countries. Father Iribarren had returned from an International Congress of the Catholic Press in Paris. He felt embarrassed in the presence of his colleagues for he wrote "they will look upon me as the editor of the only magazine in Spain that is not censored." Father Iribarren went on to project the outlines of "a policy of freedom tempered by responsibility."[14] *The New York Times* reported that "the Spanish Government was highly incensed, especially because the *Ecclesia* article was widely reproduced outside Spain." Father Iribarren was summoned to the office of Gabriel Arias Salgado, Minister of Information, and informed that his dismissal would be demanded. In November 1954, Father Iribarren resigned; for a time it was not clear whether this was a result of the tenor of his opinions or simply because "he had failed to clear his editorial with ecclesiastical authorities."[15] In the meantime, Señor Arias Salgado, undoubtedly alarmed by the newness of opinion, delivered a speech in December 1954. He called for a bill which would give the government the right to name editors of newspapers and described the role of the press as being at the service of the state. Those who "clamor for the so-called freedom of the press," he stated, "are very backward people."[16] Following this speech it became apparent that Father Iribarren's forced resignation was not a result of the tenor of his controversial editorial. A new editorial in *Ecclesia* described in *The New York Times* as "a severe attack upon censorship" maintained that the priest's statements had in fact represented the thinking of the Spanish hierarchy. The editorial went on to say that government directives "by which newspapers are obliged to present as their own the opinions of the government" violate "human rights." Insisting that there was fundamental disagreement with many of Señor Arias Salgado's views, the editorial stated: "The government acts and its actions call for an echo. If this echo . . . is fabricated by agents of the state, it is not public opinion but a fiction. Public opinion serves the common good and that not only when it applauds but also when it criticizes the actions of the government."[17] The controversy fomented by *Ecclesia* continued. The Ministry of Information repeatedly announced "that it wished to draft new laws for the press" which are to replace the laws issued on a temporary basis in 1938. In an editorial in *Ecclesia* in 1956 the editors stated that the criticism, in the government daily *Arriba*, "against certain Catholics harboring thoughts of the most liberal sort" was meant for them.[18] *Ecclesia's* editors showed themselves possessed of both realism and forbearance when they commented: "We know the difficulty at arriving at concrete solutions to the problem of freedom of the press, a problem which has been especially acute in the last decades. We also know the ineffectiveness of indefinite delays."[19]

Another important controversy, related indirectly to freedom of expression and the topics treated in Chapter II, involved Bishop Antonio Pildaín y Zapiaín of the Canary Islands. The bishop issued a statement in which he charged that Spain's state-controlled trade unions are neither true unions nor in conformity with the social teachings of the Church. He warned: "To tell Spanish workers who are unemployed, or others who are underpaid or indignant over the extravagance and wastefulness of some of their countrymen, that the existing trade unions are 'the full realization of the social doctrine of the Church' might mean causing them to experience a full disillusionment."[20] In preparing his statement the bishop relied on what he called a masterful article by Father Martín Brugarola of the Jesuit order, delivered shortly before at the Social Institute in Madrid. The article was entitled "The Present Day Unions in Spain and the Social Doctrines of the Church." According to Bishop Pildaín y Zapiaín, Father Brugarola had stressed the fact that in the teachings of the Church, trade unions are entitled to a proper autonomy and independence. The laws passed by the Spanish Government (especially those of 1941 and 1942) placed the Spanish unions under a state control so complete that all agreements are null and void unless approved by the General Labor Office.

A most bizarre and ironic controversy on freedom of the Church and freedom of expression centered around the late Cardinal Segura. While occupying the Primatial See of Toledo before the Civil War, he was (as we saw in Chapter II) diametrically and unalterably opposed to any republican concept and to liberal Catholics who entertained republican ideals. His famous pastoral letter had acted as a strong irritant in highly sensitive areas at a crucial moment in Spanish history. As a result, at least in part, he became a living incarnation of reactionary Catholicism in the minds of anticlericals like Rafael Alberti. Cardinal Segura returned to Spain in the wake of the *glorioso alzamiento nacional* (glorious national uprising) to assume the leadership of the lesser See of Seville, and found himself almost immediately in conflict with the new regime over the question of whether the Church or the state should administer ecclesiastical appointments. In other words, the Cardinal's willingness to embrace absolute confessional union of Church and state led to the point — often demonstrated in history — whereby the state began to exert pressure on the Church and use it for its own ends. The Cardinal had begun to feel the shoe pinching the other foot. Monseñor Segura then proceeded to attack the new regime "for the degree of tolerance it had been showing Spain's non-Catholics."[21] The late Camille M. Cianfarra reported to the *New York Times* in March 1955 that Cardinal Segura who could find accord neither with the liberals nor the reactionaries had begun to attack the Vatican, the Papal *nuncio,* and the Pope.[22] In a pamphlet printed in the house of the Countess Ibarra (one of the Cardinal's closest friends) and circulated privately, Monseñor Segura protested the transference of his authority to his coadjutor. He also charged that Cardinal Tedeschini, the papal *nuncio* of the early Republic, was partly responsible for his removal from the see of Toledo. He stated further that "his position was unassailable because he is known principally for his frequent attacks on Protestantism . . . Should the Vatican or the government attack him they would be aiding the Protestant cause, and this no true Catholic can do."[23] Later dispatches indicated that Cardinal Segura — a man utterly out of tune with his century, yet destined to play a vital role in it — had been excluded from the ranks of the Spanish hierarchy.[24] He spent the last few years of his life in relative obscurity.

In the last six or seven years various opposing tendencies can be noted in Spain, both concerning freedom of expression and religion and the related problem of free labor associations. Of course, the Cortes had already been re-established in 1942 along the lines of Primo de Rivera's national Assembly. But its function is merely consultative and its members are not elected but appointed along "vertical" syndicalist lines by the national and provincial governments.

In general there has been occasional unrest among the students and among the workers, particularly the miners in the North Basque provinces. There has been support for both among the Spanish hierarchy and clergy — evidence of a most desirable, long overdue change of direction. There have been repeated pleas for relaxation of the strictures against other religions — at least to make things easier for tourists and foreigners resident in Spain. Pleas in favor of such a stand have come from the more enlightened clergy and promises of action have been made by high Spanish authorities, such as Fernando María Castiella y Maíz, Spain's Foreign Minister.[25] As of this writing very little has been done. On the other side of the spectrum, some clergymen have continued in their denunciations of any progressive turn of events. A large number of ecclesiastical writers and publications condemned directly and indirectly the turn of events in the Church under the leadership of Pope John XXIII. His great encyclical *Mater et Magistra* (*Mother and Teacher*) had entire paragraphs deleted in the Spanish translation, especially passages not in accord with present governmental-ecclesiastical policy. Pope John's even greater encyclical, *Pacem in Terris* (*Peace on Earth*) was quoted only in the briefest snippets and bland paraphrases while I was in Madrid in Easter, 1963. Cardinal Montini of Milan (now Pope Paul VI) was condemned for requesting amnesty and leniency for political prisoners. And just as the Basques have continued in their traditional liberal stance, there has been a very strong renewal of ultra-extreme rightism in the North among the neo-Carlists.[26]

In recent months the Spanish Cortes (according to a report in the *New York Times* dated December 23, 1964) voted for further restrictive laws banning any organization "contrary to the fundamental principles of the National Movement." This vote was vigorously denounced by two prominent Catholic leaders. On the other hand, as is well known, the Head of the State has in recent months held talks with a leading Spanish Protestant spokesman. Also, for the first time since 1492, a leader of the Spanish Jewish community has had an official meeting with a Head of the Spanish State. Both meetings were reportedly designed to limit the restrictions against non-Catholics. As of this writing no concrete steps for implementation have been taken. Time will have to tell the story.

The following are a few specific landmarks in Spain's muted but continuing ideological battle.

1. The student riot in Madrid in 1959. This resulted in the jailing of Dionisio Ridruejo, the poet, and the expulsion of Laín Entralgo as Rector of the University of Madrid. This is particularly notable because both Entralgo and Ridruejo had been mouthpieces of the Falange who later underwent intellectual odysseies.[27]

2. The miners' strike in the Basque provinces in the Spring of 1962. These strikers demanded an increase in pay over their average rate of sixty pesetas (one dollar) a day. In this they were supported by a large number of Basque clergymen who in the fall of 1963 submitted a joint message to the Second Vatican Council denouncing the violation of basic human rights

by the present regime. *El Español* of Madrid, the organ of the Ministry of Information and a main channel of government propaganda, is leading a campaign against the outlawed Basque nationalist movement. In almost every issue the publication asserts that Basque nationalism has been infiltrated by communism.[28]

3. In 1962 a large number of Spanish intellectuals (including Dionisio Ridruejo and, surprisingly, Gil Robles, the leader of the rightist *Ceda* during the Republic) attended a conference for European integration in Munich, 1962. While at the conference the Spaniards endorsed a statement calling for immediate radical steps for social reform. Upon their return to Barajas airport those who supported the statement were given the option of going into exile immediately or recanting.[29]

4. On the seventh of December, 1962, in Geneva, The International Conference of Jurists issued a report in which it was claimed that "individual rights are still not officially recognized by the Spanish government and remain too much under the will and discretion of authority." Hope was expressed that in the future "the dignity and rights of the human person will be respected." Recent liberalization of the Spanish press laws was termed "purely symbolical."[30]

5. There has been recent overt criticism and demands on the part of workers' groups in other parts of Spain besides the North. On February 15, 1963 a Catholic workers movement demanded free elections and defended strikes, which, according to the regime's twenty-five year old Labor Charter are a crime against the nation. The organ of the movement, *Juventud Obrera* (*Working Youth*), denounced police intervention against a two-hour work stoppage in a textile plant in Seville. In July 20, 1964 *Juventud Obrera* was publicly backed by Cardinal Bueno y Monreal, Archbishop of Seville and successor to Cardinal Segura. The publication is censored by the Church but not by the state and charges against it had been made by government officials to the hierarchy. In an article in the periodical a charge was also made that "the Falangist concept

of the syndicate comes very close to the communist attitude toward labor."[31]

6. Freedom of debate and opinion has been openly upheld in at least two recent legal cases. In the week of March 14, 1963 an appeal was heard by the state against the acquittal of Dr. Francisco Herrera Oria in a six year old case involving "illegal propaganda" of a moderately left-of-center intellectual movement. Dr. Herrera Oria is the brother of the Most Rev. Angel Herrera Oria, Bishop of Málaga, who is considered to be one of the most progressive and dynamic prelates in Spain, if not the world. Dr. Herrera Oria was acquitted in 1961 after having spent five months in jail along with some of his colleagues. In the state's appeal the group was charged with "offense by tendency" and the prosecutor demanded stiffer sentences. The defense counsel, Dr. Jaime Guasp Delgado, Professor of Law at the University of Madrid, argued that "planning for an indeterminate future" was not illegal. He added that, "nobody knows what is going to happen in Spain in the future," suggesting that every Spaniard was free to look ahead. He also stated that "officials are organs of the state; they are not the state."[32]

The trial of Dionisio Ridruejo was held during the week of June 20, 1964. This time the poet was hailed before the court for a book entitled *Written in Spain* and published in Buenos Aires in 1962 while Ridruejo was in exile. The poet's defense counsel, Joaquín Ruiz Giménez y Cortes, maintained that there must be a distinction between "eternal Spain and passing political institutions." He demanded acquittal as proof that "Spain is a state based on justice." Ridruejo, for his part, pleaded not guilty and claimed that it was "essential that the right to honorable and loyal opposition be recognized."[33]

7. On May 23, 1963 a most unusual rally was held in Madrid. Radical members of the *Falange* violently denounced Spain's "capitalist oligarchy" and demanded more power for labor, the abolition of privileges and genuine land reform. There have long been splits within the *Falange* organization and Spanish socio-economic thought has exhibited tortured

convolutions. This particular vociferous rally is an example of "going left in order to keep to the right." Basically the group is alarmed at left-wing and modern Roman Catholic propaganda and its effect on the masses and is attempting an outflanking movement by adopting a violently anticapitalist line. Accordingly, their spokesman, Manuel Cantarero del Castillo, threatened to break from the *Falange* and demanded that "our anticapitalist posture . . . be recognized."[34] Compare the tenor of this stance with no. 5 (above).

8. It was reported on February 26, 1963, that the Bishop of Huelva, Pedro Cantero Cuadrado, had strongly advocated that current legal restrictions for non-Catholic religions in Spain be adjusted to conform more to "the mental and political structure of the European and Western Community." The Bishop had been queried by a priest about excusing a Protestant child from attending the usual catechism classes required in the local school. Bishop Canterero Cuadrado upheld the child's right not to attend. He stated that Catholic Spain "has nothing to fear from a legal change" in these matters and stated that "the Catholic Church respects freedom of religion, and consequently the parish is fulfilling its duty by respecting the conscience of the boy who is a person, a child of God and a Spanish citizen like his schoolmates." He added: "The Catholic unity of Spain and the *confessional character* [italics ours] of the Spanish state are perfectly compatible with the exercise of all natural rights and of all legitimate freedoms of Spaniards who do not profess the Catholic religion."[35]

9. An absolutely unprecedented attack against the policies of the present Spanish regime (in the areas we have been discussing) was made by the Benedictine Abbot of the ancient, venerable Monastery of Montserrat near Barcelona. The daring, blunt nature of the statement makes the *Ecclesia* controversy nine years earlier seem pale in comparison. The eminent Abbot, Dom Aureli M. Escarre, first charged that "the Spanish government gives a dazzling propaganda picture of material progress, not progress of liberty and justice." Then, in an interview granted to *Le Monde* of Paris, November 13, 1963,

and later published in Spain he claimed: "Spain is still divided. We have not had twenty-five years of peace. We have had twenty-five years of victory. The victors, including the Church, . . . have done nothing to close the gap . . . This is one of the most lamentable failures of a regime that calls itself Christian, but which, as a state, does not follow the basic concepts of Christianity." Dom Aureli added: "The people must be able to choose their form of government and to change it if they wish. That is the essence of liberty." He insisted that Spain needs freedom of the press and honest handling of information. He continued that "absence of information is contrary to the doctrine of the Church and this should stir the conscience of the Catholic rulers of a state which, unless it modifies its political concepts, cannot call itself Catholic." The Abbot's remarks were carried by *El Español,* the weekly published by the Ministry of Information. The editorial comment expressed sorrow for a priest who had forgotten his obligations of justice, charity, and prudence. It was amazed at "falsehoods that can be attributed only to mental aberration." It was stated further that Dom Aureli had joined ranks with the professional critics of Spain: the communists, Marxist atheists, priest-murdering anarchists, near-heretical progressives, Masonic lodges and affiliated groups, and the sectarians of the dissident churches. He had turned his back on the overwhelming majority of Spanish Catholics and the best minds of the Church.[36]

The foregoing incidents should be sufficient to indicate the cross patterns of strong opinion and sentiment lying below the surface of the Spanish body politic and the Spanish Church as of this writing. In recent trips to Spain I have talked to many Spaniards who believe that the country is becoming more open and liberal by the moment. There are others who believe that a slow but steady liberalization is taking place. There are many others who believe that the present regime, in an effort to form a more favorable image, relaxes the pressure of a few fingers while pressing down more firmly with the others. Time alone will tell who is right.

2. Government Literary Policy

Closely associated with the problem of freedom of expression and the free circulation of ideas is a sort of pre-established harmony between policy makers and the tone of post Civil War literary life in Spain. This can be seen in numerous instances, for example, literary and scholarly reviews that have dutifully followed a party line. The "Editorial Declaration" of the periodical *Escorial*, founded in 1940, reads as follows:

For some time the *Falange* has been considering the creation of a review that would be a store-house and mirror of Spanish intellectuality. Here would be gathered and exhibited certain manifestations of the undiminished work of the Spanish spirit, despite the many hardships and ruptures which year after year have impeded its life.[37]

Possibly the choice of the name "Escorial" was a conscious effort to revive and refute the interpretation which Ortega y Gasset developed in his *Meditación del Escorial*. Paradoxically, from today's standpoint, Dionisio Ridruejo was the editor with Laín Entralgo as sub-editor. The early issues contained a regular section entitled "Edifying Texts." The first was a two page selection on the Escorial and Philip II from L. Cabrera de Cordoba's *Felipe II, Rey de España* (*Philip II, King of Spain*). The second was a selection from the writings of José Antonio Primo de Rivera. José Antonio was the son of the Director, Primo de Rivera and one of the early theorists of the *Falange*. He was brutally shot by the Loyalists and became a national symbol for the insurgents. One of the main avenues of Madrid is named after him. His body has been transferred to a crypt before the high altar of the basilica of the recently completed national monument called *El Valle de los Caidos* (The Valley of the Fallen). The huge edifice is carved into the foothills of the Guadarramas, several miles from the Escorial. Fair-minded critics believe that young José Antonio's political thought was much broader than the form into which his followers have evolved it.

Similar directions appeared in other periodicals. The *Ciudad de Dios* upon resuming publication editorialized that "Spain 'has found her way' to use the beautiful words of our glorious Leader . . ."[38] The issues were often prefaced by a photograph of a military hero or governmental official to whom the number was dedicated and who in turn wrote a brief testimonial on why *La Ciudad de Dios* makes excellent reading.

The "business as usual" motif under the protective auspices of the Head of State was echoed in the introductory editorial to the resumed series of the *Boletín de la Socieded Castellonnse de Cultura* (*Bulletin of the Castillian Cultural Society*). The editorial was entitled "The Broken Thread" and was accompanied by an idealized military portrait of the Head of State, with the Latin inscription RESTITVTORI HISPANIAE.

In 1947 another literary periodical entitled *Cuardernos de la Literatura* began publication under the noted critic, Joaquín de Entrambasaguas. Passage of time accounts for a more softened dedication of the review to governmentally sponsored traditional values. The editor refers to the review as "a profoundly felt and permanent homage to the universal Spaniard . . . born four hundred years ago, whose book fills a world . . . the world of 'Hispanidad'."[39] Thomas J. Hamilton in *Appeasement's Child* attributes the word "hispanidad" to Ramiro de Maeztu. He writes: "By Hispanidad, a coined word . . . admitted to the Spanish language since Franco took Madrid, Maeztu meant the qualities that are the essence of things Spanish, the Spanish race, the Spanish language; the Catholic religion, a whole way of life . . . Maeztu's teachings were taken up immediately by the Phalanx."[40]

Literary harmony with governmental policy was not merely limited to laudatory editorials on the Head of the State and his policies. The issues of *Escorial,* for example, frequently carried sections entitled "Deeds of the Falange." The first such article in November, 1944, commented on national reconstruction. For example: "Here is a resplendent testimony of the realism, humanity and manliness of our *Falange,* our all powerful *Falange* . . . that battles with silent strength to assert its existance and thus also causes Spain to exist."[41] The following year Laín Entralgo's book, *Los Valores Morales del Nacional-*

207

sindicalismo (*The Moral Values of National Syndicalism*) was reviewed by S. Raimúndez of the Benedictine order. He wrote: "Catholicism, History, and the Falange. These three words sum up the rich content of the series of studies published by Laín Entralgo."[42]

During World War II the Spanish government frequently made claims of non-belligerency and neutrality. The incontrovertible facts of history demonstrate, however, that the totalitarian sympathy of Spain leaned heavily towards Hitler's Axis which had contributed to the nationalist victory. Labor and military manpower were given to Germany, particularly after Russia was attacked. This sympathy became increasingly obvious when the Head of the State made a premature announcement of the impending disaster of the Allies, and linked this with the defeat of world communism.[43] The pages of *Escorial* reflect this policy. The "Deeds of the Falange" section of October, 1941, treats of the exploits of the "Blue Division" on the Russian front. An unsigned review of a book entitled *Hítler y el Nacionalsocialismo* (*Hitler and National Socialism*) is strongly favorable to this abnormal monster of history and lauds the evolution of his cause. Dionisio Ridruejo, then editor of *Escorial*, became a volunteer in the Blue Division. In 1942 the issues contained excerpts from his *Poesía en Armas* (*Poetry in Arms*) written at the front. The March issue features a poetic "Memento to Dionisio Ridruejo, Soldier of the Blue Division." The contributors include Manuel Machado, Louis Felipe Vivanco, Antonio Marichalar, Luis Rosales, and Pedro Laín Entralgo. It should also be recalled here that the late brilliant and modest Catholic scholar, Carleton J. H. Hayes, was American ambassador to Spain during these years. He did heroic work in convincing the Spanish government to adopt a realistic neutrality. His record of this era can be found in his book, *A Wartime Mission to Spain.*

Anti-Semitism is an historical fact that was part and parcel of Hitler's Germany — we all know with what results. It has also been a part of Russian policy. It is a matter of unpleasant record to Catholics that the anti-Semitic spirit can also be found

208

in Spain. For example, in the January-April issue of *Ciudad de Dios,* Pedro M. Bordoy Torrents contributed an article entitled "¿Por qué los Judíos son tan Perseguidos?" (Why are the Jews so Persecuted?). The author locates his solution in the concept of "deicide." The conclusion of the article contains the following statements:

We conclude by observing that P. Manso's theory contains undeniable profound truth. It causes one to realize that there is an element here that to a certain extent offers various analogies with the transmission of original sin.

.   .   .   .

Furthermore it is undeniable that the Jews bear within themselves a hardness of heart and hate for everything Christian, which they appear to have inherited.   .   .   .   .
.   .   .   .

It is certain that the Jews have continued persevering in the imprecation: *His blood upon us and upon our children;* and that in living, concrete reality Israel is an enormous bundle of branches detached from the olive tree. She is our enemy because we exist.[44]

The close association of literature and literary scholarship with governmental policy can be seen also in the general tenor of cultural activities, such as lectures, awarding of prizes, *etc.* taken in conjunction with the public ideological stand of the participants. Three names that have been continually in the public eye for the last twenty-five years are Ramiro de Maeztu, Ernesto Giménez Caballero, and José María Pemán.

Maeztu originally was a lesser-known member of the Generation of '98. After experiencing a series of philosophical conversions, he finally turned to Catholicism which he vindicated in Spanish history in his *Defensa de la Hispanidad.* Maeztu was Ambassador at Buenos Aires at the time of Primo de Rivera; he died in Madrid in 1936, a victim of the Loyalists. We have seen that the government utilized Maeztu's concept of "Hispanidad", and his name and work are kept continually in public view. To cite but a few examples: there is a Ramiro de Maeztu Chair at the Institute of Hispanic Culture in Madrid where monthly lectures on literature and history are held in the writer's memory. In 1954 Gonzálo Fernández de la Mora, Embassy Secretary and Head of the Cultural Policy for Europe Section of the Cultural Relations department, delivered a paper on Maeztu at the Lecture Club in Valencia. Señor Fernández de la Mora stressed the fact that Maeztu is unfortunately the least known author of the Generation of '98 while in reality "he was the only one who outstripped the problems of his day."[45] In December, 1954, we read:

Public tribute has been paid at the Ramiro de Maeztu Institute, to this illustrious writer on the 18th anniversary of his death. Among other events a meeting was held in the theatre of the Institute, at which the Vice-Director don Rafael Ibarra and the Professor of Literature, Sr. Gamallo Fierros, spoke. The latter recalled the personality of Ramiro de Maeztu in all its aspects, including those of thinker, essayist, and writer.[46]

Ernesto Giménez Caballero first achieved literary attention with his *Notas Marruecas de un Soldado* (*Morrocan Notes of a Soldier*). Later he founded *La Gaceta Literaria,* a review of extreme rightist sentiments, and an even more violent weekly entitled *FE* (*Faith*); the initials also stood for *Falange Española.* A fantastic work entitled *Yo, Inspector de Alcantarillas* (*Myself, Inspector of Sewers*) was published in 1928 and records his Freudian period. Around 1932 he began to elaborate his psychopathic system of Fascist Catholicism to which I devoted several paragraphs in Chapter II. He also gathered together and amplified some of his writings on Azaña in a work entitled *Manuel Azaña* (1932), subtitled *Profecías Españoles* (*Spanish Prophecies*). It is a work of violent diatribe and frenzied personal invective. In *Genio de España* (*Genius of Spain*) published in 1934 Giménez Caballero (like Maeztu) found the essence of Spain in past national Catholic glory. The subtitle of the work is *Exaltaciones a una Resurreción Nacional y del Mundo* (*Exaltations Toward a National and World-wide Resurrection*). Here he projected a fascist program and vision of the future, amid wild nationalistic harangues and impassioned sermonizing to youth. The final "Exaltation on the Pardo Mountain" is particularly noteworthy for the fantastic halucinatory quality of his pseudo-mysticism. He also defines the outlines of Spanish fascism and what distinguishes it from other brands. *La Nueva Catolicidad* (*The New Catholicity*) published in 1933 developed the "theological" side of his program. At the end of the Civil War. Giménez Caballero published *"¡Hay Pirineos!"* which continued his wild *mèlange* of militarism, rightist extremism, the *Falange,* religion, and patriotism. The distinguished Catholic Alfred Mendizábal has called Giménez Caballero's "theology" completely absurd. Mendizábal also states that the author "organized the Phalanxes and gave them intellectual food in these books."[47] After the Civil War Giménez Caballero became a Professor at the University of Madrid. He lectures and publishes frequently and enjoys academic prominence not foreshadowed by his earlier incoherent philosophy and wild propaganda. Some indication of the scope of his more recent career and the apparent authority conceded to his literary opinions can be gained by the following biographical notes:

1. In 1952 he addressed the New Club, Tangier, on "Don Quijote and his International Zone." (He apparently believes that Side Hamete Benengeli was more than a Cervantine fiction.)[48]
2. In 1953 he continued his lectures on the *Quijote.* "Don Quijote in Spain" was delivered at the University in Barcelona. Among other things, the author stressed his conviction that the work is "the nationalist book par excellence." "Dulcinea and Catalonia" was presented at the Medina Cultural Club, Barcelona.[49]
3. In 1952 he was slated to participate in an intensive course in journalism given at Barcelona. Drawing upon his experiences as an editor he prepared three talks entitled: "Journalism and Literature in the Modern World," "Journalism as a Literary Genre," and "Cultural Roots of Journalism Throughout History."[50]
4. On November 24, 1951, he appeared with the Minister of Education at the formal opening of the Institute of Madrid Studies and gave an address entitled "The Madrid That is to be Made."[51]
5. In 1953 he was numbered among those who participated in lectures given at the *Ateneo* in Madrid. "Argentina and Spain" was the title of his talk which developed the theme that "the stages of Argentina's history were all prepared by Spain." He stressed the contributions of Catholicism.[52]

José María Pemán is a native of Cádiz where in 1931 he became involved in a public altercation with another poet of

211

the same region, Rafael Alberti. This disturbance symbolizes the complete antipathy of the ideological views of the two writers — Alberti the completely convinced, doctrinaire communist; Pemán, the equally doctrinaire proponent of traditionalism. Pemán's ideological stand can be read in numerous examples of the writings which comprise his facile, incredibly large, and rather superficial output. Of particular interest is a section of his *Complete Works* entitled *On Politics*. It consists of extended groups of essays under the general titles of "At the time of the Directorate, 1923-30"; "At the Time of the Republic"; "Concerning the National Movement"; "After the National Movement, 1934-51." The essays are derived in considerable measure from Pemán's newspaper writings and show a strong support for the rightist trends of the present government. At the conclusion of the Civil War the great Ramón Menéndez Pidal was removed from the presidency of the Spanish Academy, presumably because he had associated with liberals; Pemán, described by E. Allison Peers as "the wealthy author . . . who had lent General Franco the weight of his influence during the War" provided the replacement.[53] He was soon dismissed from the presidency, however, in the wake of a political blunder. In recent days José María Pemán has continued to occupy a prominent position on the Spanish literary scene, writing freqquently for *A.B.C.* The following are a few biographical notes that indicate the role which he has occupied in post-Civil War Spanish literary life:

1. In 1953 he lectured on Antonio Machado at the lecture club in Barcelona.[54]
2. He continued his study of the famous poet in an address entitled "The Castilian and Andalusian theme of Antonio Machado" delivered at Granada University. In this address he stressed the religious element which entered the author's late poetry.[55]
3. In 1951 he addressed the Higher Research Council at Madrid on "The Speech of Ecuador: Orators and Poets."[56]
4. In the same year some of his writings on Sor Juana Inez de la Cruz were read before the Spanish Academy.[57]
5. Recently performed theatrical works by Pemán are: *El Viejo y las Niñas, Entre el Sí y el No,* and the dramatic poem *The Destruction of Saguntum.*[58]

6. In 1951 the author lectured at the University of Santa María de la Rábida, at the conclusion of the ninth summer course. His address was entitled "The Spanish World and the Universal Attempt to Vitalize Culture." He was accompanied by the Head of the Propaganda Department, Dr. Pérez Embid and presented by the Rector of the University who in this instance was representing the Head of the State.[59]

One of José María Pemán's most important plays is entitled *El Divino Impaciente* (*A Man of Divine Impatience*). Its theme is the life of St. Francis Xavier. Valbuena Prat writes that it is "a work of noble intention whose success is due more to religio-political reasons than to literary excellence."[60]

The lectures delivered at the *Ateneo* in recent years exhibit a tone vastly different from the thought formerly expressed in that center of all shades of liberal opinion. To cite but one instance: in 1951 a series of lectures was given under the general title "Balance Sheet of Modern Culture and Actualization of Spanish Culture." In this series Manuel Fraga spoke on "The Crisis of the Liberal State."[61] Another paper was entitled "The Human Sensibilities of Philip II: A King who was a Lover of Flowers." José Vigón, author of a study entitled *Hitler Tenía Razón* (*Hitler Was Right*), delivered a third paper entitled "The Vitality of the Spanish Military Virtues." For this essay José Vigón was awarded the José Antonio Primo de Rivera prize in literature.[63]

A final symptom among the many which have been adduced to indicate the trend of governmental literary policy is the inevitable appearance of the Head of State (in person or by proxy) at literary and academic convocations. In Spain the frequency of such appearances, taken in conjunction with the pattern I have here outlined, lends strength to the conviction that the pre-established harmony is strong. One of the most significant appearances of the Head of State in this type of context was in 1954 during the festivities surrounding the seven hundredth anniversary of the University of Salamanca. During his address the Head of the State warmly evoked the spirit of Unamuno.[64] This is most ironic because, as we know, Unamuno was an implacable foe of absolutism.

Two points should be made before this section is concluded:

1. No attempt has been made to impugn the sincerity or probe the consciences of any individuals mentioned in this section. The section is an empiric observation. The body of evidence, I believe, justifies the conclusion that governmental literary policy has been and still is a fact in Spain. We go no further than the establishment of the fact.

2. In the first section of this chapter, on freedom of expression, we noted that the nineteen sixties have had experiences and trial balloons pointing toward greater liberalization than in the nineteen fifties. In literature the most prominent example is the former Republican, Buero Vallejo, whose dramatic works have been performed and well received.

3. *The Catholic Spirit in Modern Spanish Letters and the Spirit of the "Catholic Revival"*

Spanish men of letters have indubitably produced much literature which falls under such various terms as sceptical, revolutionary, anarchistic, anticlerical, antireligious, and even atheistic. But it is also indubitably true that some of the world's greatest Catholic literature has been brought into being in this same country. The Mystic school of the Sixteenth Century — unique in its claim to literary importance combined with what Catholics recognize as basically sound ascetical theology — is only one case in point. This Catholic spirit frequently (though not always) provides the idealistic trend of the literature which commentators speak of as counterpointed by a variety of more lowly themes. Thus, a blending of the idealism of Catholic doctrine and the pursuit of a more tangible this-worldly reality is frequently found in the same authors. Quevedo is at once a theologian and a master of the picaresque. During the era under investigation for the causes and directions of anticlericalism, the Catholic spirit was occasionally represented, at times even in writers who are themselves anticlerical. Unamuno as a poet is one example. Additional light can be cast upon the investigations of this chapter if a brief analysis is made of the actual directions which the contemporary Catholic spirit has been taking and the findings compared with the directions of the Catholic spirit in other lands.

Before making this analysis, however, a few general explanations of terminology are essential. The very term "Catholic literature" is vague and open to many difficulties and misinterpretations. Yet it is a legitimate term in certain critical contexts. Actually, there are many varieties of Catholic literature — almost as many as there are Catholic or even non-Catholic authors. C. Carroll Hollis has pointed out that "Christian Literature embraces much that knows not Christ." Indeed an author may be possessed of any species of Catholicism or Christianity — conservative, liberal, fervent, mystical, perfunctory — and not necessarily exhibit any particular properties of his belief in his literary output. On the other hand, there are cases where artists do not profess Catholicism (Franz Werfel, for example), or even live completely apart from all forms of organized religion; yet, for reasons both difficult and obscure, a spirit of religious commitment breathes through their work. Or, there are cases where a man's religious commitment remains concealed beneath the surface of his daily preoccupations. An excellent example of this is Dag Hammarskjold whose beautiful mystical poetry, revealed after his death, has startled the world which knew him as a master of secular affairs. There are also cases where authors, without much theological understanding, exhibit a Catholic point of view simply because it is part and parcel of an environment which they accept and articulate. The nineteenth century Spanish regional novelist, José María de Pereda, is a good illustration here, for in the last analysis Catholicism was to him an essential ingredient of a social order which he revered and upon which he looked back with nostalgia. He lived a long life in flight from his century. This type of "Catholic author" is naturally found in higher percentages in a country like Spain where in recent centuries Catholicism on the religious level has not been open to pressure from other religious beliefs as such. Again, in the literary history of the past century there are Catholic literary figures whose artistic intent is almost completely submerged by a desire to teach and illustrate the Catholic religion, or, to defend the concept and structure of the Church against non-believers. Monsignor Robert Hugh Benson can, to an extent, serve as an illustration here, as well as Cardinal Wiseman (*Fabiola,* for example). Such tendencies would be more commonly found in a country like England where the Roman Church has long been a significant but small minority. Such "apologetic" literature, was accepted in the nineteenth century and compatible within the over-all context of Victorian moralizing. It is intolerable to the deeper and more sophisticated literary standards of today. Finally, we can single out those writers who can imperfectly be called "modern" Catholic writers, or, who are referred to — again imperfectly — in some literary quarters as representative of "the Catholic revival."

The hallmarks of the Catholic revival are many and diverse. To an extent it can be said that the movement began in the last half of the nineteenth century and flowered in the twentieth. Obedient to the more precise artistic formulas which the modern age has discovered or at least more fully comprehended, these authors have produced works of literary art constructed in the context of profound theological conviction and pervaded by spiritual awareness and sensibility. At the same time they reveal little or nothing that could be called exterior motivation toward apologetics, catechetical propaganda, or religio-national chauvinism. Actually, the frequently used term "revival" is not a precise word. Renewal is better, for the Church is in a perpetual process of renewal through grace. Furthermore the achievements of the authors concerned definitely have offered an approach and a profundity that has been recognized as new and unique after several centuries of comparative sterility in Catholic literature.[65]

In England the renewal has its roots in the Oxford movement and the person of John Henry Cardinal Newman. In some aesthetic matters he is undeniably close to the Victorian tradition. But the deep generosity and high spirituality of his open approach to life and religion had a strong impact on the writers of his age, such as Coventry Patmore, Gerard Manley Hopkins, and the popular but lesser figures of Francis Thompson and Gilbert Keith Chesterton. By extension the shadow of this influence has fallen on the more contemporary figures such as Graham Greene, Bruce Marshall, and Evelyn Waugh. Cardinal Newman's essay "On Consulting the Faithful" is at last having its deserved impact in the deliberation of the Second Vatican Council.

In France the renewal has tended to be associated with the names of the philosophers Jacques Maritain, particularly, and Gabriel Marcel. Maritain in his famous studies *Art and Scholasticism* and the later, more probing *Creative Intuition in Art and poetry* clarified some of the basic principles and phenomena which lie beneath the creative process and which to a large extent have been exhibited by modern Catholic authors such as Claudel, Péguy, Bernanos, Mauriac, and Psichari — authors who are often referred to as forming the *Renouveau Catholique.* Of course, it is not my intention to imply that either Newman or Maritain initiated "schools" of literature. Rather, since the work of both was in the realm of theory which to a greater or lesser extent has been exhibited in practice by authors sharing their respective traditions, Newman and Maritain serve as focal points for convenient groupings.

Germany also has witnessed a Catholic renewal. The most prominent figure is probably the poet Gertrud von le Fort, although such names as Elisabeth Langaesser, Ruth Schaumann, Werner Bergengruen, and Jakob Kneip deserve to be better known. The German Catholics have not been conspicuously successful in novel and drama. Their poetry, however, is of a very high order and bears strong links to the "hymnic tradition" deeply imbedded in both Catholic and Evangelical German religious ceremonial.

Paradoxically, in Catholic Spain a survey over a similar historical period for parallel literary phenomena is quite unrewarding. As we have seen, bitter and often vitriolic anticleri-

calism is a frequent by-product of the concerns of Spain's greatest thinkers in this era. In other cases, as with Pereda, Catholicism is manifested to a greater or lesser extent as an occasional by-product of authors who happen to be Catholic.
Rubén Darío returned to some recognition of Spanish-Cath-
olic traditionalism, particularly in later life, and occasionally
expressed sentiments proper to this tendency. Valle Inclán
adhered somewhat to a Catholic view in matters of aesthetic
inspiration. Armando Palacio Valdés, to the extent that he
singled out the pitfalls of poorly understood or faultily applied asceticism, can be classed as a "Catholic anticlerical." In
other pages he adumbrates the pattern for a gentle Christian
humanism. Reliable writer that he was, however, Palacio
Valdés achieved his greatest success through his humor and a
specifically Spanish versatile skill as a regional novelist. His
approach to the theological implications of life reveals no
profound spiritual insights.

Other more recent Spanish writers can be submitted to some
scrutiny with regard to the Catholic spirit in their literary output. Eduardo Marquina (1879-1946) and Martínez Sierra
(1881-1947) are cases in point. Marquina utilizes a conventual
backdrop to supply color for his play *El Monje Blanco* (*The
White Monk*). More successful from the point of view of
Catholic inspiration is his *Teresa de Jesús* which brings upon
the stage the more significant episodes in the life of Thérèse
de Lisieux. Martínez Sierra achieved notice in both England
and America for his *Canción de Cuna* (*Cradle Song*) published in 1911, which portrays conventual life against a deli-
cate backdrop. (Eva le Gallienne participated in one of its
American productions.) Valbuena Prat referred to it as a
"*cromo bonito*"[66] and it is more notably a sensitive expression
of universal motherly instinct than a penetration of the spiritual
implications of Catholicism. It also presents with good taste
the truism that nuns, after all, are human beings. In *El Reino
de Dios* (*The Kingdom of God,* 1916) however the playwright probes more deeply into the meaning of conventual
life. The three well-written and powerful acts present succes-

sively the claims upon human charity made by such social outcasts as the destitute old, prostitutes, and orphans. But the message rises above mere humanitarianism. Martínez Sierra says,
in effect, that the brotherhood of man is predicated upon the
Fatherhood of God. It is Sor Gracia's true interior dedication
which causes the ugly details of her daily routine to take on
meaning. Without this dedication her life would be unbearable. With it she is building God's Kingdom. In such works
as *La Adúltera Penitente* (*The Penitent Adulteress,* 1917)
and *Lirio Entre Espinas* (*Lily Among the Thorns,* 1920) the
playwright continued to exhibit considerable insight into
spiritual conviction.

Such preoccupations alone, however, do not constitute the
quality of commitment that one has learned to associate with
the great figures of the Catholic revival. It is furthermore quite
evident that these Spanish authors are by no means of the
stature of a Claudel or a Mauriac.

Certain other authors have reached their stride in the post
Civil War era. The priest-novelist José María Martín Descalzo
gained considerable attention for his *La Frontera de Dios*
(*God's Frontier*). The novel was widely praised and won the
Premio Nadal of 1957; it exhibited some evidence that the
author had probed the deeper currents of literature. A later
brief biography entitled *Un Sacerdote se Confiesa* (*A Priest
Confesses*), despite its sincerity, is shallow and pervaded with
sentimentalism. Another newcomer among the novelists is the
woman, Carmen Laforet. She won the Nadal prize in 1944
for *Nada* (*Nothing*). In more recent years her novels show
a preoccupation with religion. She was converted to Catholicism in 1951. Her novel *La Llamada* (*The Call*) published
in 1954 shows characters who find consolation in religion. In
1955 her *La Mujer Nueva* (*The New Woman*) won the
Menorca Prize for literature and the Miguel de Cervantes
Prize. Despite considerable early promise and her modest
achievement, it is now fairly evident that Carmen Laforet is
not a major literary talent. And the sentimental tone of her
trend toward spirituality does not give her much claim to be

seriously included in the Catholic Revival. There are of course other newcomers in the field of prose. The most significant by far is José María Gironella who merits special consideration a little later in this section.

Among the post-Civil War dramatists there are none, in my opinion, who merit attention under the title of this section. José María Pemán has already been discussed in Section II of this chapter. Although strongly Catholic he has been seen to be in no way associated with the qualities of the Catholic Revival.

The development of post-Civil War poetry offers a slightly richer vein of the ore of our present quest. Prominent names associated with spiritual trends in poetry are Luis Felipe Vivanco Bergamín who has translated Claudel and Jammes (as well as Rilke), Leopoldo Panero, José María Valverde, the versatile and gifted Gerardo Diego, Luis Rosales Camacho, and Dámaso Alonso. The poetry of Dámaso Alonso is frequently intensely religious; at times almost in spite of other motivations that tug at his soul. It seems safe to say that he will always be remembered as one of the towering critics of our epoch, rather than as a poet. Luis Rosales is frankly religious in a large portion of his work. But his poetry has been said to "fail to convey a feeling of sincerity or religious conviction."[67] His sonnets have been called "placid, derivative, and uninspired."[68] Gerardo Diego has frequently undertaken religious themes. But it would be incorrect to think of him as primarily a religious poet. Luis Felipe Vivanco Bergamín, Leopoldo Panero, and José María Valverde all are to some extent religious poets who have been most successful in this generation. Of the three, Valverde is unquestionably the most powerful. His is a high talent. But again I think it fair to say that he has not reached the stature — as a religious poet — of a Thomas Merton, a Gertrud von le Fort, a Gerard Manley Hopkins or a Charles Péguy. Charles David Ley in his *Spanish Poetry Since 1939* writes that "few modern poets could be called in any full sense religious or Catholic poets. Vivanco and Garcia Nieto, though they publicly declare themselves

Catholic writers, are far less concerned with the artistic expression of their faith than the principal religious poets of England and France would be. They are Catholic poets at times, as Verlaine was."[69] In another passage Ley writes: "The lack of an inspiring body of religious poetry in modern Spain is perhaps due to the same feeling of insufficiency which troubles the revolutionary poets. Poets writing after the Civil War, whatever their ideas may be, feel that they have come too late, that they have missed the great age of literature which ended in 1936."[70]

My own observations lead me to agree with Ley. The noted Spanish critic Angel Valbuena Prat, however, has expressed a different evaluation. In the last chapter of his *El Sentido Católico en la Literatura Española* (*The Catholic Experience in Spanish Literature*) he has contributed some of the most unconvincing pages of his usually highly competent career in literary scholarship. In this chapter he makes a strenuous effort to link certain of the great writers of the century with Catholicism or, at least, with the Catholic outlook and tradition. His treatment of Ortega y Gasset and his essay "God is in Sight" is typical of the method employed throughout the chapter. He writes: "Upon casting his philosopher's glance upon the new Catholic culture he brought his disciples beyond the boundaries of the dichotomy of the nineteenth century, with open minds for the sure ground of Thomism and Augustinianism. Upon flinging forth his shout 'God is in sight' he found himself among the precursors of the new compenetration of theology and purely metaphysical speculation."[71] Similarly in treating and commenting upon many other significant literary events of the era, Valbuena Prat accumulates small details and snippets in an attempt to convey the impression that Spain possesses a highly articulate, spiritually oriented generation — in short, a Catholic Renewal. He pulls Pérez de Ayala in by the hair for his *Balarmino y Apolonio*. García Lorca, he reminds us, wrote a vibrant "Ode to the Blessed Sacrament." Manuel Machado is warmly singled out for the Catholic quality of his *Devocionario Poético*. With much more justification

221

Valbuena Prat cites the noted philosopher and esthetician, Eugenio d'Ors. It should be remembered, however, that d'Ors, whose labors have been devoted to a study of the past, does not achieve the stature of the dynamic contemporary Catholic philosophers (such as Jacques Maritain, Etienne Gilson, E. I. Watkin) who have applied the principles of Catholicism to the evolution of modernity. It would seem, further, that many of the instances which Valbuena Prat cites, instead of bolstering his thesis, prove rather the lack of the strong modern Catholic Spirit. It should be noted also that in this chapter Valbuena Prat uses the term *"nueva catolicidad"* which was first introduced in the early, pathological work of Ernesto Giménez Caballero. Much more to the point, in considering the question of Spain and the Catholic Revival, is the judgement of Matilde Pomês in "Das Katolische Schriftum der iberischen Nationen" ("The Catholic Writing of the Iberian Nations"), a chapter from her *Katolische Leistung in der Weltliteratur der Gegenwart* (*The Catholic Contribution to Contemporary World Literature*). She writes: "The interior affirmation of Catholicism in Spain degenerated into an untroubled lack of concern. People were Catholic the same way they were healthy — without giving it a thought . . . They continued to take part in ceremonies through habit, decorum, and faithfulness to family traditions . . . Concentration on mere orthodoxy had long since helped to lull to sleep any disposition toward true piety."[72]

There is one contemporary Spanish author about whom there is no doubt whether he measures up to the standards of the international Catholic Revival. He is, of course, José María Gironella, and his greatest novel is unquestionably *Los Cipreses Creen en Dios* (*The Cypresses Believe in God*), published in 1953. Paradoxically, from certain points of view the novel is not unlike Arturo Barea's *The Forging of a Rebel*. The historical scope is much the same: both writers concentrate heavily on the years leading up to the Civil War. Barea, however, carries his readers through the conflict itself, while Gironella stops in the midst of the first awful days of full scale bloodshed. Both writers, as their narratives unfold, probe profoundly into the underlying causes of the conflict. Also, certain external details are similar: Ignacio's days at the bank, the people he meets at work, the arguments he engages in — all these are strongly reminiscent of Barea's real-life experiences. Like Barea, too, Ignacio sought early sexual experience with women of easy morals. In the Calle de la Barca, the slum area of Gerona, the at once colorful and pitiful dregs of humanity (whom we meet so frequently in *The Forging of a Rebel*) again rise up to assume flesh and blood amid picaresque surroundings. We meet them now as César, the seminarist, hurries toward them on his errands of mercy and as Ignacio wanders about to assuage his social curiosity. Once again, yet with more precision, the student of Spanish history is given insight into the specific *élan* of such movements as the CNT, the "Ceda," the FAI, and the *Falange*. Like Barea, Gironella strongly underlines the various formative influences, intellectual convictions, human prejudices, and psychological states which entered into the composite of a given individual's choice of one of these, or other conflicting movements.

It is at the point where the similarity between the two writers breaks off, however, that the specific differentiating quality in Gironella's novel emerges. This difference constitutes the work's unquestioned greatness, even if considered merely from the viewpoint of historical interpretation. This specific difference is precisely what has been called the work's "godlike impartiality."[73] Gironella affords his readers a slice of life of every conceivable political, economic, and social element. Aristocrats, derelicts, the bourgeoisie, conservatives, pure republicans, reactionaries, masons, liberals, communists, priests, anarchists, Catalonian nationalists, socialists, anticlericals, etc., are all portrayed. From time to time we see certain of these various elements coalesce around a specific issue. Thus, the Costa brothers, liberal republicans and industrialists, make common cause with the anarchists and the masons on the question of Catalonian autonomy. With another turn of political fortune, the anarchists make a pragmatic alliance with their arch-enemies, the communists, and people like the Costas will be lucky if they do not lose their lives at the hands of their erst-while cell mates. Thus, "the Spanish labyrinth" is revealed in all its conflicting and criss-crossing passages which in this his-torical moment led but to chaos. Ignacio, unable to make a clear choice on the political level, focuses our attention upon the confusion of issues and overlappings of good and evil. He seems surrounded by a many-headed dilemma. Above the confu-sion is Gironella, the master of *chiaroscuro*, offering insights — not practical solutions. It is here that his godlike impar-tiality is evidenced. He shows the legitimacy of the claims of the down-trodden; he mitigates the guilt of their radical ex-cesses by exposing the squalor that spawned them. He portrays the military class and the aristocrats, but does not condemn them with a doctrinaire allegiance to class antipathy. On the other hand, he does not exculpate them from negligence and costly mistakes. He shows the formation of the Falangist spirit and emphasizes its dangers. Yet he cannot help evoking sym-pathy for its young adherents' sincere enthusiasm. But this sympathy is mingled with sadness as he contemplates their erroneous idealism and vague, fanatical mystique. At other times — and here he treads on ground pertinent to the main lines of our investigation — he would seem to be on the side of the anticlericals. He is not afraid to show the failings of the clergy, yet he does not depict most priests as monsters of iniquity; rather, in his hands, they are human beings with fail-ings, many of them serious. With the opening of a new chap-ter, however, the author's skill shapes a portrait of a true mystic soul, consumed with the love of God and mankind. Thus, a constant balance pervades the work with the author continually showing good mixed with evil — in short, a pic-ture neither black nor white but multi-shaded and tragic grey. Binding the disparate elements together in the unity of the work is a never-failing, all-pervading Christian charity.

Gironella has also proved himself to be a master-artist in matters of style. Throughout one thousand pages he maintains a never failing level of interest. His characters are warm, eminently human, and credibly motivated. A superbly endowed poetic personality is revealed by his descriptions, where sporadic flashes of simile and metaphor connote startlingly original visions of beauty. Gironella obviously writes from the viewpoint of a Catholic. He is not chauvinistic; neither does he put art to the service of the catechism. Yet, the high spirituality of his outlook pervades every corner of his tremendous structured edifice. He belongs in every sense to the new generation of Catholic writers who have entered the stream of the world's great literature.

Los Cipreses Creen en Dios was conceived as the first part of a trilogy. The second part, *Un Millión de Muertos (One Million Dead)* appeared in 1961. Gironella begins this second part with Ignacio searching for César's body in the cemetery where the young boy had been shot by the leftist extremists. The author then carries his characters through the Civil War. The locale expands from Gerona and environs to take in all of Spain in the throes of the most violent convulsion in her history. The novel is the result of intense concentration and focussing of creative energy. Not the least part of that energy is directed toward maintaining the supreme impartiality that marked *Los Cipreses. Gironella* claims that he is not trying to make out an historical or sociological case for either side. Rather, he leans over the body of his bleeding country and embraces it with a tender compassion, accepting it totally in all its aspects, whether they be brutal, stupid, or sublime. He tells us in the introduction that the novel can definitely be considered an answer to Andre Malraux' *L'Espoir,* Hemingway's *For Whom the Bell Tolls,* Koestler's *Spanish Testament,* Bernanos' *Les Grands Cimetières Sous la Lune,* and Barea's *The Forging of a Rebel.* Certainly Hemingway's inferior, sensation-seeking, novel leaves much to be desired. The Maria-Roberto love theme is nineteenth century Romanticism re-adapted with an eye toward Hollywood — and Hollywood royalties. The pseudo-Spanish argot and the portrayals of the subsidiary characters and situations show that Hemingway knew Spain and Spanish literature just well enough to give an unsatisfying interpretation, an "uncomfortable feeling," as Gironella says. But I would not extend this disapproval to the other four works, as Gironella does. Certainly he is correct in his implied estimation that all five tell but one side of the story; they narrate the suffering of but one sector of a people in the toils of a total tragedy. I can see no error in this provided that it is done truthfully. On the other hand — now that Gironella has pushed his narrative into the Civil War — I question whether any author can successfully remain preoccupied with the mere human tragedy and really remain removed from the socio-historical implications. Is not the socio-historical picture the sum of individual human experience? I also feel that *Un Millón de Muertos* does not face squarely the problem of the closed society — which seems to be the key to great segments of Spanish history — and the rising expectations against such a society which seems to be the consensus of theologians of most denominations and of free men the world over. Thus, many critics feel that *Un Millón de Muertos* has not lived up to the expectations of *Los Cipreses*. And it is probably true that the first part of the trilogy will remain Gironella's masterpiece. There is evidence on record that the author encountered considerable difficulty getting both books passed through censorship. The fact that they did so pass is another indication of the softening of the closed rigidity that has characterized this epoch of Spanish history. And — apart from these observations — it should be noted that Gironella will most likely go down in Spanish literary history as the most powerful novelist since Pérez Galdós.

4. *Negative Spanish Evaluations of the Catholic Revival*

I believe that I have established the point that there has been very little great literature in Spain that can lay claim to significant participation in the Catholic Revival. This is, of course, an open judgement subject to some qualification (as in the case of Gironella) and subject to change as authors mature and newer writers arrive on the scene. A very interesting corollary to this situation is the evidence that the literature of the Catholic Revival has been received in some quarters in Spain as the object of harshly negative criticism.

In the first place it is only recently that names such as Bernanos, Mauriac, Patmore, Greene, etc., have begun to appear in the book lists or review sections of literary journals. There is as yet no body of criticism on such figures as Claudel and Péguy. Indeed, the great revolutionary movement in French poetry beginning in the second half of the nineteenth century is an unopened chapter in Spanish literary criticism, although creative artists and professors in Madrid and other centers are of course familiar with it. A reviewer of Leopoldo Rodríguez Alcalde's *Antología de la Poesía Francesa* admitted that "some of the poets in the collection are almost totally unknown in Spain, in matters touching upon their Catholic side; thus, this brief anthology will be fulfilling an educational task."[74]

A critic named Floris Delattre used the pages of the *Escorial* for an article on what he considered to be the inadequacies of English Catholic letters. In an essay entitled "Un Poeta Católico Francisco Thompson," he writes not only of the beloved poet but also of Cardinal Newman and Coventry Patmore. All are singled out for the unwholesome tendencies they supposedly represent. Patmore is dismissed as inconsequential because of his "minute, thorough-going sentimentalism." Thompson is down-graded for "his attraction to ritual and independence with regard to doctrinal principles" and the entire Oxford Movement is subjected to the same stigma: "Independence regarding doctrinal principles emerges with sufficient clarity along with the rebirth of Catholicism in England during the second half of the nineteenth century. It comes in a direct line from the Oxford Movement and the considerable influence of the personality of Newman." Thompson's doctrinal limitations are thus an extension of Newman's: "Francis Thompson recalls Newman's aristocracy of soul, his harmonious elegant refinement. The totality of his precise intellectuality together with his sympathies for the sciences and his constant

227

preoccupation for strict truth threw certain of his ideas into contradiction with the principles of the Church he adopted." Again Newman's personal influence "in large part aided the unfolding of a Catholicism which was, to sum up, severely limited. An ideal . . . had opened up with Newman. It was an ideal of piety . . . of fervor, of ascetcism. It found its perfect expression not in dogmatic principles, certainly, but rather in the pious customs of Catholicism."[75]

French Catholic letters suffered a worse fate. Jesús Saínz Mazpule has the following comments on Jacques Maritain in an essay entitled "De la Teología a la Política" ("From Theology to Politics"): "If we were to express with a single word the political doctrine of Jacques Maritain, so much discussed in recent years, that word is 'abdication.' Theology abdicates to his philosophy; his philosophy abdicates to his sociology; his sociology abdicates to the sociology of the mob. Thus, by a series of debasements he is able to posit both a dialectic point of departure and a point of historical arrival, a terminus of permanence in the social order — the level of conformity with the non-Catholic world." A motif as anti-Semitic as it is obviously erroneous emerges when the same critic, condemning the philosopher for his efforts to seek the foundation for his "social order distinct from those that preceded," announces what he believes to be the partial cause of Maritain's defection: "Here we find a feature that renders facile a desireable comparison between the convert Jew, Maritain, and the atheistic Jew, Marx." The conclusion is resounding condemnation: "We fear that some day his doctrine will have to be condemned [by the Church]; in anticipation of this condemnation] we hereby condemn it now."[76]

Further evidences of this attitude, with overtones of the Spanish Sixteenth Century controversies over Erasmus, appear in an article entitled "Christianity is not a Humanism" by Raimundo Pániker. The writer tries to prove the "radical incompatibility of humanism with the Christian conception of man."[77] The article is also aimed at Maritain, who in his *Integral Humanism* establishes principles precisely for the pur-

228

pose of achieving a compatibility between Christianity and Humanism.

Maritain is in good company. Gabriel Marcel, the venerable French philosopher who has explored the Christian implications of existentialism, is roundly condemned in a monograph entitled *Crítica de la Objetividad en el Existencialismo de Gabriel Marcel* (*Critique of the Objectivity in Gabriel Marcel's Existentialism*) by Ambrosio Rebollo Peña. Rebollo Peña criticizes the attempts "to reconcile Marcel's theories with traditional thought."[78]

It is hardly necessary to refute these erroneous charges and misinterpretations. Jacques Maritain, whose political philosophy has had a profound influence on liberal democratic movements the world over, is not a convert Jew. The philosopher's maternal grandfather was the French statesman, Jules Favre (of the same family as Blessed Pierre Le Fèvre); Favre embraced Protestantism as did his daughter, Geneviève, Maritain's mother. Maritain's father, Favre's secretary, was a Catholic but the wishes of the mother prevailed and the boy Maritain was baptized a Protestant. Maritain's wife, the late highly gifted poet and writer, Raissa, was a Jew. She and Jacques both became converts to Catholicism as did several members of Raïssa's family. A great deal of Raïssa's prose work has helped to spread knowledge of the Renouveau Catholique. Two of her books in particular, *We Have Been Friends Together* and *Adventures in Grace,* give an excellent insight into various figures of this movement against the backround of the Maritain home which served as a crossroads of Catholic intellectual life in our epoch. Maritain and Gabriel Marcel are of course controversial figures. But certainly not unorthodox.

There has existed for some time in Spain a continuing *polémica* between thinkers who are pro-Maritain and anti-Maritain. The latter group's attitude has been expressed by Leopoldo Eulogio Palacios in a book significantly entitled *El Mito de la Nueva Cristiandad* (*The Myth of the New Christianity*), published in 1951. The polarities of the two groups are crystallized by two other books — the now liberally inclined Laín Entralgo's *España Como Problema* (*Spain as a Problem*) published in 1948 and *España Sin Problema* (*Spain Has No Problem*) published in 1949 by Rafael Calvo Serer, a member of the Opus Dei.

Newman, during his life was subjected to much unfair criticism. This criticism was dispelled when Pope Leo XIII created him a Cardinal. The orthodoxy of Thompson and Patmore has never been in doubt and it is difficult to imagine how Delattre arrived at his highly unusual conclusions. I had the pleasure of studying Thompson and Patmore under the late Terrence L. Connolly, S.J., of Boston College. Father Connolly was one of the world's greatest Patmore scholars and unquestionably the greatest Thompson scholar since the time of Wilfrid Meynell. The world's greatest collection of manuscripts and "Thompsoniana" are preserved in the Francis Thompson room at Boston College Library, a Jesuit University. The charge that the poet exhibited "independence with regard to doctrinal principles" is completely absurd.

5. *A Theological Evaluation of the Trends Studied in this Chapter*

It is obvious from the trends studied in this chapter that freedom of expression and liberal opinion (Catholic or otherwise) have been in a state of slow flux. The post-Civil War laws governing the press and publication were more stringent then under the Directorate. There have been some recent relaxations, but it is difficult to say how far they have gone, or how deep and lasting they will be. The Spanish hierarchy itself, which originally sanctioned the heavily restrictive measures, is showing signs of genuine impatience, and perhaps the fear that restrictions may likewise be extended to them. Literary expression has been channelized with many indications that the men of letters who have most vigorously championed the existing government have been singled out for preferential treatment. Catholic thought, meagre in the twentieth century in a country that has produced some of the world's greatest Catholic literature, frequently exhibits tendencies emotionally associated with the efforts of the present regime. Catholic thought in general has not yet produced the combined open and spiritual approach found in other countries. It is therefore not surprising that numerous Catholic intellectuals were forcibly exiled or have voluntarily sought exile.

The patterns we have noted are a manifestation of the new "confessional state." Father John Courtney Murray, S.J., quotes a complaint of the Spanish bishops in this matter:

The Spanish bishops . . . undertook to complain: "It is astonishing that there are Catholics outside of Spain who attack Catholic unity in itself and hold doctrines which are completely incompatible both with the *Syllabus* of Pius IX and with the encyclical *Libertas* of Leo XIII." And they express their wish "that Catholics in all lands would keep before their minds [the] principle of Leo XIII" concerning religious toleration. For their own part: "We Catholic Spaniards will avoid criticizing our brethren, who are a minority in other states and nations, because they shelter themselves under the banner of liberty. However, they will never lead us to grant, as a thesis, the same rights to error as to truth. And let Catholics in all countries, if they wish truly to be Catholics, if they wish to be faithful to papal teachings — let them be on their guard against ridiculing as backward and intransigeant, the Catholics of Spain or of any other country which has the great fortune of preserving Catholic unity, because of their defense of this unity."[79]

Father Murray comments as follows:

This is indeed a sharp rebuke and a rude lesson in orthodoxy. However, if I may say it under all respect for their Excellencies, the sharpness of the rebuke is not matched by clarity and completeness in the statement of an issue that concerns not merely the Spanish nation but the universal Church; similarly the lesson in orthodoxy in regard to the Catholic "thesis" on Church-state relationships is (again *sit venia verbo*) just a bit too rude, in the Latin sense of the word. Those who know something of the results reached in medieval times or even in the sixteenth century by sheerly dialectical interpretation of the *Decretum Gratiani* will not antecedently have confidence in the results that may be reached by application of the same method to the *Syllabus* or to the Leonine *corpus*.[80]

CHAPTER VI

CONCLUSIONS AND IMPLICATIONS

1. *Conclusions*

This study gathers together most of the ideas appearing in most of the important Spanish anticlerical writers of the twentieth century and has analyzed them in juxtaposition to the national problems which created them. The following intimately related conclusions are fairly obvious:

1. *There was a long psychological preparation for anticlericalism centered chiefly in the struggle between old and new.* This conclusion is derived from the material treated in the first chapter.

2. *Twentieth century anticlericalism is similarly rooted in the struggle between old and new and differs from earlier manifestations only in intensity and quantity.* This conclusion is supported by the historical and literary evidence adduced throughout Chapters II, III, and IV.

3. *The charge that clerical pressure resisted the flow of change and the reasonable aspirations of modernity is justfiable from a Catholic standpoint.* This conclusion is documented by examination, in Chapter II, of the climate of opinion. The interpretation "justifiable" is supported by the opinion of leading Catholic scholars, such as Jacques Maritain, John Courtney Murray, S.J., and Conrad Bonacina (to name but a few) who make the same charges both in a general sense and, at times, in consideration of the very topics treated in this study.

4. *The anticlerical controversy was generated to some extent by "cultural lag" whereby one component of culture tends to lag behind others.* Cultural lag is a term used by contemporary sociologists and political scientists. W. F. Ogburn and M. F. Nimkoff define it as: "The strain that exists between two correlated parts of culture that change at unequal rates of

speed."[1] Pitirim Sorokin describes it in the following terms: "What is styled 'culture' is in a permanent process of change. However, various parts of a culture do not change simultaneously. Some parts of it, especially material culture, may change, while other parts, especially non-material culture, forms of social organization, religion, arts, and mores may remain, at least for a time, unchanged . . . This results in cultural lags and disharmony between various parts of material and non-material culture."[2] Thus, religio-political social theory in Spain has tended to lag behind the changes wrought by industrialism. Controversial heat became generated in some proportion to the degree of lag. This conclusion is adduced as a corollary from the implications of conclusions 1 and 2. It has been seen that the controversy is centered in the struggle between old and new; it has also been seen that the old (considered as the religio-political element) need not be considered (from a Catholic point of view) as fixed and rigidly incapable of change or adaptation. Consequently, a sustained clerical effort to recognize and reduce the cultural lag would have reduced the bitterness of the anticlerical controversy.

5. *Anticlericalism does not exist in a vacuum; rather, it develops as a by-product of heated disagreement over some national problem.* Thus, the priority of motivation in a given work or author is usually to be assigned to the national problem. It is rarely that an author takes his pen for the express purpose of either discrediting religion or discussing clerical influence in abstract terms. This conclusion derives from the examination of the individual authors treated in Chapters III and IV.

6. *The revival of restrictive religio-political measures has worked to the detriment of contemporary literature.* This conclusion is supported by the trends brought together and examined in Chapter V.

7. *General criticism is an area where the anticlericals' views are often shared by Catholic thinkers.* This conclusion is supported by parallels drawn throughout the study between the views of the anticlericals and the thought of such Catholic

figures as Francisco de Osuna, Cisneros, Ludwig von Pastor, Georges Bernanos, and François Mauriac.

8. *The objections of the anticlerical writers on the specific issue (clerical power exerted in the political and social order) is shared by many of the world's leading Catholic philosophers, theologians, etc.* This conclusion is supported particularly by the writings of Maritain, Courtney Murray, Bonacina, and Alfred Mendizábal, which have been adduced throughout the study at critical junctures. Although these four authors have been relied upon most consistently, other writers (such as John Cogley, Father Jesús Iribarren and Bruce Marshall) have been referred to in passing. Canalejas' liberal struggle in the early part of the century is symptomatic of this conclusion. To the list of authors actually used could be added the following, among many others, not directly cited but whose writings have influenced the evolution of this most important conclusion: Emanuel Mounier, Etienne Gilson, Yves Simon, John Lukas, and the Dominican editor of *La Vie Intellectuelle,* Father Yves Congar, O.P.

The study in no sense establishes a total evaluation of all phases of the Spanish Church. Rather, it seeks to discover what the great anticlerical writers said, why they said what they did, and whether or not their statements have good reason. In so doing it probes the background and sources of the phenomenon. Thus, notice has been taken of the development of anticlerical thought in the history of the literature. The sociological and intellectual background of the twentieth century has been given special treatment. In studying the various authors it has been observed that the anticlerical phenomenon is proportioned to their backgrounds. Thus we have the anticlericalism of the Ateneo mentality, anticlericalism associated with agnosticism, with atheism, with republicanism, with communism; there is intellectual anticlericalism, there is folkloric anticlericalism, etc. Chapter V examines the revival in recent history of the attitudes that helped create anticlericalism. The overt expression of anticlericalism has had to cease.

One hope is that this study will facilitate in students of

Spanish literature an awareness that statements critical of the Church and the clergy do not necessarily have to be ascribed *a priori* to malice or personal bias on the part of the critic. A second hope is that an awareness can be created that the theory of the confessional state is by no means a dogma of the Catholic Church. A third hope is that the whole problem of anticlericalism has been elucidated in general — not only in Spanish literature. A general overriding conclusion reads in a word: *Apart from frequent anti-religious or biased overtones, the basic anticlerical position is understandable and justifiable, even from a Catholic critique.*

2. Implications

Now that the conclusions have been drawn a few other considerations are vital. Anticlericalism is accepted in this study as a reaction to undue intrusion of clerical power and pressure in the political and social order. But in the last analysis this definition — though adequate for the development of the Spanish phenomenon — remains inadequate in a more universal perspective. Ultimately questions must be asked: What kind of pressure? What constitutes *undue pressure?* What political or social order is involved? In recent years, for example, the position of the German clergy (both Protestant and Catholic) during the Hitler years has undergone searching re-examination. This criticism has extended even to the motivations of Pope Pius XII. Without entering into any of the subtle points in this debate, I feel it at least safe to say that a consensus is growing among fair-minded men to the effect that the German (and Roman) clergy did not do enough. They did not *exert* enough *moral authority.* They did not *intrude* their *leadership* against a malignant socio-political order.

Or let us take a hypothetical case. Let us imagine that a serious threat were mounted against the great cluster of traditions and institutions that have (despite many imperfections and unfinished business) created the unparalleled human achievement of American freedom. Let us suppose that a threat came from either the left or — what is more likely — the right extreme, and the clergy were to remain silent. The clergy would then be excoriated for remaining within the sanctuary, for closing their eyes, for timidity, for being out of step with events, for failing to exert their great moral authority in the socio-political arena at a time of national danger. Thus, it would seem that clericalism is not the mere intrusion of the clergy into the sociol-political order but rather *an intrusion for the purpose of demanding exclusive preference for a specific religious formula,* as was the case in Spain. The nineteenth century Jesuit and minor novelist, Luis Coloma, was never condemned for his efforts to disturb the corrupt Spanish society of his day. Nor would many thinking people condemn the efforts of the clergy in the early 1960's to help the beleagued miners in the north of Spain; nor the many strong — nay daring — criticisms by liberal clergymen in Spain in recent years; nor the efforts all over the world of clergymen to try to secure bread, justice, and freedom for the poor of the world.

The entire problem of clerical influence, however, remains a difficult area. There will always be controversy as to when and how it should be exerted. And certainly thinking men do not envision it in the sense of back-stage power ploys. Rather they expect moral authority — a bearing of witness to truth. But, again, truth must be witnessed within a pluralistic context which recognizes the freedom of the individual conscience. The old saw that "error has no rights" will not work, particularly if "error" is formulated in terms of practises which do not coincide with an official Catholic "line."

In the United States the exercise of Catholic clerical power has had a checkered career. In the 1930's Father Coughlin was widely respected for joining in the war against the depression. But he quickly allowed his vast influence to be prostituted into rightwing extremism and anti-Semitism. The Coughlin era and "Coughlinism" is an historical fact that most intelligent American Catholics — I think — prefer to forget. A generation later, America again suffered one of her chronic rightwing extremist convulsions in the McCarthy era. Here the moral authority of the American Church made another very poor showing. Blinded by real or imagined dangers from the left, American Catholics, along with millions of other self-righteous souls, failed to realize that ruthless abuse of power would lead to the extinction of the very freedoms they wanted to preserve. During the present-day right-wing rumblings, such as the John Birch Society and similar outlandish groups, the Catholic Church (and other denominations) have done fairly well.

One of the problems of the American Church is that its understanding of the great cluster of American institutions and traditions has had to undergo a maturing process. Along with many other segments of American life, the Catholic community has had to acquire a more profound understanding and appreciation of the deeper meaning of our civilization. Democracy once meant bread, opportunities, governmental aid in time of need. The clergy did not take full cognizance of our unparalleled history of intellectual freedom and (with the exception of the Negroes) the steady gains in Civil Rights — our almost two centuries of development that has truly provided a better and free life on an increasingly broad basis. A generation or so ago democracy also meant freedom of worship for Catholics who had suffered persecution in other lands. But until the recent work of John Courtney Murray and a few others no meaningful Catholic research was done on the problem of other religions, should Catholicism in America ever become numerically predominant. Twenty years ago when this problem was posed, the typical answer of American Catholic spokesmen was: We need not examine this question because it is purely academic; it could never happen. Will Herberg has shown how woefully inadequate this answer is.[3]

The foregoing raises the question of the American Presidency. America has had her first Catholic President and no serious problem of a religio-political nature marred the brilliant brief years of John Kennedy in that office. (I prescind from the question of Federal aid to parochial schools, and disagree with Kennedy's position.) But during the campaign of 1960 Kennedy's religion was raised as an objection by large segments of non-Catholic laymen and clergy. Most Catholics were indignant. If Catholic spokesmen ever challenged a candidate on the grounds of religion, it was claimed, Catholics would be branded with the stigma of crude, unwarranted clerical intrusion. I agree. So they would be. But I do not think the situations are entirely parallel. Nor do I think that the non-Catholic desire for Kennedy to declare himself on Church-State relationships was (apart from concommitant scurrilous vitriol in some quarters) entirely unjustified. The Catholic experience with the confessional state is too contemporary! The Spanish experience — the content of this study — is enough to prove my point. Catholic candidates for the American Presidency will continue to run into trouble until the theological status of the confessional state is fully clarified — once and for ever.

Ten years have passed since I began to study Spanish anticlericalism. In those ten years the Church (and the world) has passed through "the Johannine era." Two men called John envisioned a new world and symbolized the best of the old and the new through the exuberance and intellectual vitality of a man called John, who was young, and the fatherly wisdom and charity of a man called John, who was old. The Church has experienced Pope John, the Good. He convened Vatican Council II. He gave to the World (and to the Church) his immortal *Peace on Earth*. A man called Paul must execute the Papal Johannine legacy — for weal or for woe.

With the coming of John XXIII I was convinced that the general tone of the body of modern Catholic thought that I have accepted in this study would become imbedded in the matrix of contemporary Catholicism. It would no longer remain the property of a Catholic elite. As of this writing, I have some doubts. I do not doubt that these attitudes will come into their inheritance eventually. But there has been recent ground to fear that they have been in danger of being postponed — again. It is certainly no secret that progressive Catholic opinion and opinion throughout the world was disappointed by the Second Session of Vatican II. The session closed, for example, without a declaration on anti-Semitism. The new draft resolution published September 5, 1964 was highly unsatisfactory in intellectual Catholic circles and to most Jews. Furthermore, the Second Session included a poorly prepared and quite evidently superficially studied decree *On Instruments of Social Communication.* Dr. Robert McAfee Brown, a most sympathetic Protestant ecumenist and observer at Vatican II finds it on the surface, "banal and innocuous"; below the surface he finds it deeply disturbing and a likely source of fuel for anti-Catholics. Reactionary Catholics, he feels, "are going to be able to use the decree to impose a type of control that will jeopardize Catholic creativity in the arts, let alone good community relations." The official Church in its administrative function, according to the literal reading of the decree, becomes a supreme arbiter of esthetics. And, under many paragraphs of the text, there is ample room to invoke a most rigorous program of censorship and thought-control.[4] The liberal Catholic, John Cogley, was also disturbed by this decree. He treated it rather lightly however, and admitted that the Fathers had not given it the study it deserved. He and others feel that it is so ambiguous and ambivalent that it is not worth making a fuss about it. If we don't think about it, John Cogley seems to say, maybe it will go away.[5]

The Third Session of Vatican II was held during the final writing of this chapter. It appears that progressive opinion may well prevail in Vatican II. Cardinal Cushing of Boston and other progressive churchmen (especially Cardinal Bea) have spear-headed drives for a meaningful declaration on anti-Semitism. They have also championed a strong statement on religious liberty and the dignity of the human conscience (from this country the late Cardinal Meyer of Chicago has been a great leader). Such declarations, if finally promulgated, will largely offset the ambiguous clauses in the communications decree.

In all these and other related matters the Church can be guided by the sad experience and bitter resentment of anti-clericalism in Spain and other countries.

The conclusion to this study of Spanish anticlericalism, again, is: "Apart from frequent anti-religious or biased overtones, the basic anticlerical position is understandable and justifiable, even from a Catholic critique." I wish that I could amend the conclusion and make it more affirmative. I wish I could say that "the basic anticlerical position *has now been indisputably established by a general consensus in the Church on certain theological topics* as understandable and justifiable from a Catholic critique."

This is not yet possible. But it may be soon. The Fourth and last Session of Vatican II has been very interesting.

NOTES

CHAPTER I

Section 1: In the Early Years of the Literature

[1] Juan Ruiz (Archpriest of Hita), *The Book of Good Love*, tr. Elisha K. Kane (Private publication, 1933), pp. 312-13.

[2] *Webster's International Dictionary of the English Language*, 2nd ed., unabridged (Springfield, Mass., 1953).

[3] J. D. M. Ford, *Old Spanish Readings* (New York, 1939), p. 152.

[4] Juan Ruiz (Arcipreste de Hita), *El Libro de Buen Amor*, ed. Cejador y Frauca (Madrid, 1913), II, 145-7.

[5] Juan Ruiz, II, 77.

[6] Arnold Toynbee, *Civilization on Trial* (New York, 1948), p. 257. Edward Ingram Watkin, *Catholic Art and Culture* (New York, 1944), p. 5ff.

[7] Pero López de Ayala, *Rimado de Palacio*, ed. Albert F. Kuersteiner (New York, 1920), II, strophes 227, 224, 226, 196.

[8] Francisco de Osuna, *Abecedario Espiritual, Primera-Sexta Parte* (Çaragoça, 1546-56), p. 161.

[9] See for example the use of the term anticlericalism in Boak, Hyma, and Slosson, *The Growth of European Civilization*, 4th printing (New York, 1939), p. 366; Hayes and Moon, *Modern History*, 4th edition (New York, 1952), p. 845.

[10] Terence L. Connolly, S.J., "Coventry Patmore", *Renascence*, X, 53.

[11] "Recent Events," obituary for Georges Bernanos in *The Catholic World*, Aug., 1948, p. 466.

Section 2: The Inquisition

[12] Luis Bertrand and Sir Charles Petrie, Bart., *The History of Spain, 711-1931*, trans. Ware B. Wells (New York, 1937), p. 228.

[13] Rafael Altamira y Crevea, *Historia de España y de la Civilización Española* (Barcelona, 1902), II, 423.

[14] Ludwig von Pastor, *Geschichte der Päpste* (Freiburg im Breisgau, 1889), II, 583.

[15] *The Catholic Encyclopedia* (1910), VIII, 36.

[16] Joseph Lortz, *History of the Church*, trans. Edwin Kaiser (Milwaukee, 1939), p. 236.

[17] Lortz, p. 380.

[18] Lortz, p. 236.

[19] Lortz, p. 236.

[20] Philip Hughes, *A Popular History of the Catholic Church* (New York, 1953), p. 112.

[21] William Shirer, *The Rise and Fall of the Third Reich* (New York, 1960), pp. 22-26.

[22] See such recent works as Xavier Rynne's *Letters from Vatican City* (New

York, 1963) and Michael Serafian's *The Pilgrim* (New York, 1964) for a full treatment of this attitude in the deliberations of the first two sessions of the Second Vatican Council.

Section 3: Some Sixteenth Century Erasmista Controversies

[23] William E. Campbell, *Erasmus, Tyndale, and More* (Milwaukee, n.d.); see especially Campbell's treatment of Father Villosolada's work on Erasmus.

[24] Altamira y Crevea, II, 423.

[25] *Enciclopedia Universal Ilustrada*, XX, 402.

[26] Henry Charles Lea, *The Inquisition in Spain* (New York, 1906), I, 158.

[27] Juan Hurtado y Angel González Palencia, *Historia de la Literatura Española* (sexta ed., Madrid, 1949), p. 364. (Hereafter all references to this volume will be simply Hurtado y Palencia.) See also *The Encyclopedia Britanica* (1952 edition), XII, 383.

[28] Lea, III, 418.

[29] Lea, III, 419.

[30] Altamira, III, 382.

[31] Altamira, III, 385.

[32] *Encyclopedia Britanica* (1952), XII, 383.

[33] *Dos Diálogos Escritos por Juan de Valdés* (place of publication not given, 1850), p. 220. Until recently the words of the Valdés brothers have been confused. It is now definitely established that Alfonso is the author of the *Diálogo de Lactancio* (see Hurtado y Palencia, pp. 416-17).

[34] *Dos Diálogos*, p. 390.

[35] Various cited opinions of Alfonso in *Dos Diálogos*, pp. 331-2, 335-6, 392-3, 426, 444, 448.

[36] Signor Valdés à Baldessar Castiglione in *Lettere del Conte Baldessar Castiglione Ora per la Prima Volta Data in Luce con Annotazioni Storiche Ilustrate*. Dall' Abate Pierantonio Serassi (Padua, 1769), p. 173.

[37] Castiglione, p. 176.

[38] Castiglione, p. 201.

[39] Castiglione, p. 199.

[40] Castiglione, pp. 201-202.

[41] Marcelino Menéndez y Pelayo, *Historia de los Heterodoxos de España* (Madrid, 1880), II, 121.

[42] Intimate details of the personality of "el Brocense" in *Colección de Documentos Inéditos para la Historia de España*, eds. M. F. Navarrete, Miguel Salva, Pedro Sáinz de Baranda (Madrid, 1843), tomo II.

[43] *Documentos Inéditos*, II, pp. 59-60.

[44] *Doc. Inéd.*, II, p. 82.

[45] *Doc. Inéd.*, II, p. 89.

[46] *Doc. Inéd.*, II, p. 81.

[47] *Doc. Inéd.*, II, p. 88.

[48] *Doc. Inéd.*, II, p. 57.

[49] Further details on life of "el Brocense" in Aubrey F. G. Bell, *Francisco Sánchez, el Brocense* (Milford: Ox. Un. Press, 1925), *passim*.

[50] Hurtado y Palencia, p. 310.

[51] Hurtado y Palencia, p. 215.

[52] *Teatro Español Anterior a Lope de Vega*, ed. Böhl de Faber (Hamburg, 1832), pp. 69-70.

53 Menéndez y Pelayo, II, 28n.
54 Menéndez y Pelayo, II, 123.
55 Gerald Brenan, *The Spanish Labyrinth* (Camb. Un. Press, 1950), pp. 40-41.

Section 4: Toward the Modern Context

56 Angel Valbuena Prat, *La Novela Picaresca Española* (Madrid, 1943), p. 1065.
57 Altamira, IV, 148-9; 201-245.
58 Fernando Díaz-Plaja, *La Historia de España en sus Documentos; El Siglo* xviii (Madrid, 1955), pp. 142-4.
59 Brenan, p. 205.
60 *Encyclopedia Britanica* (1952) XII, 383.
61 Menéndez y Pelayo, II, 259-262.
62 See *Historia de la Censura Literaria Gobernativa en España* (Madrid, 1940).
63 Frederich D. Wilhelmsen, "Forces at Work in Today's Spain," *America*, CIX, 306-14.
64 Brenan, p. 204.
65 Quoted by Brenan, p. 212.
66 All quotations from Castelar in *Discursos Parlamentarios de Don Emilio Castelar en la Asamblea Constituyente* (Madrid, 1871), pp. 257-286.

CHAPTER II

(For the sake of brevity, all references to the periodicals *La Ciudad de Dios* and *Razón y Fe* will be abbreviated *CDD* and *RYF*, after their first entry.)

Section 1: The General Pattern

1 John Courtney Murray, S.J., "Contemporary Orientations on Church and State," (reprinted from *Theological Studies*, June, 1949), *Cross Currents*, Fall 1951, p. 18.
2 Murray, p. 49.
3 Murray, pp. 46-7.
4 Conrad Bonacina, "The Catholic Church and Modern Democracy," *Cross Currents*, Fall 1951, p. 1.
5 Bonacina, p. 2.
6 See discussion of Emilio Castelar in Chapter I, section 4.
7 Bonacina, p. 3.

Section 2: New Educational Trends and the Church

8 See José Castillejo, *War of Ideas in Spain* (London, 1937) for further information on the *Institución* and allied programs.
9 Francisco Giner de los Ríos, *Obras Completas* (Madrid, 1925), VII, 41-2.
10 Richard Pattee, *This is Spain* (Milwaukee, 1951), p. 55.
11 Gerald Brenan, *The Spanish Labyrinth* (Camb. Un. Press, 1950), p. 50.
12 José Castillejo, p. 101.
13 John Cogely, "Things That are Caesar's," *Commonweal*, LXI, 118.

[14] "Past and Present" by the Editors, *Commonweal*, LXI, 113.
[15] Quote in Pattee, pp. 54-5.
[16] R. Ruiz Amado, "La Iglesia y la Escuela," *Razón y Fe*, XXVII, 14-15.
[17] Jeronimo Montes, O.S.A., "Las Reformas en la Enseñanza," *La Ciudad de Dios*, LII, 39.
[18] Unsigned review, *RYF*, XXVI, 388.
[19] "Variedades — Programa de la Unión de los Católicos", *RYF*, XXVI, 273-4.
[20] "Las Injusticias del Estado Español," *CDD*, LIII, 510. Signed P. M. A.
[21] "Las Reformas en la Enseñanza," *CDD*, LII, 46. Signed Montes.
[22] *CDD*, LIII, 130. An unsigned review.
[23] V. Minteguiaga, "La Real Orden Circular Sobre las Escuelas Laicas," *RYF*, XXVI, 451.
[24] Benito R. González, O.S.A., "Naciones Católicas y Naciones-Protestantes," *CDD*, LIV, 173. The series begins in LII, 481.
[25] "Revista de Revistas," *CDD*, LIII, 123. An unsigned digest of Eduardo Sanz y Escartín's article "De la Enseñanza," which had originally appeared in *La Revista Contemporánea*, Aug. 15, 1900.
[26] "Crónica General — España," *CDD*, LIV, 574. Unsigned.
[27] "Variedades," *RYF*, XXVI, 137. Unsigned.

Section 3: The Monarchy; the Directorate; the Liberals and the Church

[28] V. Minteguiaga, "La Real Orden de 10 de Junio Sobre Manifestaciones del Culto," *RYF*, XXVII, 440.
[29] Minteguiaga, as in note 28.
[30] Minteguiaga, as in note 28, p. 441.
[31] Quoted in P. Villada, "Sobre la Real Orden contra las Asociaciones Religiosas," *RYF*, XXVII, 347.
[32] Villada, as in note 31.
[33] A. Pérez Goyena, "Noticias Generales — España," *RYF*, XXVIII, 261-2.
[34] P. Villada, "¿Ha admitido Roma la Libertad de Culto en España?" *RYF*, XXVIII, 357-8.
[35] Jacques Maritain in his Introduction to Alfred Mendizábal's *The Martyrdom of Spain*, trans. Charles Hope Lumley (London, 1938), p. 2.
[36] "Crónica General — España," *CDD*, CXXVII, 76. Signed P. G.
[37] Brenan, p. 23.
[38] Brenan, p. 165.
[39] Jerónimo Montes, O.S.A., "Ferrer, su Obra y sus Cómplices," *CDD*, LXXX, 353.
[40] "Los Patrones y las Sociedades Obreras," *CDD*, LV, 292-293.
[41] "Revista de Revistas — La Democracia Cristiana," *CDD*, LII, 288.
[42] See note 41.
[43] "Revista de Revistas," *CDD*, LIII, 129.
[44] Francisco Rivas Moreno, "Las Cajas Rurales," *CDD*, CXXIV, 40.
[45] Rivas Moreno, "Cómo se Funda una Cooperativa de Consumo," subtitled "Cartas a un Obrero," *CDD*, CXXIV, 452-466.
[46] J. M. Vicuña, "Notas de Información — Los Sindicatos Católicos-agrarios en Vizcaza," *CDD*, CXXV, 143-155.
[47] Brenan, p. 55.
[48] Teodoro Rodríguez, O.S.A., "Teorías y Realidades Sociales (conclusión)," *CDD*, CXXVI, 323.

49 An unsigned review of Georges Fonsgrieve's *La Crisis Social*, *CDD*, LIV, 56.

50 Teodoro Rodríguez, "Teorías y Realidades Sociales," *CDD*, CXXVI, 246-7.

51 Pattee, pp. 58 and 66.

52 Salvador Madariaga, *Spain* (New York, 1930), p. 243.

53 Personal experience of Dr. Samuel M. Waxman, who was present at Salamanca when Unamuno made the remark publicly.

54 Brenan, p. 82.

55 Alfred Mendizábal, *The Martyrdom of Spain* (London, 1938), p. 64.

56 P. Gutiérrez, "Crónica . . . de España," *CDD*, CXXV, 397.

57 "Crónica General — España," *Religión y Cultura*, XIII, 472.

58 Gutiérrez, "Crónica . . . de España," *CDD*, CXXVII, 312.

59 Gutiérrez, "Crónica . . . de España," *CDD*, CXXV, 236-7.

60 Gutiérrez, "Crónica . . . de España," *CDD*, CXXIX, 458.

61 Gutiérrez, "Crónica . . . de España," *CDD*, CXXVII, 154-5.

62 Teod. Rodríguez, O.S.A., "Intelectualismo y Educación," *CDD*, CXXVII, 261.

63 Gutiérrez, "Crónica . . . de España," *CDD*, CXXIX, 469.

64 "Crónica General — España," *CDD*, CLI, 144. Signed R. V.

65 "Crónica General — España," *Religión y Cultura*, XIII, 154.

66 Conrad Bonacina, *The Catholic Church and Modern Democracy*, *Cross Currents*, Fall 1951, p. 3.

67 William Clancy, "The Area of Catholic Freedom," *Commonweal*, LXI, 129.

Section 4: The Republic and the New Constitution

68 Brenan, p. 236.

69 Mendizábal, p. 111.

70 Quoted in Mendizábal, p. 159.

71 Quoted in Mendizábal, p. 156.

72 Mendizábal, p. 155.

73 Maritain: Intro. to Mendizábal, p. 12.

74 Quoted in E. A. Peers, *The Spanish Tragedy, 1930-1936* (London, 1937), p. 53.

75 Peers, p. 53.

76 Brenan, p. 236.

77 Mendizábal, pp. 157-8.

78 Peers, p. 72.

79 Peers, p. 72.

80 Brenan, pp. 242-6.

81 Quoted in Carlton J. H. Hayes, *The United States and Spain* (New York, 1951), pp. 90-91.

82 Peers, p. 196.

83 See Peers, pp. 190-191; Brenan, 298-9; Hayes, pp. 98-9.

84 Peers, p. 205f.

85 Peers, p. 206.

86 Brenan, pp. 303-5.

87 These and other names are listed in a pamphlet entitled *Catholics Speak* (a rare bibliographical item) included in a special collection at Widener Library, Harvard Un., entitled "Spanish Civil War Tracts." Widener Catalogue number: Span. 745. 19. 37.

88 Maritain, p. 6.

89 See Georges Bernanos, *Les Grands Cimetières sous la Lune* (Paris, 1938). For a fuller understanding, the Bernanos work should be read *in toto* along with Mendizábal-Maritain.

90 See the *Commonweal*, 1931-1939, for a rich collection of thoughtful articles pertinent to this area.

91 William Cardinal O'Connell, *A Memorable Voyage* (private publication, 1939), p. 32.

92 Mendizábal, p. 178f. "Fascist Catholicity Facing Christian Catholicity."

93 Mendizábal, especially p. 176.

94 Brenan, pp. 291-3.

95 Peers, *passim.*

96 Mendizábal, p. 270.

97 Maritain, p. 47.

98 Maritain, p. 47.

CHAPTER III

The following notes are divided by authors' names into sections corresponding to the text. For the sake of brevity, after the first entry, all references to the *Obras Completas* of any anticlerical author studied in the text will be abbreviated *O.C.;* the author's name will be omitted or reduced to obvious initials when possible.

BENITO PÉREZ GALDÓS

1 See my treatment of Giner and the *Institución Libre de Enseñanza* in the second section of Chapter II of this study.

2 The term *"cristiano viejo"* also implies the notion that a person's blood is not mixed with Moorish or Jewish strains.

3 Benito Pérez Galdós, *Gloria*, in Federico Sáinz de Robles' edition of the *Obras Completas* (Madrid, 1941), IV, 510.

4 P. G., *Gloria, O. C.,* IV, 519-520.

5 *O.C.,* IV, 520.

6 *O.C.,* IV, 535.

7 The views of Padre Silvestre and Don Horro: *O.C.,* IV, 543-5.

8 Gloria's cultural formation: *O.C.,* IV, 510-13.

9 See Bonacina's views in the first section of Chapter II of this study.

10 *O.C.,* IV, 549.

11 *O.C.,* IV, 549.

12 *O.C.,* IV, 589.

13 *O.C.,* IV, 575.

14 *O.C.,* IV, 609.

15 P. G., *Doña Perfecta,* O.C., IV, 464.

16 *O.C.,* IV, 499.

17 *O.C.,* IV, 465.

18 *O.C.,* IV, 502.

19 César Barja, *Libros y Autores Modernos* (Los Angeles, 1933), pp. 344-355.

20 José Balseiro, *Novelistas Españoles Modernos* (New York, 1933), pp. 173-80.

21 See François Mauriac's *La Pharisienne* (Paris, 1941).

22 Georges Bernanos, *Les Grands Cimetières sous la Lune* (Paris, 1938), pp. 102-3.

23 P. G., *La Familia de León Roch, O.C.,* IV, 805.
24 *O.C.,* IV, 808.
25 See S. Griswald Morley, Intro. to *Mariucha* (N. Y., 1921), p. XXXIVf.

VICENTE BLASCO IBÁÑEZ

26 Camilo Pitollet, *Vicente Blasco Ibánez, Sus Novelas y la Novela de su Vida,* versión española de Tulio Moncada (Valencia, n.d.), p. 47.
27 Pitollet, p. 47.
28 V. Blasco Ibáñez, *La Barraca,* 2da. edición (Espasa-Calpe, 1944), pp. 52-9.
29 *La Barraca,* pp. 112-130.
30 Sagonereta views: Blasco Ibáñez, *Cañas y Barro* in *Obras Completas* (Madrid, 1946), I, 850-852.
31 B. I., *Cañas y Barro, O.C.,* I, 861.
32 B. I., *La Catedral, O.C.,* I, 921.
33 *O.C.,* I, 912.
34 *O.C.,* I, 912.
35 *O.C.,* I, 924.
36 *O.C.,* I, 931.
37 *O.C.,* I, 938.
38 *O.C.,* I, 941.
39 *O.C.,* I, 945.
40 *O.C.,* I, 954.
41 Don Martín's remarks: *O.C.,* I, 1000f.
42 *O.C.,* I, 1006.
43 B. I., *Arroz y Tartana, O.C.,* 327ff.
44 B. I., *Flor de Mayo, O.C.,* 405ff.
45 B. I., *Sangre y Arena, O.C.,* 231ff.
46 B. I., *El Intruso* (Valencia, 1904), p. 340.
47 *El Intruso,* p. 343.
48 *El Intruso,* p. 346.
49 *El Intruso,* p. 345.
50 B. I., *La Bodega* (Valencia, 1905), p. 36.
51 B. I., *La Horda* (Valencia, 1905), p. 371.
52 B. I., *El Papa del Mar* (Valencia, 1925), pp. 109-110.
53 B. I., *A los Pies de Venus* (Valencia, 1926), p. 41.
54 See the Renaissance era in Ludwig von Pastor, *Geschichte der Päpste* (Freiburg in Breisgau, 1889).
55 Arturo Barea, *The Forging of a Rebel,* trans. Ilsa Barea (New York, 1946), p. 82.

MIGUEL DE UNAMUNO

56 Barea, *Unamuno* (Cambridge, 1951), p. 32.
57 Unamuno, *En Torno al Casticismo* (Buenos Aires, 1943), pp. 106-9.
58 *En Torno al Casticismo,* p. 127.
59 John A. Mackay, in his Foreword to *Poems of Miguel de Unamuno,* trans. Eleanor L. Turnbull (Baltimore, 1952), p. VIII.
60 Unamuno, *Vida de Don Quijote y Sancho* (Madrid, 1905), p. 19.
61 Unamuno, "Mi Religión," in *Ensayos* (Madrid, 1951), II, 372.
62 *Ensayos,* II, p. 371.
63 II, p. 371.
64 II, p. 371.

65 Unamuno, *Del Sentimiento Trágico de la Vida* (B's Aires, 1947), p. 70.
66 Barea, *Unamuno*, p. 50.
67 *Ensayos*, II, p. 374.
68 Unamuno, *Poesías* (Bilbao, 1907), pp. 53-4.
69 *Sentimiento Trágico*, p. 62.
70 Barea, *Unamuno*, p. 19.
71 Unamuno, "Materialismo Popular," *Ensayos*, II, 526.
72 Unamuno, *Torno al Cast.*, p. 129.
73 Unamuno, *De Fuerteventura a Paris* (Paris, 1925), pp. 13-14.
74 *De Fuerteventura*, p. 72.
75 *Sentimiento Trágico*, p. 262.

PIO BAROJA NESSI

76 Pío Baroja, *Las Horas Solitarias* in *Obras Completas* (Madrid, 1948), V, 321.
77 P. B., *Nuevo Tablado de Arlequín*, O.C., V, 96.
78 *Las Horas Solit.*, O.C., V, 320.
79 P. B., "Las Ideas de Santa Cruz," in *Divagaciones Apasionadas*, O.C., V, 541.
80 P. B., *Aurora Roja*, O.C., I, 602-3.
81 P. B., *La Sensualidad Pervertida*, O.C., II, 853.
82 P. B., *Juventud, Egolatría*, O.C., V, 158.
83 *Las Horas Solit.*, O.C., V, 236.
84 *Juventud, Egolatría*, O.C., V, 159.
85 *Juv., Ego.*, O.C., V, 158.
86 *Las Horas Solit.*, O.C., V, 345.
87 P. B., *Las Veleidades de la Fortuna*, O.C., I, 1286.
88 *Las Veleidades*, O.C., 1274.
89 *Las Horas Solit.*, O.C., V, 319.
90 P. B., *César o Nada*, O.C., II, 629.
91 *César o Nada*, O.C., II, 630.
92 *O.C.*, II, 630.
93 *O.C.*, II, 606.
94 P. B., *El Arbol de la Ciencia*, O.C., II, 483.
95 P. B., *Camino de Perfección* (Buenos Aires, 1944), p. 144.
96 *César o N.*, O.C., II, 605.
97 P. B., *El Mayorazgo de Labraz*, O.C., I, 1507-9.
98 P. B., *Los Amores Tardíos*, I, 1388.
99 *César o N.*, O.C., II, 651-76.
100 *Las Horas Solit.*, O.C., V, 320.
101 *La Sensualidad Per.*, O.C., II, 986ff.
102 *Veleidades*, O.C., I, 1285.
103 *O.C.*, I, 1281.
104 *O.C.*, I, 1287.
105 *O.C.*, I, 1273.
106 *Las Horas Solit.*, O.C., V, 345.
107 *César o N.*, O.C., II, 627.
108 *Veleidades*, O.C., I, 1281.
109 *O.C.*, I, 1273.
110 *César o N.*, O.C., 641.
111 *O.C.*, 641.

112 P. B., *La Dama Errante, O.C.*, II, 302.
113 P. B., *Vitrina Pintoresca, O.C.*, V, 739-43.
114 *César o N., O.C.*, 661.

MANUEL LINARES RIVAS

115 Manuel Linares Rivas, *Aire de Fuera* in *Obras Completas* (Madrid, 1931), I, 230.
116 *Aire de Fuera, O.C.*, I, 230.
117 *O.C.*, I, 229.
118 *O.C.*, I, p. 378.
119 Linares Rivas, *La Garra, O.C.*, XI, 40.
120 *La Garra, O.C.*, XI, 68.
121 *O.C., XI*, 41-2.
122 George D. Smith, "Christian Marriage," *The Teachings of the Catholic Church* (New York, 1949), II, 1096.
123 *La Garra, O.C.*, XI, pp. 110-113.
124 All additional judgements in *O.C.*, XI, between pp. 116-122.

JOSE ORTEGA Y GASSET

125 E. A. Peers, *The Spanish Tragedy* (London, 1937), p. 117.
126 Gerald Brenan, *The Spanish Labyrinth* (Comb. Un. Press, 1950), p. 235.
127 José Ortega y Gasset, *España Invertebrada* in *Obras Completas*, III, 76.
128 *Esp. Inv., O.C.*, III, 78.
129 *Esp. Inv., O.C.*, III, 79, 81.
130 *O.C., III*, 69.
131 *O.C.*, III, 70.
132 *O.C.*, III, 70.
133 Christopher Dawson, *Religion and Culture* (New York, 1948), p. 3.
134 Ortega y G., *La Rebelión de las Masas*, "Epílogo para Ingleses," (Buenos Aires, 1944), p. 210.
135 Ortega y G., *Meditación del Escorial* in *O.C.*, II, 554.
136 *Meditación del Escorial, O.C.*, II, 557.
137 *O.C.*, II, 554-7.
138 *O.C.*, II, 555.
139 *O.C.*, II, 556.
140 *O.C.*, II, 557.
141 *Revista de Occidente*, I (no. 1), 3.
142 Bertrand Russell, "Icaro o el Porvenir de la Ciencia," *Rev. de Occ.*, V, 161.
143 *A. B. C.*, Madrid, 20 de octubre de 1955.
144 My documentation on this point is personal and rests on the opinion of numerous friends in the intellectual community in Madrid.

RAMON PEREZ DE AYALA

145 Ramón Pérez de Ayala, *Los Trabajos de Urbano y Simona* (Madrid, 1923), p. 109.
146 *Los Trabajos*, pp. 85-6.
147 *Los Trabajos*, p. 186.
148 *Los Trabajos*, pp. 53-4.
149 Hieronymus Noldin quoted in *Jubilee*, August 1964, p. 44.
150 *Los Trabajos*, pp. 55-6.

151 *Los Trabajos*, p. 57.
152 *Los Trabajos*, p. 124.
153 Ramón Pérez de Ayala, *A. M. D. G.*, pp. 233-4.
154 *A. M. D. G.*, p. 138.
155 *A. M. D. G.*, p. 147.
156 *A. M. D. G.*, p. 151.
157 *A. M. D. G.*, pp. 197-9.
158 *A. M. D. G.*, p. 231.
159 *A. M. D. G.*, p. 250.
160 *A. M. D. G.*, p. 253.
161 *A. M. D. G.*, p. 255.
162 Valbuena Prat, *Historia de la Literatura Española* (Barcelona, 1952), III, 521.
163 Quoted in E. A. Peers, *The Spanish Tragedy*, p. 93n.

CHAPTER IV

ARTURO BAREA

1 Arturo Barea, *The Forging of a Rebel* (New York, 1946), p. 692.
2 *The Forging*, p. 106.
3 See the first section of Chapter II of this study.
4 *The Forging*, p. 461.
5 *The Forging*, pp. 460-61.
6 *The Forging*, p. 691.
7 *The Forging*, pp. 494-5.
8 Barea's argument with his mother: *The Forging*, p. 218.
9 *The Forging*, p. 705.
10 *The Forging*, p. 705.

RAMON SENDER

11 Ramón Sender to Charles L. King, quoted in *PMLA*, LXIX, 993.
12 Ramón Sender, *The King and the Queen*, trans. Mary Loro (New York, 1948), the dedication.
13 Ramón Sender, *Contraataque* (Madrid-Barcelona, 1938), p. 304.
14 Georges Bernanos, *Les Grands Cimetières sous la Lune* (Paris, 1938), p. 128.
15 Bernanos, p. 128.
16 R. S., *Contraataque*, p. 22.
17 Arturo Barea in the Introduction to Sender's *The Dark Wedding*, p. 13.
18 *Contraataque*, p. 11.
19 *Contraataque*, p. 16.
20 *Contraataque*, pp. 10-11.
21 *Contraataque*, p. 11.
22 *Contraataque*, p. 11.
23 R. S., *Crónica del Alba*, ed. Florence Hall (New York, 1946), p. 106f.
24 *Contraataque*, pp. 50-51.
25 *Contraataque*, p. 300.
26 R. S., *Crónica del Pueblo en Armas, Historia para Niños* (Madrid-Valencia, 1936), p. 20.

27 Ramón Sender, author's introduction to *Siete Domingos Rojos* (Barcelona, 1932), p. 7.
28 *Siete Domingos*, pp. 5-6.
29 The anti-litany: *Siete Domingos*, pp. 266-70.
30 *The King and the Queen*, p. 126.
31 See John Devlin on Joyce's manipulation of feminine symbolism: "On Reading Joyce," *America*, XCIX, 195-7.
32 Charles L. King, "Sender's Spherical Philosophy," *PMLA*, LXIX, 999.
33 R. S., *Mosén Millán* (Mexico, 1953), p. 56.
34 *Mosén Millán*, p. 66ff.
35 *Mosén Millán*, p. 74.
36 R. Sender, *Hipogrifo Violento* (Mexico, 1954), p. 15.
37 *Hipogrifo Violento*, p. 9.
38 *Hipogrifo Violento*, p. 85.
39 See our final evaluation of Pérez Galdós, Chapter II. Karl Pfleger's *Geister die um Christus Ringen* was published in Salzburg, 1934.
40 *Hipogrifo Violento*, p. 223.

RAFAEL ALBERTI

41 Quoted in Valbuena Prat, *Historia de la Literatura Esp.* (Barcelona, 1950), III, 636.
42 Angel Flores, editor in the introduction to Alberti's *A Spectre is Haunting Europe*, trans. A. Flores and Ira Jan Wallach (New York, 1936), p. 9.
43 Rafael Alberti, *Poesía 1924-39* (Buenos Aires, 1940), p. 263.
44 Angel Flores, *A Spectre is Hauting Europe*, pp. 23-4. The translation quoted is by Flores and Wallach.
45 Alberti, "Colegio (S.J.)," *De un Momento a Otro* (Buenos Aires, n.d.), p. 160.
46 Alberti, *El Poeta en la España del 1931* (Buenos Aires, n.d.), p. 52.
47 Alberti, *El Poeta en la Esp. del 1931*, p. 7.
48 *El Poeta — 1931*, pp. 13-14.
49 *El Poeta — 1931*, p. 16.
50 *El Poeta — 1931*, p. 21.
51 *El Poeta — 1931*, p. 13.
52 *El Poeta — 1931*, p. 14.
53 *El Poeta — 1931*, p. 15.
54 *El Poeta — 1931*, p. 15.
55 Alberti, *Romancero General de la Guerra Española* (Buenos Aires, 1944), pp. 20-21.
56 Alberti, *De un Momento a Otro*, pp. 222-3.

CHAPTER V

The New York Times and the *Spanish Cultural Index* are abbreviated *NYT* and *SCI* respectively, after their first entry.

Section 1: Church and State and Freedom of Expression

1 Bruce Marshall, *The Fair Bride* (London, 1953).
2 Marshall, p. 8.
3 Marshall, p. 89.

4 Marshall, p. 247.

5 Marshall, p. 249.

6 Juan Soto de Gangoiti, *Relaciones de la Iglesia Católica y el Estado Español* (Madrid, 1940), p. 11.

7 Soto de Gangoiti, p. 9.

8 Soto de G., p. 9.

9 Soto de G., p. 9.

10 Soto de G., p. 291.

11 Soto de G., p. 304.

12 E. A. Peers, *Spain in Eclipse, 1937-43* (London, 1943), pp. 113-114.

13 Peers, p. 114.

14 Reports in *The Pilot* (Boston Diocesan Newspaper), Jan. 15, 1955.

15 Report in *The New York Times*, Tuesday, Nov. 9, 1954. Camille Cianfara reporting.

16 Delgado's remark: *NYT*, Jan. 8, 1955.

17 *The Pilot*, Jan. 15, 1955.

18 *The Pilot*, Jan. 16, 1956.

19 *The Pilot*, Jan. 16, 1956.

20 *The Pilot*, Jan. 15, 1955.

21 *The Pilot*, March 26, 1955.

22 Camille Cianfara reporting in the *NYT*, March 20, 1955.

23 *The Boston Herald*, March 18, 1955.

24 *The Boston Globe*, March 25, 1955.

25 *Time* (Paris edition), Feb. 8, 1963, p. 31.

26 Frederich D. Wilhelmsen, "Forces at Work in Today's Spain," *America*, CII, 306-314.

27 See our remarks on Ridruejo and Laín Entralgo in Sections II and III of this chapter.

28 *NYT* (Paris), July 28, 1963. Report by Paul Hofmann.

29 Paul Hofmann, *NYT*, June 21, 1964.

30 *Il Corriere de la Sera*, Dec. 8, 1962.

31 Paul Hofmann, *NYT* (Paris), Feb. 16, 1963; P. H., *NYT* (Paris), April 22, 1963; P. H., *NYT* (Paris), July 21, 1963.

23 Paul Hofmann, *NYT* (Paris), March, 1963.

33 Paul Hofmann, *NYT* (Paris), June 21, 1963.

34 P. Hofmann, *NYT*, May 29, 1964.

35 *The Denver Register* (American Catholic Sunday periodical), Feb. 26, 1963.

36 *The New York Post*, Dec. 16, 1963.

Section 2: Governmental Literary Policy

37 *Escorial*, editorial comment; I, 7.

38 *La Ciudad de Dios*, "A Nuestros Lectores," CXLIII, 7.

39 "Editorial," *Cuadernos de la Literatura*, I, 4.

40 Thomas J. Hamilton, *Appeasement's Child* (New York, 1943), p. 85.

41 "Hechos de la Falange," *Escorial*, I, 157.

42 S. Raimúndez, O.S.B., "Catolicismo, Historia, y Falange," *Escorial*, V, 287.

43 Peers, *Spain in Eclipse, 1937-43*, p. 203.

44 Pedro M. Bordoy-Torrents, Pbro., "¿Por qué los Judíos son tan Perseguidos?" *La Ciudad de Dios*, CXLIV, 98-9.

45 *Spanish Cultural Index*, No. 99, pp. 377-8.

46 *SCI*, No. 107, p. 1,244.

[47] Alfred Mendizábal, *The Martyrdom of Spain*, trans. Charles Hope Lumley (London, 1938), p. 179.
[48] *SCI*, No. 76, p. 31.
[49] *SCI*, No. 89, p. 580.
[50] *SCI*, No. 81, p. 35.
[51] *SCI*, No. 72, p. 31.
[52] *SCI*, No. 90, p. 691.
[53] Peers, *Spain in Eclipse*, p. 152.
[54] *SCI*, No. 87, p. 366.
[55] *SCI*, No. 98, p. 254.
[56] *SCI*, No. 90, p. 700.
[57] *SCI*, No. 71, p. 30.
[58] *SCI*, No. 102, p. 741.
[59] *SCI*, No. 70, p. 28.
[60] Valbuena Prat, *Hist. de la Lit. Esp.*, III, 732.
[61] *SCI*, No. 64, p. 29.
[62] *SCI*, No. 61, p. 41.
[63] *SCI*, No. 61, p. 57.
[64] *SCI*, No. 101, p. 574.

Section 3: The Catholic Spirit in Modern Spanish Letters and the Spirit of the "Catholic Revival"

[65] The American literary review *Renascence* is devoted to the renewal in Catholic letters.
[66] Valbuena Prat, *Hist. de la Lit. Esp.*, III, 419.
[67] Richard E. Chandler and Kessel Schwartz, *A New History of Spanish Literature* (Louisiana State Un. Press, 1961), p. 405.
[68] Chandler & Schwartz, p. 406.
[69] Charles D. Ley, *Spanish Poetry Since 1939* (Washington, 1962), p. 132.
[70] Ley, p. 140.
[71] Valbuena Prat, *El Sentido Católico en la Literatura Española* (Barcelona, 1940), p. 174.
[72] Matilde Pomès, "Das Katolische Schriftum der iberischen Nationen" in *Katolische Leistung in der Weltliteratur der Gegenwart* (Herder, 1934), p. 247.
[73] Quoted from the box cover of the first English translation.

Section 4: Negative Spanish Evaluations of the Catholic Revival

[74] Leopoldo Alcalde Rodríguez, reviewer, "Antología de la Poesía Francesa," *Escorial* (julio-agosto 1947), p. 177.
[75] Floris Delattre, "Un Poeta Católico Francisco Thompson," *Escorial*, XVII, 182-87.
[76] Jesús Sáinz Mazpule, "De la Teología a la Política," *Escorial*, XX, 169-79.
[77] *SCI*, No. 107, p. 1,227.
[78] *SCI*, No. 107, p. 1,226.

Section 5: A Theological Evaluation of the Trends Studied in This Chapter

[79] John C. Murray, S.J., "Contemporary Orientations on Catholic Thought on Church and State in the Light of History," *Cross Currents*, No. 5, p. 46.
[80] Murray, S.J., pp. 46-47.

CHAPTER VI

[1] W. F. Ogburn and M. F. Nimkoff, *Sociology* 2nd. ed. (Boston, 1946), p. 561.
[2] Pitirim Sorokin, *Contemporary Sociological Theories* (New York, 1928), p. 742.
[3] Will Herberg, "A Jew Looks at the Catholic Church," *Commonweal* LXXIX, LVIII, 174-77.
[4] Robert McAfee Brown, "A Protestant Assessment," *Commonweal*, LXXIX, 396-8.
[5] John Cogley, "Grounds for Hope," *Commonweal*, LXXIX, 399.

BIBLIOGRAPHY

Sources marked with an asterisk were used to establish the Catholic literary, philosophical, or theological points of view utilized in this study.

A. Primary Sources

I. BOOKS

Alas, Leopoldo ("Clarín"). *La Regenta.* 2 vols. Madrid, 1900.

Alberti, Rafael. "Colegio (S.J.)" in the collection entitled *De un Momento a Otro.* Buenos Aires, n. d.

—— *Poesía 1924-39.* Buenos Aires, 1940.

—— *El Poeta en la España del 1931.* Buenos Aires, 1942.

—— "Romancero de Fermín Galán y los Sublevados de Jaca" in *El Poeta en la España del 1931.* Buenos Aires, 1942.

—— "Vida Bilingüe de un Refugiado Español" in the collection entitled *De un Momento a Otro.* Buenos Aires, n. d.

Alemán, Mateo. *Guzmán de Alfarache.* Edited by Gili Gaya. 5 vols. Madrid, 1927-1936.

Barea, Arturo. *The Forging of a Rebel.* Translated from the Spanish by Ilsa Barea. New York, 1946.

—— Introduction (translated by Ilsa Barea) to Ramón Sender's *The Dark Wedding.* Translated by Eleanor Clark. London, 1948.

Baroja Nessi, Pío. *Los Amores Tardíos.* Tomo I of *Obras Completas.* 6 vols. Madrid, 1948.

—— *El Arbol de la Ciencia.* Tomo II of *Obras Completas.* 6 vols. Madrid, 1948.

—— *Aurora Roja.* Tomo I of *Obras Completas.* 6 vols. Madrid, 1948.

—— *Camino de Perfección.* Buenos Aires, n. d.

—— *César o Nada.* Tomo II of *Obras Completas.* 6 vols. Madrid, 1948.

—— *La Dama Errante.* Tomo II of *Obras Completas.* 6 vols. Madrid, 1948.

—— *Divagaciones Apasionadas.* Tomo V of *Obras Completas.* 6 vols. Madrid, 1948.

—— *Las Horas Solitarias.* Tomo V of *Obras Completas.* 6 vols. Madrid, 1948.

—— *Juventud, Egolatría.* Tomo V of *Obras Completas.* 6 vols. Madrid, 1948.

—— *El Mayorazgo de Labraz.* Tomo I of *Obras Completas.* 6 vols. Madrid, 1948.

—— *Nuevo Tablado de Arlequín.* Tomo V of *Obras Completas.* Madrid, 1948.

—— *La Sensualidad Pervertida.* Tomo II of *Obras Completas.* 6 vols. Madrid, 1948.

—— *Las Veleidades de la Fortuna.* Tomo I of *Obras Completas.* 6 vols. Madrid, 1948.

—— *Vitrina Pintoresca.* Tomo V of *Obras Completas.* 6 vols. Madrid, 1948.

—— *Zalacaín el Aventurero.* Tomo I of *Obras Completas.* 6 vols. Madrid, 1948.

*Bernanos, Georges. *Les Grands Cimetières Sous la Lune.* Paris, 1938.

Blasco Ibáñez, Vicente. *A los Pies de Venus (Los Borgia).* Valencia, 1926.

Blasco Ibáñez, Vicente. *Alfonso XIII Unmasked.* Translated from the Spanish by Leo Ongley. New York, 1924.

—— *La Barraca.* Segunda edición. Buenos Aires, 1944.

—— *La Bodega.* Valencia, 1905.

—— *Cañas y Barro.* Tomo I of *Obras Completas.* 3 vols. Madrid, 1946.

—— *La Catedral.* Tomo I of *Obras Completas.* 3 vols. Madrid, 1946.

—— *Los Cuatro Jinetes del Apocalipsis.* Tomo II of *Obras Completas.* 3 vols. Madrid, 1946.

—— *Flor de Mayo.* Tomo I of *Obras Completas.* 3 vols. Madrid, 1946.

—— *La Horda.* Valencia, 1905.

—— *El Intruso.* Valencia, 1904.

—— *El Papa del Mar.* Valencia, 1925.

—— *Sangre y Arena.* Tomo II of *Obras Completas.* 3 vols. Madrid, 1946.

Cánovas Cervantes, S. *Apuntes Históricos de Solidaridad Obrera.* Barcelona, n. d. This work consists of varied selections reprinted from *Solidaridad Obrera,* a radical newspaper of the 1930's.

Castelar, Emilio. *Discurso Leído en La Academia Española Seguido de Otros Varios Discursos del Mismo Orador.* Madrid, n. d.

—— *Discursos Parlamentarios.* Tomo I. Madrid, 1871.

—— *La Fórmula del Progreso.* Madrid, 1870.

*Denziger, Henricus. *Enchiridion Symbolorum: Definitionum et Declarationum de Rebus Fidei et Morum.* Herder & Co., Typog. Editores Pontificii, 1937.

Diaz-Plaja, Fernando. *La Historia de España en sus Documentos: El Siglo XVIII.* Madrid, 1955.

Diego, Gerardo. *Poesía Española, Antología 1915-1931.* Madrid, 1932.

Echegaray, José. *En el Pilar y en la Cruz.* Madrid, 1878.

—— *La Muerte en los Labios.* Cuarta edición. Madrid, 1880.

*Evans, Joseph W. and Ward, Leo R. *The Social and Political Philosophy of Jacques Maritain.* Selected Readings. New York, 1955.

Fernández de Moratín, Leandro. *El Sí de las Niñas.* Valencia, 1877.

Flores, Angel. *Spanish Writers in Exile.* Sausalito, California, 1950.

—— (ed.). *A Spectre is Hauting Europe.* Poems of Revolutionary Spain. Translated from the Spanish by Ira Jan Wallach and Angel Flores. New York, 1936.

Ganivet, Angel. *Idearium Español.* Buenos Aires, 1944.

Giménez Caballero, Ernesto. *España y Franco.* Guipuzcoa, 1938.

—— *Genio de España (Exaltaciones a una Resurrección Nacional y del Mundo).* Segunda edición. Madrid, 1934.

—— *¡Hay Pirineos!* Barcelona, 1938.

—— *Lengua y Literatura de España.* Madrid, 1946.

—— *Manuel Azaña* (Profecías Españolas). Madrid, 1932.

—— *Notas Marruecas de un Soldado.* Madrid, 1923.

—— *La Nueva Catalicidad,* Madrid, n. d.

—— *Yo, Inspector de Alcantarillas.* Madrid, 1928.

Giner de los Ríos, Francisco. "En la Institución Libre de Enseñanza." Tomo VII (*Estudios Sobre Educación*) of *Obras Completas.* 19 vols. Madrid, 1922.

—— "La Enseñanza Confesional y la Escuela." Tomo VII (*Estudios Sobre Educación*) of *Obras Completas.* 19 vols. Madrid, 1922.

—— "La Iglesia Española." Tomo VI (*Estudios Filosóficos y Religiosos*) of *Obras Completas.* 19 vols. Madrid, 1922.

—— "El Problema de la Educación Nacional." Tomo XII (*Educación y Enseñanza*) of *Obras Completas.* 19 vols. Madrid, 1925.

Gironella, José María. *Los Cipreses Creen en Dios.* Madrid, 1953.

Gironella, José María. *Un Millón de Muertos*. Madrid, 1961.

*Karrer, S.J., Otto. *The Religions of Mankind*. Translated from the German by E. I. Watkin. New York, 1945.

Lazarillo de Tormes. Edited by Adolfo Bonilla y San Martin. Madrid, 1915.

Lettere de Conte Baldessar Castiglione Ora per la Prima Volta Date in Luce con Annotazioni Storiche Illustrate. Dall' Abate Pierantonio Serassi. Padua, 1769.

El Libro de los Gatos. Edited by G. T. Northup. Chicago, 1908.

López de Ayala, Pero. *Rimado de Palacio*. Edited by Albert F. Kuersteiner. 2 vols. New York, 1920.

Machado, Manuel. *Poesía (Opera Omnia Lyrica)*. 2da. edición. Barcelona, 1942.

Mackay, John A. Foreword to *Poems of Miguel de Unamuno*. Translated by Eleanor L. Turnbull. Baltimore, 1952.

Maeztu, Ramiro de. *Defensa de la Hispanidad*. Tercera edición. Valladolid, 1931.

—— *Ensayos*. Buenos Aires, 1948.

*Maritain, Jacques. *Art and Scholasticism*. With other essays by Jacques Maritain. Translated from the French by J. F. Scanlan. New York, 1930.

*—— *Christianisme et Démocratie*. New York, 1943.

*—— *Humanisme Intégral*. Problèmes Temporels et Spirituels d'une Nouvelle Chrétienté. Paris, 1936.

*—— *Man and the State*. Chicago, 1951.

*—— Introduction to Alfred Mendizábal's *The Martyrdom of Spain*. Translated from the French by Charles Hope Lumley. London, 1938.

*—— *Trois Reformateurs, Luther - Descartes - Rousseau*. Paris, 1925.

*Maritain, Raïssa. *Adventures in Grace*. Translated from the French by Julie Kernan. New York, 1945.

*—— *We Have Been Friends Together*. Translated from the French by Julie Kernan. New York, 1942.

Marquina, Eduardo. *El Monje Blanco*. Tercera edición. Madrid, 1930.

—— *Teresa de Jesús*. Segunda edición. Madrid, 1933.

*Marshall, Bruce. *The Fair Bride*. London, 1953.

Martínez Sierra, Gregorio. *Canción de Cuna*. Edited by Aurelio M. Espinosa. Boston, 1921.

—— *El Reino de Dios*. Madrid, 1916.

Martínez de Toledo, Alfonso (Arcipreste de Talavera). *Corvacho ó Reprobación de Amor Mundano*. Madrid, 1901.

*Mendizábal, Alfred. *The Martyrdom of Spain*. Introduction by Jacques Maritain. Translated from the French edition by Charles H. Lumley. London, 1938.

Miró, Gabriel. *Figuras de la Pasión del Señor* in *Obras Completas*. 1 vol. Madrid, 1943.

—— *Los Tres Caminantes* in *Obras Completas*. 1 vol. Madrid, 1943.

Mugueta, Doctor [sic]. *Los Valores de la Raza* (contains excerpts by Victor Pradera, Ramiro de Maeztu, José Calvo Sotelo, J. A. Primo de Rivera). San Sebastián, 1938.

Navarrete, M. F., Salva, Don Miguel, y Sáinz de Baranda, Don Pedro. *Colección de Documentos Inéditos para la Historia de España*. Tomo II. Madrid, 1843. 112 vols.

Navarro, Martín. *Vida y Obras de Don Francisco Giner de los Ríos*. Mexico, 1945.

O'Connell, William Cardinal. *A Memorable Voyage*. Private Publication, 1939.

Old Spanish Readings. Selected on the Basis of Critically Edited Texts. Edited by J. D. M. Ford. New York, 1939.

Ortega y Gasset, José. *La Deshumanización del Arte*. 2da edición. Madrid, 1928.

Ortega y Gasset, José. *España Invertebrada.* Tomo III of *Obras Completas.* Segunda edición. 3 vols. Madrid, 1950.

—— *Meditación del Escorial.* Tomo II of *Obras Completas.* Segunda edición. 3 vols. Madrid, 1950.

—— *La Rebelión de las Masas.* Buenos Aires, 1944.

—— *Rectificación de la República.* Madrid, 1931.

—— *El Tema de Nuestro Tiempo.* Sexta edición. Buenos Aires, 1947.

Osuna, Francisco de. *Abecedario Espiritual Primera-Sexta Parte del Abecedario Espiritual.* Colophon: Çaragoça, 1546-56.

Palacio Valdés, Armando. *La Hermana San Sulpicio.* Tomo IV of *Obras Completas.* 15 vols. Madrid, 1906.

—— *José.* Tomo VII of *Obras Completas.* 15 vols. Madrid, 1902.

—— *Marta y María.* Tomo II of *Obras Completas.* 15 vols. Madrid, 1895.

Patmore, Coventry. *Mystical Poems of Nuptial Love.* "The Wedding Sermon," "The Unkonwn Eros," and Other Odes. Edited with Notes by Terence L. Connelly, S.J. Boston, 1938.

Pemán, José María. *Del Movimiento Nacional.* Tomo V (*Doctrina y Oratoria*) of *Obras Completas.* Madrid, 1953.

—— *De Religión.* Tomo V (*Doctrina y Oratoria*) of *Obras Completas.* Madrid, 1953.

—— *El Divino Impaciente.* Trece edición. Cádiz, n. d.

—— *En la Hora de la Dictadura* (1923-1930). Tomo V. (*Doctrina y Oratoria*) of *Obras Completas.* Madrid, 1953.

—— *En la Hora Posterior al Movimiento Nacional.* Tomo V (*Doctrina y Oratoria*) of *Obras Completas.* Madrid, 1953.

—— *En la Hora de la República.* Tomo V (*Doctrina y Oratoria*) of *Obras* Completas. Madrid, 1953.

Pereda, José María. *Don Gonzalo González de la Gonzalera.* Tomo III of *Obras Completas.* Segunda edición. 17 vols. Madrid, 1889.

—— *Peñas Arriba.* Buenos Aires, 1942.

—— *Sotileza.* Buenos Aires, 1938.

Pérez de Ayala, Ramón. *A. M. D. G.* Madrid, 1923.

—— *Luna de Miel, Luna de Hiel* (*novela*). Madrid, 1923.

—— *Los Trabajos de Urbano y Simona* (*novela*). Madrid, 1923.

Pérez Galdós, Benito. *El Abuelo.* Tomo VI of *Obras Completas.* Edited by Federico Carlos Sáinz de Robles. 6 vols. Madrid, 1941.

—— *El Doctor Centeno.* Tomo IV of *Obras Completas.* Edited by Federico Carlos Sáinz de Robles. 6 vols. Madrid, 1941.

—— *Doña Perfecta.* Tomo VI of *Obras Completas.* Edited by Federico Carlos Sáinz de Robles. 6 vols. Madrid, 1941.

—— *Electra.* Tomo VI of *Obras Completas.* Edited by Federico Carlos Sáinz de Robles. 6 vols. Madrid, 1941.

—— *La Familia de León Roch.* Tomo IV of *Obras Completas.* Edited by Federico Carlos Sáinz de Robles. 6 vols. Madrid, 1941.

—— *Gloria.* Tomo IV of *Obras Completas.* Edited by Federico Carlos Sáinz de Robles. 6 vols. Madrid, 1941.

—— *Mariucha.* Tomo VI of *Obras Completas.* Edited by Federico Carlos Sáinz de Robles. 6 vols. Madrid, 1941.

—— *Nazarín.* Tomo VI of *Obras Completas.* Edited by Federico Carlos Sáinz de Robles. 6 vols. Madrid, 1941.

—— *Sor Simona,* Tomo VI of *Obras Completas.* Edited by Federico Carlos Sáinz de Robles. Madrid, 1941.

Pérez Galdós, Benito. *Tormento*. Tomo IV of *Obras Completas*. Edited by Federico Carlos Sáinz de Robles. 6 vols. Madrid, 1941.

Pérez de Urbel, Fray Justo. *El Monasterio en la Vida Española de la Edad Media*. Barcelona, 1942.

—— *Semblanzas Benedictinas*. Madrid, 1925.

Romancero General de la Guerra Española. Selección y Prólogo de Rafael Alberti. Buenos Aires, 1944.

Ruiz, Juan (Arcipreste de Hita). *Libro de Buen Amor*. Edited by Cejador y Frauca. Madrid, 1913.

—— *The Book of Good Love*, tr. Elisha K. Kane. Private publication, 1933.

Sender, Ramón. *Contraataque*. Madrid-Barcelona, 1938.

—— *Crónica del Alba*. Edited by Florence Hall. New York, 1946.

—— *Crónica del Pueblo en Armas, Historia para Niños*. Madrid-Valencia, presumably 1936.

—— *Epitalamio del Prieto Trinidad*. México, 1942.

—— *Hipogrifo Violento* (novela). México, 1954.

—— *Imán* (novela). Madrid, 1930.

—— *The King and the Queen*. Translated from the Spanish by Mary Loro. New York, 1948.

—— *Míster Witt en el Cantón*. Madrid, 1936.

—— *Mosén Millán*. México, 1953.

—— *Siete Domingos Rojos*. Barcelona, 1932.

Soto de Gangoiti, Juan. *Relaciones de la Iglesia Católica y el Estado Español*. Madrid, 1940.

Teatro Español Anterior a Lope de Vega. Por el editor de la *Floresta de Rimas Antiguas Castellanas*, Böhl de Faber. Hamburgo, 1832.

Thompson, Francis. *Complete Poems*. New York, n. d.

*Toynbee, Arnold J. *Civilization on Trial*. New York, 1948.

Unamuno, Miguel de. *Contra Esto y Aquello*. Madrid, 1912.

—— *El Cristo de Velázquez*. Madrid, 1920.

—— *Del Sentimiento Trágico de la Vida en los Hombres y en los Pueblos*. Buenos Aires, 1950.

—— *De Fuerteventura a París*. Paris, 1925.

—— "El Materialismo Popular." Tomo II of *Ensayos*. 4 vols. Madrid, 1951.

—— "Mi Religión." Tomo II of *Ensayos*. 4 vols. Madrid, 1951.

—— *Niebla* (*nivola*). Madrid, 1914.

—— *Poesías*. Bilbao, 1907.

—— *Poesías Místicas*. Selección de Jesús Nieto Pena. Madrid, 1941.

—— *Rosario de Sonetos Líricos*. Madrid, 1911.

—— *San Manuel Bueno, Mártir*. In *De Unamuno a Ortega Gasset*. Edited by Luis J. Navascués. New York, 1951.

—— *La Tía Tula*. Madrid, 1921.

—— *En Torno al Casticismo*. Buenos Aires, 1943.

—— *Vida de Don Quijote y Sancho*. Madrid, 1905.

Valbuena y Prat [sic], Angel. *La Novela Picaresca Española*. Selección, Prólogo, y Notas. Madrid, 1913.

—— *El Sentido Católico en la Literatura Española*. Barcelona, 1940.

Valdés, Alfonso de. *Diálogo entre Lactancio y un Arcediano* in *Dos Diálogos Escritos por Juan de Valdés* [sic]. n.p., 1850.

Valera, Juan. "Los Jesuítas de Puertas Adentro," *A Vuela Pluma*. Madrid, 1897.

—— *Pepita Jiménez y Cuentos y Romances*. Madrid, 1875.

Villalón, Fernando. *Poesías*. [Prólogo de José María De Cossío; dibujos de José Martínez del Cid.] Madrid, 1944.

Vivanco, Luis Felipe. *Introducción a la Poesía Española Contemporánea*. Madrid, 1957.

*Watkin, Edward Ingram. *Cathólic Art and Culture*. New York, 1944.

II. PERIODICALS

"A Nuestros Lectores, Decíamos Ayer," *La Ciudad de Dios*, CLIII (1941), 5-8. Signed "La Dirección."

Baroja Nessi, Pío. "The Mistakes of the Spanish Republic," *Living Age*, CCCLI (Jan., 1937), 422-427. Translated from the Buenos Aires *Nación*.

*Bonacina, Conrad. "The Catholic Church and Modern Democracy," *Cross Currents*, Fall, 1951, pp. 1-14. Reprinted from *The Wind and the Rain*, Summer, 1951.

Bordoyes-Torrents, Pedro M. "¿Por qué los Judíos son tan Perseguidos?" *La Ciudad de Dios*, CLIV (1942), 85-99.

The Boston Globe, March 25, 1955.

The Boston Herald, March 18, 1955.

"Catholics Speak for Spain." New York; Published by the North American Committee to Aid Spanish Democracy, 1937.

La Ciudad de Dios. Volumes 1945 and the following consulted *passim* for dedications and photographs.

*Clancy, William P. "The Area of Catholic Freedom" (subtitled "It is wider than those outside the Church can see or understand"), *Commonweal*, LXI (Nov. 5, 1954). 129-134.

*Cogley, John. "Grounds for Hope," *Commonweal*. LXXIX, 399.

*——— "Things That Are Caesar's," *Commonweal*, LXI (Nov. 5, 1954), 117-120.

*Congar, O.P., Ives. "Attitudes Toward Reform in the Church," *Cross Currents*, Summer, 1951, pp. 80-102. Selections from the Author's *Vraie et Fausse Réforme dans l'Eglise;* translated from the French by Bernard Gilligan.

——— "Vraie et Fausse Réforme dans l'Eglise," *Cross Currents*, III (Summer, 1953), 358-365. Reprinted from the *Downside Review;* selections made and translated from the French by Launcelot C. Sheppard.

Connolly, Terence L., S.J. "Coventry Patmore," *Renascence*, X, 53.

Corpus Barga, Andrés de. "Venus Novissima," *Revista de Occidente*, III (1924), 332ff.

Il Corriere de la Sera, Dec. 8, 1962.

"Crónica General — España," *La Ciudad de Dios*, LIV (5 de abril, 1901), 572-576. Unsigned.

"Crónica General — España," *La Ciudad de Dios*, CXXVII (5 de oct., 1921), 74-77. Signed P. G.

"Crónica General — España," *La Ciudad de Dios*, CLI (20 de oct., 1927), 141-146. Signed R. V.

"Crónica General — España," *Religión y Cultura*, XIII (enero, 1931), 152-160. Unsigned.

"Crónica General — España," *Religión y Cultura, XIII* (marzo, 1931), 470-477. Unsigned.

Delattre, Floris. "Un Poeta Católico Francisco Thompson," *Escorial*, XVII (enero, 1949), 163-193.

The Denver Register (An American Catholic Sunday Periodical), Feb. 26, 1963.

Devlin, John J. "French Influences on Gertrud von le Fort," *Renascence*, VII (Winter, 1954), 63-69.

Devlin, John J. "On Reading Joyce," *America*, XCIX, 195-97.

"Editorial," *Cuadernos de la Literatura, Revista General de Letras*, I (enero-febrero, 1947), 3-4. Unsigned.

García Acuña, J. "Inglaterra y los Estados Unidos," *Revista Contemporánea*, CXX (oct.-dic., 1900), 239-248.

González, O.S.A., Benito. "Naciones Católicas y Naciones Protestantes," *La Ciudad de Dios*, LIV (5 de feb., 1901), 161-176.

González Palencia, Angel. "La Divina Comedia y el Islam," *Revista de Occidente*, IX (1925), 100ff.

Gutiérrez, P. "Crónica . . . de España," *La Ciudad de Dios*, CXXV (5 de mayo, 1921), 236-238.

────── "Crónica . . . de España," *La Ciudad de Dios*, CXXV (5 de junio, 1921), 396-398.

────── "Crónica . . . de España," *La Ciudad de Dios*, CXXV (20 de junio, 1921), 458-460.

────── "Crónica . . . de España — La Religión en las Escuelas Nacionales," *La Ciudad de Dios*, CXXVII (20 de oct., 1921), 153-155.

────── "Crónica . . . de España," *La Ciudad de Dios*, CXXVII (20 de nov., 1921), 311-313.

────── "Crónica . . . de España," *La Ciudad de Dios*, CXXIX (20 de junio, 1922), 468-471.

"Hechos de la Falange," *Escorial*, I (nov., 1940), 157-159.

"Hechos de la Falange; En Tierra de Rusia," *Escorial*, V (oct., 1941), 113-115.

Herberg, Will. "A Jew Looks at the Catholic Church," *Commonweal*, LVIII, 174-77.

"El Hilo Roto," Boletín de la Sociedad Castellanense de Cultura, XVIII (1943), 1-3. Unsigned editorial.

"Hítler y el Nacionalsocialismo por O. Scheid," *Escorial*, IV (agosto, 1941), 321. An unsigned review.

"Las Injusticias del Estado Español," *La Ciudad de Dios*, LIII (20 de nov., 1900), 510. Signed P. M. A.

*Kuehnelt-Leddihn, Erik von. "The Catholic Reactionary," *"Commonweal* LVIII (June 19, 1953), 267-270.

"Manifiesto Editorial," *Escorial*, I (nov., 1940), 7-12.

*McAfee Brown, Robert. "A Protestant Assessment," *Commonweal*, LXXIX, 396-8.

Minteguiaga, V. "La Real Orden Circular sobre las Escuelas Laicas," *Razón y Fe*, XXVI (abril, núm. 4, 1910), 450-456.

Montes, O.S.A., Jerónimo. "Ferrer, su Obra y sus Cómplices," *La Ciudad de Dios*, LXXX (5 de nov., 1909), 356-364.

────── "Las Reformas en la Enseñanza," *La Ciudad de Dios*, LII (5 de mayo, 1900), 34-46.

*Mounier, Emmanuel. "Christian Faith and Civilization," *Cross Currents*, Fall, 1950, pp. 3-23. A lecture given in 1949 at the Semaine des Intellectuels Catholiques in Paris; translated from the French by Edwin W. Geissman.

*Murray, S.J., John Courtney. "Contemporary Orientations of Catholic Thought on Church and State in the Light of History," *Cross Currents, Fall*, 1951, pp. 15-55. Reprinted from *Theological Studies*, June, 1949.

*────── "Governmental Suppression of Heresy." Paper read before the American Catholic Theological Association, 1949. Private Notes.

The New York Post, Dec. 16, 1963.

The New York Times. Nov. 9, 1954 (report by Camille M. Cianfarra).

The New York Times. Jan. 8, 1955.

The New York Times. March 20, 1955.
The New York Times (Paris). Feb. 16, 1963.
The New York Times (Paris). March 23, 1963.
The New York Times (Paris). April 22, 1963.
The New York Times (Paris). June 21, 1963.
The New York Times (Paris). July 28, 1963.
The New York Times. May 29, 1964.
The New York Times. June 21, 1964.
"Past and Present" by the Editors, *Commonweal*, LXI (Nov. 5, 1954), 113.
Pérez Goyena, A. "Noticias Generales — España," *Razón y Fe*, XXVIII (oct., núm. 2, 1910), 261-264.
The Pilot. Jan. 1, 1955.
The Pilot. Jan. 15, 1955.
The Pilot. March 19, 1955.
The Pilot. Jan. 15, 1956.
*Pomés, Professor Mathilde. "Das Katholische Schrifttum der iberischen Nationen," *Katholische Leistung in der Weltliteratur der Gegenwart*. Freiburg im Breisgau: Herder, 1934.
"El Problema de la Enseñanza — Carta Pastoral que el Excmo. y Rvmo. Sr. Arzobispo de Valencia Dirige a sus Amados Fieles." Unsigned review in Razón y Fe, XXVI (marzo, núm. 3, 1910), 338.
"Un Prólogo de José Antonio," *Escorial*, II (enero, 1941), 7-13.
Raimúundez, O.S.B., S. "Catolicismo, Historia y Falange." (Containing a review of Laín Entralgo's *Los Valores del Nacional-sindicalismo*.) *Escorial*, V (nov., 1941), 287-292.
Real Orden: "La Religión en las Escuelas Nacionales," *La Ciudad de Dios*, CXXVII (20 de oct., 1921), 159.
"Recuerdo del Poeta Dionisio Ridruejo" por Manuel Machado, Luis F. Vivanco, Antonio Marichalar, Luis Rosales, Pedro Laín Entralgo; *Escorial*, VI (marzo, 1942), 393-407.
"Revista de Revistas — la Democracia Cristiana," *La Ciudad de Dios*, LII (20 de junio, 1900), 287-289. An unsigned discussion of the implications of Armando Castroviejo's article entitled "La Democracia Cristiana," which had recently appeared in *La Revista Contemporánea*.
"Revista de Revistas," *La Ciudad de Dios*, LIII (20 de sept., 1900), 121-123. An unsigned digest of Eduardo Sanz y Escortín's article, "De la Enseñanza," which had appeared in *La Revista Contemporánea* (15 de agosto).
"Revista de Revistas," *La Ciudad de Dios*, LIII (20 de sept., 1900), 128-130. An unsigned discussion of Georges Fonsgrieve's article, "La Condition du Travailleur dans le Catholicisme" which had appeared in *La Quinzaine* (16 août, 1900).
"Revista de Revistas — Los Patrones y las Sociedades Obreras," *La Ciudad de Dios*, LV (20 de junio, 1901), 292-293.
Ridruejo, Dionisio. "Poesía en Armas, Campaña de Rusia," *Escorial*, VI (marzo, 1942), 377-389.
Rivas Moreno, Francisco. "Como se Funda una Cooperativa de Consumo," subtitled "Cartas a un Obrero," *La Ciudad de Dios*, CXXIV (20 de marzo, 1921), 452-466.
———"Las Cajas Rurales," *La Ciudad de Dios*, CXXIV (enero, 1921), 40-54.
Rodríguez, O.S.A., Teodoro. "Intelectualismo y Educación," *La Ciudad de Dios*, CXXVII (20 de nov., 1921), 261-293.
———"Teorías y Realidades Sociales," *La Ciudad de Dios*, CXXVI (20 de agosto, 1921), 241-152.

Rodríguez, O.S.A., Teodoro. "Teorías y Realidades Sociales" (conclusión), *La Ciudad de Dios*, CXXVI (5 de sept., 1921), 321-331.

Ruiz Amado, R. "La Iglesia y la Escuela," *Razón y Fe*, XXVII (enero, 1910), 5-19.

Russell, Bertrand. "Icaro o el Porvenir de la Ciencia," *Revista de Occidente*, V (no. 14), 161ff.

Sáinz Mazpule, Jesús. "De la Teología a la Política de Maritain," *Escorial*, XX (sept., 1949), 169-181.

Schoeningh, Franz Josef. "What is Christian Politics?" *"Cross Currents*, Fall, 1950, pp. 55-65. Reprinted from *Hochland*, April, 1949; translated from the German by Sally Cunneen.

Spanish Cultural Index. Published by the Cultural Relations Department, Madrid. Entire series consulted *passim with specific references as* follows: Nos. 49, 60, 61, 62, 63, 64, 70, 71, 72, 73, 76, 79, 81, 102, 106, 107.

Time (Paris edition), Feb. 8, 1963, p. 31.

Unsigned review of Georges Fonsgrieve's *La Crisis Social, La Ciudad de Dios*, LIV (5 de enero, 1901), 55-56.

Unsigned review of R. P. Laberthonière's, "Le Problème de l'Education," *La Ciudad de Dios*, LIII (20 de sept., 1900), 130. The article had originally appeared in *La Quinzaine* (1er sept., 1900).

"Variedades," *Razón y Fe*, XXVI (enero, núm. 1, 1910), 135-138.

"Variedades — Programa de la Unión de los Católicos," *Razón y Fe*, XXVI (feb., núm. 2, 1910), 273-274.

Vicuña, J. M. "Notas de Información — Los Sindicatos Católicos-agrarios en Vizcaya," *La Ciudad de Dios*, CXXV (20 de abril, 1921), 143-155.

Villada, S.J., P. "¿Ha admitido Roma la Libertad de Cultos en España?" *Razón y Fe*, XXVIII (nov., núm. 3, 1910), 354-358.

—— "Sobre la Real Orden Contra las Asociaciones Religiosas," *Razón y Fe*, XXVII (julio, núm. 3, 1910), 340-348.

White, Peter. "The Church and the Nazis," *Jubilee*, August, 1964, p. 44.

B. *Secondary Sources*

I. BOOKS

Altamira y Crevea, Rafael. *Historia de España y de la Civilización Española.* 4 vols. Barcelona, 1906.

Amo, Julián y Shelby, Charmion. *La Obra Impresa de los Intelectuales Españoles en América.* Prólogo de Alfonso Reyes. California, 1951.

Agustín, Francisco. *Ramón Pérez de Ayala. Su Vida y Obras; Crítica.* Madrid, 1927.

Balseiro, Jose A. *Novelistas Españoles Modernos.* New York, 1933.

Barea, Arturo. *Unamuno.* Cambridge, 1951.

Barja, César. *Libros y Autores Modernos, Siglos XVIII y XIX.* Los Angeles, 1933.

Bell, Aubrey F. G. *Francisco Sánchez, El Brocense.* Milford, 1925.

Bertrand, Louis and Petrie, Sir Charles Bart. *The History of Spain.* Translated from the French by Ware B. Wells. New York, 1937.

Boak, A. E. R., Hyma, Albert and Slosson, Preston. *The Growth of European Civilization.* 4th printing. New York, 1939.

Brenan, Gerald. *The Spanish Labyrinth.* 2d ed. London, 1950.

*Campbell, Edward William. *Erasmus, Tyndale, and More.* Milwaukee, n. d.

Castillejo, José. *Wars of Ideas in Spain.* London, 1937.

Chandler, Richard E. and Schwartz, Kessel. *A New History of Spanish Literature.* Louisiana State Un. Press, 1961.

Chapman, Charles E. *A History of Spain.* New York, 1918.

Clough, James. *Spain in the Modern World.* London, 1952.

Codex Iuris Canonici. Westminster, Maryland, 1944.

Connolly, S.J., Terence (ed.). *Mystical Poems of Nuptial Love by Coventry Patmore.* Boston, 1938.

Del Río, Angel. *Historia de la Literatura Española.* 2 vols. New York, 1948.

Diez-Echarri, R. and Roca Franquesa, J. M. *Historia General de la Literatura Española e Hispanoamericana.* Madrid, 1960.

Farrow, John. *The Pageant of the Popes.* London, 1943.

Foulché-Delbosche, R. and Barrau-Dihigo. *Manuel de L'Hispanisant.* 2 vols. New York, 1920.

Grismer, Raymond L. *A New Bibliography of the Literature of Spain and Spanish America.* 6 vols. Minneapolis, 1941.

Hamilton, Thomas J. *Appeasement's Child.* New York, 1943.

Hayes, C. J. H., and Moon, F. J. *Modern History,* 4th ed. New York, 1942.

Hayes, Carlton J. H. *The United States and Spain.* New York, 1951.

Hughes, Philip. *A Popular History of the Catholic Church.* New York, 1953.

Hurtado de la Serna, Juan J., and González-Palencia, Angel. *Historia de la Literatura Española.* Sexta edición, corregida y aumentada. Madrid, 1949.

Lea, Henry Charles. *A History of the Inquisition of Spain.* 4 vols. New York, 1906.

Leo XIII, Pope. *On the Condition of Workers.* Washington, D.C., 1943.

Ley, Charles David. *Spanish Poetry Since 1939.* Washington, 1962.

Longhurst, John E. *Erasmus and the Spanish Inquisition.* Albuquerque, 1950.

Madariaga, Salvador de. *Spain.* New York, 1930.

Menéndez y Pelayo, Marcelino. *Historia de los Heterodoxos Españoles.* 3 vols. Madrid, 1880.

Morley, S. Griswold. Introduction to *Mariucha.* New York, 1921.

Ogburn, W. F. and Nimkoff, M. F. *Sociology,* 2d. ed., Boston, 1946.

Pastor, Ludwig von. *Geschichte der Päpste.* Band II. Freiburg im Breisgau, 1889.

Pattee, Richard. *This is Spain.* Milwaukee, 1951.

Peers, E. Allison. *The Church in Spain 1737-1937.* London, 1938.

——*Spain, the Church, and the Orders.* London, 1939.

——*Spain in Eclipse 1937-1943; A Sequel to the Spanish Tragedy.* London, 1943.

——*The Spanish Tragedy 1930-1936.* London, 1937.

Pitollet, Camilo. *V. Blasco Ibáñez, Sus Novelas y la Novela de Su Vida.* Versión española de Tulio Moncada. Valencia, n. d.

Reid, John T. *Modern Spain and Liberalism. A Study in Literary Contrasts.* California, 1937.

Rodríguez, José Francas. *La Vida de Canalejas.* Madrid, 1918.

Romera Navarro, M. *Miguel de Unamuno.* Madrid, 1928.

Rynne, Xavier. *Letters from Vatican City.* New York, 1963.

Sáinz de Robles, Federico. *Censo de Personajes Galdosianos.* In tomo VI de *Obras Completas de Benito Pérez Galdós.* Edited by Federico Carlos Sáinz de Robles. 6 vols. Madrid, 1941.

Sánchez Alonso, B. *Fuentes de la Historia Española e Hispano-Americana.* 3 vols. Tercera edición. Madrid, 1952.

Serafian, Michael. *The Pilgrim.* New York, 1964.

Serís, Homero. *Manual de Bibliografía de la Literatura Española.* Primera Parte. Syracuse, New York, 1948.
Shirer, William. *The Rise and Fall of the Third Reich.* New York, 1960.
Smith, George D. (ed.). *The Teaching of the Catholic Church.* New York, 1949.
Sorokin, Pitirim. *Contemporary Sociological Theories.* New York, 1928.
Trend, John Brande. *The Origins of Modern Spain.* New York, 1934.
—— *A Picture of Modern Spain.* Boston, 1921.
Valbuena Prat, Angel. *Historia de la Literatura Española.* Tercera edición. 3 vols. Barcelona, 1950.
Webster's International Dictionary of the English Language. 2d ed., unabridged. Springfield, Mass., 1953.
Welling's Press Guide. London, 1953.
Zabala Lera, Pío. *Historia de España y de la Civilización Española, Edad Contemporánea, 1808-1923.* A continuación of Altamira's *Historia.* 2 vols. Barcelona, 1930.

II. PERIODICALS

King, Charles L. "Sender's Spherical Philosophy," *PMLA,* Dec. 1955, 993.
Wilhelmsen, Frederich D. "Forces at Work in Today's Spain." *America.* CIX, 306-314.

III. ENCYCLOPEDIAS

Encyclopedia Britannica. 1952 edition. Vol. XII. Article, "Inquisition."
Catholic Encyclopedia. 1907 edition. Vol. v. Article, "Erasmus."
Catholic Encyclopedia. 1907 edition. Vol. VIII. Article, "Inquisition."
Enciclopedia Universal Ilustrada. 1912. edición. Tomo VIII. Article, "Blasco Ibáñez."
Enciclopedia Universal Illustrada. 1912 edición. Tomo XX. Article, "Erasmistas."
Enciclopedia Universal Illustrada. 1912 edición. Tomo XL. Article, "Ortega y Gasset."
Enciclopedia Universal Illustrada. 1912 edición. Tomo XLIII. Article, "Pérez de Ayala."
Enciclopedia Universal Illustrada. 1912 edición. Tomo XLIII. Article, "Pérez Galdós."

C. *Miscellaneous: Works Referred to in Passing or Relied Upon Indirectly*

Alberti, Rafael. *Marinero en Tierra.* Madrid, 1925.
Blasco Ibáñez, Vicente. *Cuentos Valencianos.* Buenos Aires, 1921.
Bernanos, Georges. *Sanctity Will Out. An Essay on St. Joan.* Translated from the French by R. Batchelor. New York, 1947.
Boccaccio, Giovanni. *Il Decamerone.* Milano, 1914.
Broncensis, Francisci Santii. *Opera Omnia una cum ejusdem Scriptoris Vita Autore.* Genevae, MDCCLXVI.
Castro, Américo. *El Pensamiento de Cervantes.* Madrid, 1925.
Chaucer, Geoffrey. *The Canterbury Tales.* Edited by Thomas Wright. London, 1853.

Darío, Rubén. *Poema del Otoño y Otros Poemas.* Tercera Edición. Buenos Aires, 1946.

Dawson, Christopher. *The Making of Europe.* An Introduction to the History of European Unity. New York, 1945.

—— *Religion and Culture.* Gifford Lectures delivered in University of Edinburgh in the year 1947. New York, 1948.

Erasmus, Desiderius. *Colloquia Selecta.* With an English translation by John Clark. Worcester, Mass., 1801.

—— *In Praise of Folly.* With life of Erasmus and his epistle addressed to Sir Thomas More; illustrated by Hans Holbein. London, 1876.

Feijóo, Fray Benito Jerónimo. *Teatro Crítico Universal.* Selección, prólogo y notas por Agustín Millares Carlo. 3 vols. Madrid, 1923.

Fernández Ardavín, Luis. *A Mitad del Camino (Selección de Poesías).* Colección Crisol, núm. 20. Madrid, 1944.

García Lorca, Federico. *Romancero Gitano, 1924-1927.* Buenos Aires, 1933.

Jovellanos, Gaspar Mechor de. *Obras Escogidas.* 3 vols. Madrid, 1935-1946.

López de Ubeda, Francisco. *La Pícara Justina.* Edited by Puyol. 3 vols. Madrid, 1912.

Lubac, Henri de. *Catholicism.* A Study of Dogma in Relation to the Corporate Destiny of Mankind. New York, 1950.

Maritain, Jacques. *Education at the Crossroads.* New Haven, 1943.

Pérez de Ayala, Ramón. *La Paz del Sendero.* Madrid, 1924.

Pope Pius X. *"Motu Proprio" on Sacred Music.* Included in Dom. Gregory Suñol, O.S.B., *Textbook of Gregorian Chant.* Translated from the Sixth French Edition by G. M. Durnford. Tournai (Belgium), 1930. pp. 164-172.

Quevedo, Francisco de. *Historia de la Vida del Buscón.* Edited by Américo Castro. Madrid, 1927.

Rumeu de Armas, Antonio. *Historia de la Censura Literaria Gobernativa en España.* Madrid, 1940.

Sachs, Hans. *Ausgewählte Poetische Werke.* Sprachlich erneuert und mit Einleitung und Anmerkungen versehen von Karl Pannier. Leipzig, 1879.

Sargent, Daniel. *Thomas More.* New York, 1938.

Valdés, Alfonso de. *Diálogo de Mercurio y Carón.* Edición y notas por José F. Montesinos. Madrid, 1947.

Valdés, Juan de. *Diálogo de la Doctrina Cristiana.* Coimbra, 1925.

—— *Diálogo de la Lengua.* Madrid, 1860.

Valle Inclán, Ramón de. *Obras Completas.* 2 vols. Madrid, 1944.

Wiseman, Nicholas P. S. Cardinal. *Fabiola* or *The Church of the Catacombs.* New York, 1860.

INDEX

A

Aguirre, José Antonio, 78
Alarcón, Pedro Antonio, 43
Alas, Leopoldo, 43
Alberti, Rafael, 43, 80, 146, 183-192, 199, 212
Albigensian Heresy, 21, 22
Alcalá Zamora, 76, 77
Aleixandre, Vicente, 146, 184
Alemán, Mateo, 34
Alfonso XIII, 60-80, *passim*, 81, 122, 123, 161, 189
Altolaguirre, Manuel, 190
Anti-Semitism, 23, 86, 95, 129-131, 208, 228, 237
Arcipreste de Hita, see Juan Ruiz
Arcipreste de Talavera, see Martínez de Toledo
Ateneo, 62, 69, 81, 91, 189, 213
Augustine, Saint, 17, 152
auto da fe, 28, 29, 35-36
Azaña, Manuel, 75-76, 210
"Azorín", 59

B

Bails, Benito, 37
Barea, Arturo, 42, 80, 111, 112, 114, 119, 121, 161-168, 169, 172, 173, 188, 222-223
Baroja, Pío, 43, 113-133, 154, 173
Benson, Monsignor Robert Hugh, 216
Bergamín, José, 78, 190
Bernanos, Georges, 19, 26, 78, 90, 95, 171, 217, 225, 227, 235
Birch Society, 238
Blasco Ibáñez, Vicente, 42, 44, 72, 96-113, 121, 130, 132, 146, 163, 166, 173, 190, 194
Bonacina, Conrad, 42, 50-52, 65, 71, 85, 163, 233, 235
Bosch, Hieronimus, 18
Brenan, Gerald, 33, 36, 64, 73, 79, 163
"Brocense," see Francisco Sánchez
Bueno y Monreal, Cardinal, 202

C

Canalejas, José, 60-63, 235
Canterbury Tales, 16

Carafa, Cardinal, see Pope Paul IV
Carlos de Borbón and *carlismo*, 37-40, 48, 81, 100, 101
Castelar, Emilio, 39-43, 51, 141
Castiella y Maíz, Fernando María, 200
Castiglione, Baldassare, 27-29
Castillejo, José, 54, 56
Castro, Américo, 33, 34
Ceda, 79, 223
Cejador y Frauca, Julio, 158
Centro de Estudios Históricos, 55
Céspedes, Pedro de, 31
Clancy, William, 72
"Clarín", see Leopoldo Alas
Claudel, Paul, 217, 219, 220, 227
Clavigo y Fajardo, José, 37
Cogley, John, 52, 235, 240
Coloma, S.J., Louis, 237
Comisión de Reformas Sociales, 60, 67
communism and communists, 171, 172, 175, 183-192, 196
"Confessional state" and confessionalism, 49-52, 57, 104, 111, 147, 158, 195, 204, 235-241
Congar, O.P., Yves, 52, 235
Connolly, Terrence L., S.J., 19, 230
Cossío, M. B., 59
Cruz, San Juan de la, 26, 115
"Coughlinism", 237

D

Dança General, 18
Danse Macabre, 18
Dato, Eduardo, 49, 67, 68
Da Vinci, Leonardo, 145
Dawson, Christopher, 144, 145, 146
Decameron, the, 16
Diego, Gerardo, 146, 183, 220
Dieste, Rafael, 190

E

Ecclesia, 197-198
Echegaray, José, 43, 44
Encina, Juan del, 32
Entrambasaguas, Joaquín de, 207
Erasmus, Desiderius, and *erasmismo*, 24-33, 94
Escarre, Dom Aureli, 204-205

F

Falange, 77, 79, 196, 202, 203, 204, 207, 208, 210-211, 224
Farrow, John, 110
Feijóo, Benito, 35
Fernando VII, 38, 101
Fernando and Isabella, 20-23, 194
Ferrer, Francisco, and the escuela laica, 64, 65, 71
French Catholic Authors, 217
French Enlightenment, 35

G

García, Rev. Félix, 148
García Lorca, Federico, 146, 184
German Catholic Authors, 217
Giménez Caballero, Ernesto, 78, 79, 147, 209, 210
Giner de los Ríos, Francisco, 53-60, 64, 82, 87, 141
Gironella, José María, 81, 220, 222-226
Greene, Graham, 217, 227

H

Hammarskjold, Dag, 215
Hayes, Carleton J. H., 208
Hemingway, Ernest, 108, 112, 225
Herberg, Will, 238
Herrera Oria, Bishop Angel, 197, 203
Herrera Oria, Francisco, 203
hispanidad, 50, 207
Hitler, 23, 208, 213, 236
Hughes, Philip, 20
humanism, 16, 17, 228, 229
Hollis, C. Carroll, 215

I

Irene, Princess (of the Netherlands), 38
Iriarte, Tomás de, 37
Iribarren, Rev. Jesús, 197-198, 235
Inquisition, 20-23, 24-33, 90, 101, 121, 122
Institución Libre de Enseñanza, 53-60, 62
Instituto Escuela, 54, 55

J

Joyce, James, 149, 159, 179
Junta para Ampliación de Estudios, 54-57, 69

K

Kennedy, John F., 238-239
Kraus and krausismo, 39, 86, 94, 141

L

Labré, Saint Benedict, Joseph, 182
Laforet, Carmen, 219
Laín Entralgo, Pedro, 201, 206, 208, 230
Largo Caballero, Ernesto, 68, 77
Lazarillo de Tormes, 32
León, Fray Luis de, 26
Lerma, Pedro de, 25
Ley, Charles David, 220, 221
Linares Rivas, Manuel, 133-141
Lobo, Don Leocadio, 78, 165, 166
López de Ayala, Pero, 17-18
Lortz, Joseph, 21, 22
Lucas Fernández, 32

M

McAfee Brown, Dr. Robert, 240
Machado, Antonio, 59
Machado, Manuel, 221
Mackay, John A., 115
Maeztu, Ramiro de, 207, 209, 210
Madariaga, Salvador, 159
Mal Lara, Juan de, 25
Malraux, André, 225
Manicheans, 17
Manterola, Vicente, 39-43
Marañón, Gregorio, 141, 149
Marcel, Gabriel, 217, 229
Maritain, Jacques, 42, 62, 73, 78, 79, 217, 222, 228-230, 233, 235
Marquina, Eduardo, 218, 219
Marshall, Bruce, 193, 194, 217, 235
Martín Descalzo, José María, 219
Martínez Sierra, Gregorio, 218, 219
Martínez de Toledo, 18
Maura, Antonio, 60, 64, 65, 162
Mauriac, François, 89, 217, 219, 227, 235
Mendizábal, Alfred, 72, 74, 77, 78, 79, 211, 235
Menéndez Pelayo, Marcelino, 29, 33, 35, 37, 56, 81
Menéndez Pidal, Ramón, 147, 212
Moratín, Fernando F., 37
Moreno, Enrique, 78
Moreno Villa, José, 191
Michaelangelo, 145
Murray, S.J., John Courtney, 42, 49-52, 231, 233, 238

N

Nakens, 111, 190
Nebrija, Antonio, 25
neo-Platonists, 17

Newman, John Henry Cardinal, 216, 217, 227, 230

O

O'Connell, William Cardinal, 78
Oldenbourg, Zoe, 178
Ortega y Gasset, José, 42, 55, 59, 72, 76, 102, 110, 111, 112, 121, 141-148, 190, 194, 221
Osuna, Francisco de, 18, 235

P

Palacio Valdés, Armando, 44, 157, 218
Panero, Leopoldo, 220
Pastor, Ludwig von, 110, 235
Patmore, Coventry, 217, 227, 230
Pattee, Richard, 54, 67
Peers, E. Allison, 74, 77, 79, 196, 212
Péguy, Charles, 217, 227
Pemán, José María, 189, 209, 211, 213, 220
Pereda, José María de, 81, 215, 218
Pérez de Ayala, Ramón, 102, 103, 138, 141, 148-159, 181, 221
Pérez Galdós, Benito, 42, 44, 58-95, 96, 104, 105, 112, 121, 133, 140, 147, 162, 173, 183, 194, 195, 226
Pildaín y Zapiaín, Bishop Antonio, 198
Pomès, Mathilde, 222
Pope Adrian VI, 24
Pope John XXIII, 22, 52, 94, 200, 201, 239, 240
Pope Leo XIII, 65, 67, 230
Pope Paul III, 24
Pope Paul IV, 21
Pope Paul VI, 201, 239
Pope Pius IX and *The Syllabus of Errors*, 71, 72
Pope Pius XII, 236
Portocarrero, Bishop Pedro, 30, 31, 33
Primo de Rivera, José Antonio, 206, 213
Primo de Rivera, Miguel, 68-72, 122, 123, 169, 170, 196, 200, 206
Psichari, Ernest, 217

Q

Quevedo, Francisco de, 34, 35, 85, 154, 190, 214

R

Republic, the Second, 48, 52, 54, 70, 71, 72-80, 107, 140, 141, 142, 149, 159, 161, 163-168, 171-180, 190-191, 194
Residencia de Estudiantes, 55

Ridruejo, Dionisio, 201, 202, 203, 206, 208
Right-wing extremism, 236
Robles, Gil, 77, 79, 163, 164, 202
Rocaful, Canon, 78
Rosales, Luis, 208, 220
rotativismo, 48, 63
Ruiz, Juan, 15-17

S

Sachs, Hans, 16
Sánchez, Francisco, 29-31
Santa Teresa, 26
Segura, Cardinal, 42, 73, 74, 188, 199, 200
Semprún y Gurrea, José María de, 73, 74, 78
Sender, Ramón, 42, 80, 157, 168-183, 188
Schoenigh, Franz Joseph, 52
Simon, Yves, 235
Sorokin, Pitirim, 234
Sturzo, Don Luigi, 50

T

Thompson, Francis, 227-230
Torres Naharro, 32
Totentanz, 18
Toynbee, Arnold, 17
Trend, John Brande, 55
Trent, Council of, 18

U

Unamuno, Miguel de, 39, 42, 55, 60, 68, 72, 113-123, 124, 125, 133, 213

V

Valbuena Prat, Angel, 159, 184, 213, 218, 221
Valera, Juan, 44, 157
Valdés, Alfonso de, 26-29
Valdés, Juan, 26-29
Valverde, José, 220
Vergara, Francisco de, 25
Vergara, Juan de, 25
Vicente, Gil, 32
Virués, Fray Alonso de, 25
Vivanco, Luis Felipe, 208, 220

W

Watkin, Edward Ingram, 17, 222
Waugh, Evelyn, 217
Wiseman, Nicholas Cardinal, 216